TARGET

GUITTA KARUBIAN

BOOKS BY GUITTA KARUBIAN

THE MOON TRILOGY
Persian Moon - Layla's Story - *Book 1*
Moon Child - Jolie's Story - *Book 2*
Moonlight - *Book 3*

Target

You, Me, and I

Target is a work of fiction. All names, characters, businesses, places, events, locales, and incidents are the product of the author's imagination and used only in a fictitious manner. Any resemblance to actual entities, either living or dead, past or present (or to actual events) is purely coincidental.

ISBN: 978-1-7330151-5-8

"What for centuries has raised man above the beast is not the cudgel but the irresistible power of unarmed truth."

— Boris Pasternak

"Three things cannot be long hidden: the sun, the moon, and the truth."

— Buddhist saying

ACKNOWLEDGEMENTS

It takes a small village to turn out a finished book. When the book is self-published, that is doubly true.

The author writes and rewrites. But were it not for the help of others, that writing would not evolve into a book. My thanks to all those who participated in the creation of **Target**.

Thanks to family and friends who provided encouragement and support from the inception of this story and along the way, even taking it upon themselves to read drafts, offer suggestions, and assure me that the trial sequence didn't put them to sleep. To all these people, I extend my gratitude.

The result of this collaborative effort is presented to you in the hope that you will enjoy **Target** and pass along the good word to others in your village.

Thank you.
Guitta Karubian
Los Angeles, California

1

At two minutes before nine on a clear Monday morning in April, Rafael Villa Lamon parked his five-year old black Volvo in his assigned space in the subterranean garage on North Camden Drive in Beverly Hills, took the elevator up to the ground level, and headed for what he thought would be a typical day at work. He walked across the manicured courtyard, enjoying the multi- colored flowers and saluted as he passed the uniformed security guard posted at the bank's main entrance.

"Good morning, Ed."

"Morning, Mr. Lamon."

In fact, Rafael's life would change forever that day.

Pushing through the glass double doors emblazoned with the logo of TriWorld Bank scripted in gold, he entered the bank's sumptuous reception area where employees, well-groomed and dressed to the nines, went about their business with quiet grace. Rafael gave his usual greeting to the receptionist.

"Good morning, Bright Eyes."

She returned a dazzling smile. The other men and women in the office greeted him as he passed.

The consensus was that Rafael was appealing in a sexy way. At forty-eight, it seemed the older he got, the more appealing he became. He was slim and tall, but not too tall, and broad-shouldered without appearing muscle-bound. His Latin complexion made him look perpetually tanned. His suits, though not expensive, fit him well, and his few silver hairs added to his distinguished appearance.

He turned the corner, continued down a hall and stopped at Selena's desk. They exchanged pleasantries and she handed him several pink slips. "I'm not finished sorting your mail yet," she said. "I'm about to get a cup of coffee. Can I bring a cup in to you with your mail?"

"If you don't mind," he said, "that would be great."

He came to a door marked "Rafael V. Lamon, Director," opened it and entered the relatively modest office with no-nonsense furnishings. There was a cloth-covered couch and a simple walnut desk with a comfortable executive chair behind it and two chairs placed in front. Rafael had never bothered to hang anything on the walls. On the single shelf behind his desk was paraphernalia he had collected through the nearly eight years he'd been at TriWorld. There was also a miniature red Ferrari positioned between a small glass plaque of gratitude for excellent service and a glass paperweight, both branded with the company slogan, *We are wherever you are*. The model red Ferrari had been a birthday gift from her.

Rafael put his briefcase down and placed his messages on his desk then rubbed his neck. Just carrying his briefcase from the car to his office had heightened the pain. He took off his jacket, set it on one of the chairs and rotated his left shoulder as his physical therapist had instructed, first forward then backward. He put his suit jacket back on, sat at his desk and brought out his smart phone. He turned to that day's calendar. As he found what he was looking for, Selena knocked and came in with his mail and a mug of coffee, also emblazoned with the bank's slogan.

"Here you go. It's just the way you like it, freshly brewed, hot and naked." Rafael smiled.He enjoyed knowing they could banter like that with clear boundaries in place.

He brought out two tablets of Aleve from a bottle in his pocket and downed them with the coffee.

Selena noticed. "Still bad, huh?"

"Yeah, guess I'm getting old. I'm doing my exercises religiously but they say it takes a few months."

"Okay. Let me know if you need me." With that she left his office.

Using the company landline, Rafael dialed the first number of the day. While he waited for someone to pick up, he cleared his throat and lit a Marlboro.

A woman answered, "Bueno."

"Good morning, Monica. I'm not waking you up?"

"Who is this?"

"It's Rafael Lamon."

Monica answered in Spanish. "Oh, amore, I wish you had spent the night. We'd have had a lovely night together and you'd have awakened me with a lovely kiss."

Raphael laughed and replied in Spanish as well. "Yes, that *would* have been lovely. But I'm afraid my wife would have missed me."

"Claro," Monica said then reverted to English. "So, tell me, why are you calling me so early?"

"I'm returning your call from yesterday. We're meeting today and I'm wondering if you've made a decision about that three-million-dollar letter of credit." Rafael said.

"Yes, amore, but I have some silly questions first. Perhaps we can have lunch and you can explain these to me?"

Just then the door to Rafael's office burst open and the bank's General Manager, Bob Stamen charged in. Behind him, Rafael's immediate supervisor, Jason Alandro, closed the door. The two men stood in front of Rafael's desk.

Believing their unceremonious entry signaled that something urgent was in the works, Rafael was eager to end his call with Monica. "Yes, of course. Let me call you back in a few minutes, Monica."

"I will wait for you, amore. Ciao."

Rafael hung up the phone and looked up at the two men. "Good morning, Bob, Jason. What's up?"

Bob Stamen, with his hands in his pockets, his fingers wiggling around in them, answered without hesitation. "You're fired," he said.

2

Rafael stared at the General Manager with squinted eyes. "What?"

Stamen repeated himself. "You heard me. You're fired. Effective immediately."

"You're kidding, right?" Rafael laughed nervously. He was sure Bob was kidding; he had to be. This was a prank the two men had cooked up. He rubbed his aching neck. "This is a joke?"

"It's no joke," Stamen said.

Rafael stopped laughing. He turned his attention to his immediate supervisor. Jason was standing rock still, biting his upper lip, his eyes fixed on the carpet by his feet. He and Rafael spent hours talking. Rafael reasoned that if Bob had been planning to fire him, Jason would have known and warned him. *Why hadn't he?*

Rafael looked back at the General Manager. Bob's fingers were still in his pants pocket, moving faster inside them now. Rafael sat back in his chair and tried to make sense of what was happening; it made no sense. His heart began pumping. *Fired why?*

He squinted again, as though the problem was his vision. "What are you talking about?" he asked Stamen. "What the hell for? What's this about?"

Stamen's response was deadpan. "You'll be told everything in due time. Right now, gather your things and leave the premises. Immediately. You'll be escorted off the property."

Dumbfounded, Lamon tried to stay calm as he pressed for an explanation. "Can't I know what this is about? Bob, I have a right to know. Why am I being fired?"

Stamen was through talking. He was heading for the door.

"You need to go. Now," he said. He opened the office door and motioned to Ed, the security guard waiting outside Rafael's door, to enter. Then he turned back to Rafael. "Give Ed your key. He'll see you out." He looked at his wristwatch and spoke to Rafael one last time. "Go. Leave right away." Then, to Ed, he said, "Take him now." With that, he was gone, Jason, following behind.

Rafael was caught between shock and confusion. He wanted to jump out of his chair and run after Bob. He wanted to grab him and demand an explanation right then and there. But dumbfounded and in shock, he couldn't move. Stamen had said he would find out in due time. *What did that mean?*

Ed spoke softly. "Your key, please, Mr. Lamon." When Rafael remained motionless, Ed repeated, "Mr. Lamon?" Rafael looked up at him, aroused out of a daze. "I'll need your key."

Rafael slowly fished in his pocket and brought out his keys, but his hands were shaking so badly that he couldn't take the office key off the keyring.

"Let me help you with that, Mr. Lamon."

Rafael let Ed take the keys from his hand. He moved to pick up the cigarette he'd left in the ashtray, but saw it had burned out, and so he sat dumbly, with his hands on his lap, staring ahead at the blank wall.

"I'll get a couple of boxes and be right back," Ed said.

When the security guard opened the office door, Rafael noticed the staff milling around in the hall outside his office. Having gotten a whiff that something was up, they were craning their necks to see what they could. A concerned Selena was about to enter his office when Ed, carrying two legal-sized boxes, returned and closed the door.

"If there's anything you'll want," he said to Rafael, "You need to take it with you now." He spoke gently. "You won't be allowed access after this, Mr. Lamon."

Rafael looked up at the guard. It took a moment to register what he'd said. He thought to ask Ed if he knew why he was being fired, but, of course, Ed wouldn't know. In any event, even if he did know, Rafael was certain he'd been instructed not to tell him.

Rafael shook his head and began opening his desk drawers one at a time. He needed time to digest what had just happened before he could catch up to the present minute – and Stamen wasn't giving him time to think. *How can I know what to take when I can't think straight?*

He picked up TriWorld Bank's daily rate sheet, then shook his head and dropped it back onto the desk. "I won't be needing this." He walked around the office, then came back to the desk and threw some odds and ends from the top desk drawer into the box. He deposited the paperweight and the plaque inside. Gently handling the small red Ferrari, he wrapped it in several sheets of that day's Wall Street Journal before placing it into the box, then added the small colored photograph on his desk. He had taken that photo of his wife and daughter on a trip to San Francisco three years ago. The last thing he put in the box was the black-and-white photograph of her he'd cut out of a newspaper and had kept in the bottom drawer of his desk.

Everything fit in one box. He looked at Ed and rubbed his neck. The Aleve had not yet taken effect. It hadn't yet been twenty minutes since he'd taken it.

"Is that everything, Mr. Lamon?" Rafael barely nodded. "Okay, come with me, please."

When Rafael picked up the box and his attaché, it proved to be too much of a strain. He put the box down and asked Ed to carry it. When they exited Rafael's office, those milling about in the hallway quickly dispersed without a word. Selena stood watching, her hand at her mouth. Rafael, too humiliated to make eye contact with anyone, kept his gaze planted on Ed's back as he followed him down the hallway and through the impressive reception area, exited the glass doors, walked down the cement path in the courtyard with the lush gardens on either side, and entered the elevator. Together they rode down to the garage and approached his Volvo. Ed waited until his charge was seated in his car and had turned on the ignition before he left him.

On his way to the elevator, Rafael had not seen the three men enter the Bank.

3

Dressed in jeans and a plain white T-shirt, Alexa Starr was packing up her law office and listening to Elton John on her iPod. As always, the volume was turned up to max. She looked around her office. She'd started packing over the weekend and had finally finished this Monday morning.

The movers would be coming at ten. Sealed and marked boxes were everywhere. Some held framed licenses, diplomas, and certificates of admission into various courts. Others were filled with either law books or plants. The file cabinet stood ready to be carted away.

Alexa had been in practice in Beverly Hills since her admission to the California State Bar almost fifteen years earlier, and she'd been successful as a sole practitioner from the first week she began her practice. Her first case had been a personal injury case, a family friend who had been hit by an SUV as she passed through a crosswalk on Venice Boulevard.

The woman had been badly injured. She'd had two broken legs, two broken ribs, and had lost a kidney. Alexa had been able to get her policy limits on the driver's insurance policy and a handsome amount from the driver himself. Pursuant to the client's wishes, Alexa deposited all the money into an account, solely for the benefit of her client's teenage son.

After lying on her back in the UCLA hospital for six months with her two legs held up at a ninety-degree angle, a rod going through both, without ever voicing a single complaint, the woman went home. Soon her second kidney failed. She was put on dialysis and died within a year. Alexa was heartbroken. Since then, she had handled an array of legal matters but never took on another personal injury case.

Early on, the young lawyer had specialized in criminal defense work, and though she enjoyed it and did well, her sudden hearing loss had made her uncomfortable in the courtroom; she felt insecure, unsure she could hear the judge or the witnesses. So, she transitioned to transactional law, a practice outside the courtroom. She did fine with administrative hearings and arbitrations; the venues were smaller, so she had no problem hearing witnesses as well as the arbitrator. She also became an expert in contracts, handled immigration cases, some family law and real estate matters, and consulted on an array of subjects.

Alexa had gotten clients out of all sorts of jams. She loved the law. She loved helping people and had always made time to take on worthy pro bono cases for needy clients. She loved seeing justice take its course. Sometimes it just needed a push, and she had no problem being the one to give it that gentle nudge. She also loved being her own boss. She couldn't fathom working for another attorney, doing things the way someone else told her to. She had to do things her way or not at all. Aware that her approach was sometimes a bit unconventional, she always made sure to explain to her clients what her strategy would be and let them choose: Alexa or another attorney. So far, those who had chosen to go with Alexa were glad they had, which made her wonder if it was a matter of time before the odds went the other way.

There were two things about the practice of law that Alexa did not like at all: lawyers and office buildings. She found lawyers to be generally myopic, arrogant, and – all too often – simply greedy. As for office buildings, she was glad to be leaving this one. Even after 15 years, she still hated elevators, fluorescent lights, and having a receptionist act as a buffer between her and her clients. She had always made it a point to greet her clients in the reception area and let them know when she was running late. *Never again!* This was the last day her office would be in an eight-story building with four elevators and lots of bells and lights. After today, the Law Office of Alexa Starr would be located in what had previously been her guesthouse.

Her cell phone vibrated in her jeans pocket. Seeing that the call was coming from her house, she quickly turned off the music and answered it. It was Savannah, her five-year-old daughter. "Hi, sweetheart."

"Mommy?"

"Yes, baby?"

"Mommy, when are you coming home?"

"Soon."

"Oh, goodie. Mommy? Reggie's been so good today."

What Alexa heard didn't make sense. "Reggie's been sawing wood today?"

Savannah fell into peals of laughter, and Alexa joined her, knowing she was off mark. "Reggie, Mommy thought I said you were sawing wood today." Alexa heard Reggie's screams of laughter. Then Savannah spoke more distinctly. "Mommy, I said, Reggie's been so good today."

"That's great. Sorry, honey," Alexa said, "It's my hearing."

"I know," Savanna said. "It's okay, Mommy."

Savannah was always ready to make everyone feel better.

She was a natural-born caretaker, especially of her brother. Even though Savannah and Reggie were twins, Alexa would often say she had a five-year-old daughter who had a five-year-old son.

"Thanks, Sweets. What's he doing?"

"He's playing with his Lego. Making Superman."

Alexa could picture her son in his room. Once finished making the superhero, he would hold him high in the air in one hand and Batman or Spider-Man in the other. He'd wave his arms until the two heroes collided, mimicking a fight. When Superman inevitably knocked a Lego block off his opponent, the fight would be over, and Superman would once again be declared the winner.

"Okay, Cookie, let's hang up now so I can finish packing and get home."

Within the hour, the movers had emptied out Alexa's office, and she'd said goodbye to the other attorneys and staff in her suite.

"I'll miss you, honey," her receptionist said. She hugged Alexa. "Don't be a stranger."

Julia had been the suite receptionist for the last five years and knew all of Alexa's clients. A year earlier, Julia and her live-in partner, Paula, had married. Their wedding ceremony in Malibu was so beautiful that Alexa was almost envious. As she had sat at her table watching the two women take their vows on the sand, she'd actually thought about dating a lesbian. Why bother trying to please a man? Julia and Paula could go shopping together, borrow one another's clothing – and they'd be so much more forgiving of cellulite.

"I'm sure we'll talk," Alexa said. "Come visit me."

She took the elevator down to her car for the last time. As she entered the garage, she saw the elderly optometrist whose office was on her floor. She was moving large cans stacked between the wall and her car, parked across the way. Alexa could see she was grumbling. She called out. "Hi, Jane. Is something wrong?"

Jane didn't look up. With her back to Alexa and a can in her arms, she muttered, "Someone's putting garbage in front of my car!"

Alexa had another one of those moments when she knew what she heard was probably wrong, but maybe not; after all, Jane was grumbling. "Someone's putting garlic in front of your car?"

Jane put the can down, put her hands on her hips, and turned around. The look on her face confirmed that Alexa had misunderstood her. "I said, someone's putting garbage in front of my car."

Alexa tried not to show her embarrassment. "Sorry. You should report it to security."

Had I really thought she'd said someone was putting garlic in front of her car?

She really had to do something about her hearing aids.

4

When Alexa turned the lock of her front door and entered her living room, Reggie and Savannah rushed to greet her.

"Hi, chickies," Alexa greeted them, then called to the nanny. Lupe had been with Alexa since her divorce three years ago and was absolutely indispensable in her life. "Hi, Lupe. The movers are outside. Would you please show them to the guesthouse? They can go in through the driveway and put everything there. They've already been paid." Lupe nodded and left to take charge of the movers.

Now that the move was done, Alexa was ready to relax. She plopped down on the couch. Immediately, the twins were all over her, vying for her attention.

"Mommy, can we go to American Girl? Please, Mommy? I want a doll, and I know her," Savannah said. She was clapping her hands and jumping excitedly. "Her name is Isabella. She's so pretty! And she does ballet! Please, Mommy?"

"Mommy, there's a new PlayStation," Reggie said, pulling at her jeans. "Can we have that? And, and, and can we go to the video store?" He hadn't yet fully mastered his Rs yet, and 'store' came out as 'stow.' It seemed unfair that he had a name he couldn't yet pronounce correctly. Of course, he would outgrow it. Meanwhile, it didn't seem to bother him, and it melted her heart. "Please, Mommy?"

Alexa had recently gone shopping to buy a birthday gift for Savannah's classmate at American Girl in the Grove. So she knew that Isabella, like the other dolls there, cost well over a hundred dollars; and that was without the branded accouterments so tempting to little girls – Isabella's multiple costumes, her dollhouse, furniture, and books...Isabella had an entire life in storage at American Girl waiting to be bought and put into a little girl's room. And PlayStation cost several hundred dollars. Regardless of their cost, Alexa was determined to stop catering to her children's material desires.

When their divorce was fresh, Alexa and Ben had drowned both children in toys. Maybe it was guilt. Maybe it was carelessness. In any event, there was nothing the children didn't have. And, because of their different interests, few toys were shared. Furthermore, they spent time in two houses – hers and Ben's – so they doubled up on almost everything. She came to realize her children were becoming accustomed to having everything they wanted and were having a hard time accepting that there was anything they couldn't have.

Alexa had brought the topic to Ben's attention. They discussed that the twins were starting kindergarten and would have to learn they could not and would not have everything they saw on television or that their classmates had. It was time they learned that things were not as important as they believed them to be and that they could do fine without having everything they asked for thrown at them. Mother and father began practicing moderation and simultaneously launched a campaign to replace material rewards with verbal praise and greater physical affection.

"No, guys, I'm sorry, but the answer is no to American Girl and no to PlayStation." She looked at Savannah. "You have enough dolls, and you," she said, looking at Reggie, "have a new game system at Dad's house, and the one you have here is good enough to keep you and your friends busy."

Just then, her cell phone rang. She pulled it out of her purse. It was a call from Julia. She smiled. "Julia. I'm not even gone an hour. You miss me already?"

"Alexa, I thought you should know. Rafael Lamon just called. He sounded awful. He wanted to see you. When I said you were at home, he said he was on his way to your house. I guess he knows where you live."

Alexa didn't explain why he had her address.

5

It alarmed Alexa to hear Julia say that Rafael had sounded awful. He was a man that always had it together, always appeared cool, in control and incredibly, seductively, charismatic. She wondered what could have happened to make him sound so bad and why he would head for her house without even a call. She would soon know; he'd be there any minute. She got up off the couch. "Chickies, I have a client on his way here. I need to go change so I can meet with him." She started off towards her bedroom.

"But Mommy!" Savannah wailed. "We're going out!"

Alexa turned to her children and spoke sternly. "There will be no whining!" She continued in a softer tone. "You both need to understand what we've discussed many times. As of today, I don't go to the office anymore, but I'm still working, just like always. Remember? The only difference is that I'll be working at home now. And I expect you both to act like big children and be well-behaved. When I'm working – and especially when I have a client here – I expect you to keep yourselves busy. If you need anything at all, ask Lupe. Please don't disturb me. Do you understand?"

Both children sulked, but Alexa refused to feel guilty. She had made certain that the children hadn't been home the one time that Rafael had been there. Now he was on his way to her house, and she didn't want the children underfoot. She had never represented him, but he was probably in need of some sort of legal advice.

"Reggie? Savannah? Look at me. Remember, we talked about this? We all agreed before I decided to stop going to the office and work at home instead. Right?" The children cast their mournful eyes at their mother and nodded. "Okay then. We're clear?" They nodded again, resigned to their fate. Alexa sealed the deal. "This is a day that you have no school. But it's a workday for adults, and a client is coming here who needs my help. So, I'm sorry, but I can't buy dolls or go to the video store or anything else. I'd like to, but I have to help my client. I'm really sorry. Okay?" They nodded reluctantly. "Okay," Alexa said and hurried to her room.

No sooner had she changed into a skirt and blouse, brushed her hair, and applied a touch of lipstick than the doorbell rang. Lupe was on her way to the front door, but stopped short in the living room when she heard Alexa call out. "I'll get it."

Opening the door, Alexa saw Rafael Lamon standing there, his complexion ashen and his face sagging, his eyes red. She could have sworn he'd been crying.

"Rafael, you look awful! What's wrong?" When Rafael just stood there looking at Alexa as if he'd forgotten everything he ever knew, Alexa became even more alarmed. "Rafael? What is it? What's happened?"

Rafael looked at Alexa as if pleading for mercy and spoke as if uttering his last words. "I was fired."

6

That same Monday morning at precisely ten o'clock, five men entered the conference room of TriWorld Bank on Camden Drive.

Bob Stamen and Jason Alandro sat on one side of the long table. The three men sitting across from them wore hats and trench coats, obviously not dressed for Los Angeles weather and with good reason: they had arrived at the Bank directly from LAX and New York. They had taken their hats off on entering the bank, but kept their trench coats on.

Once they were all seated at the conference table, Stamen felt that as General Manager, he should preside over the meeting. Wanting to create an atmosphere of informality, he decided not to stand while speaking.

"Good morning, gentlemen. I understand that the three of you are from the Federal Reserve. I'm Bob Stamen, the General Manager of this branch, and this," he said, gesturing to Jason, "is Jason Alandro, the Executive Director in Charge of New Accounts. I've asked Mr. Alandro to join us because I believe he can shed some light on the matter we're discussing here. Mr.

Alandro has been with our bank for a long time, and I vouch for his integrity."

The man sitting in the middle of the three New Yorkers spoke without inflection or emotion. "I'm Jones, Federal Reserve." He nodded to the man sitting at his right. "This is Dave Mandon, my colleague." He pointed his head to the man sitting to his left. "And Mr. Martin here is from Justice." As he spoke, he reached into his wallet, brought out a card, and slid it across the table towards Stamen. Mr. Martin followed suit.

The General Manager stretched to pick up the two cards and read aloud. "John Jones, Federal Reserve Bank, Field Investigator," and "S. Martin, Department of Justice, Chief, Special Task Force." He nodded and looked across the table. "Well, Mr. Jones, I must say, this is not a meeting we welcome here at TriWorld." He smiled broadly. "It's nothing personal, of course, but TriWorld prides itself on having an excellent relationship with the Federal Reserve."

Mr. Jones answered dryly. "That may be, but this present breach of the regulations is a matter of grave concern both to us and Justice."

"Yes, of course," Stamen said, daring a smile, and quick to reassure. "It is to us as well. I've been in constant communication with our President, Mr. Han, and I want to assure you we've made this unfortunate turn of events our top priority. I'm certain you'll find we've taken care of the problem." He paused then and switched into host mode. "Before we continue, let me get us all some coffee." He clicked the intercom on. "Ask Judy to kindly bring in coffee for our guests, five cups."

John Jones, all business, turned to the trench coat on his right. "Give us a brief summary, Dan."

Dan Mandon opened the briefcase that lay at his side. He brought out a legal pad and turned to a page he referred to now and then as he spoke. "As you've been informed, we're here because, following your last audit, our auditor reported certain irregularities in procedures followed at your branch. In particular, violations of the U.S. Code section that strictly prohibit an international bank such as TriWorld from loaning money to U.S. citizens.

"As an international bank, TriWorld Bank's charter allows lines of credit to be established and loans to be extended only to non-U.S. nationals. Apparently, according to the auditor, the breach of the regulations was carried out through paperwork that enabled fraudulent practices on behalf of certain clients, including the use of matching funds, which was also illegal. This has occurred in more than one case in the Beverly Hills branch.

"Further, we believe that the branch has intentionally neglected to process certain required paperwork, thereby engaging in fraud and possible money laundering." Mandon put his pad down and looked pointedly at Stamen for an instant before he went on. Bob took the opportunity to refresh his smile.

"In short, our auditor has reported irregularities in procedures followed at your branch, irregularities that are violations of established banking regulations. In particular, regulations forbid TriWorld Bank, as an international bank, from establishing lines of credit or lending money to U.S. nationals." He closed the legal pad and looked up at Stamen. "Beyond that, several other illegal practices were discovered."

Bob Stamen hoped his broad smile, still in place, didn't look strained. He noticed that Jason had paled during Dave's oration and hoped his guests hadn't noticed. He tried to sound confident, but was only unnecessarily loud, so that Jason jumped slightly in his chair, startled. "That is our understanding as well," Stamen said to the three men. "And believe me when I say we were shocked! However, as I said, as soon as we were apprised of the situation, we conducted an in-depth internal investigation – very thorough. As sorry as we are that such a thing could have happened at TriWorld, I can report – both on Mr. Han's behalf as well as my own – that we have been able to successfully get to the bottom of this." The three New Yorkers glanced at one another.

There was a knock on the conference room door, and Judy entered holding a tray bearing five mugs all bearing the Bank slogan, *We are wherever you are,* a carafe of coffee, cream, and assorted sweeteners. She set the tray down on the conference table. "Would you like me to pour?" she asked Stamen.

Impatient with the interruption, John Jones answered for him. "We don't want anything."

"No, thank you," Stamen said. Judy lingered, looking at the three visitors. "That's all, Judy." Judy nodded and exited the room, leaving the tray untouched.

Stamen began again. "As I was saying, I can assure you that the seriousness of this situation is not lost on us. As President, Mr. Han has been personally involved in our internal investigation. The party responsible for the questionable activity you have described – and, I might add, solely responsible – has been terminated. He was the Director of South American accounts and directly responsible for the irregularities in question. He was responsible for those files, and we deeply regret that his illegal activity was undetected by us for so long."

Again, Dave and John Jones made eye contact. Dave asked, "And who is that person?"

"Rafael Villa Lamon," Bob Stamen answered.

"And did Mr. Lamon compose the paperwork used in processing those loans to U.S. citizens?" Dave asked.

Jason's head snapped up as Steman answered. "Absolutely. Mr. Alandro here was his direct superior. They went over the paperwork together, as all division heads are required to do. Apparently, it seems that Mr. Lamon saw fit to increase his pool of clients by altering some of those papers after they'd gone over them."

"And did Mr. Lamon orchestrate the illegal matching of funds with the Bank of Taiwan?" Dave asked.

Stamen nodded, "Yes, sir. He's the one." Jason Alandro turned to look at him but said nothing.

Jones took over from Dave. "We'd like to speak with Mr. Lamon," he said. "Please ask him to join us."

Bob shook his head and clasped his hands. "I'm afraid that's not possible. As I said, he's been terminated. But we can get you his contact information."

"Yes, do that," Dave said dryly.

"We'll want that right away," John Jones added. He stood and took his hat off the table. His colleagues followed suit.

"All right," Stamen said as he got to his feet. He turned to Alandro. "Jason, please get these gentlemen Mr. Lamon's contact information." Jason hurried out of the conference room. Stamen rubbed his palms together. "Well, gentlemen, now that we're done here, let me invite you to an early lunch. There's a wonderful new restaurant that's opened up right next door. Their fish is excellent. I think they'll open at eleven thirty."

The men weren't interested in eating. "We'll be heading back to the airport. They'll want a report today."

The three visitors made their way out of the conference room, and Stamen followed, nodding and smiling

7

Alexa took Rafael by the hand and led him inside her house.

"Come in. Tell me what happened." She sat on the living room couch. Rafael remained standing in the entry hall. "Sit down," she said. His blank look upset her greatly. "Rafael, sit," she repeated, patting the couch by her side. Finally, he sat. "Now, tell me what happened," she coaxed. Rafael was silent. "You were fired today?" He nodded. She continued cuing him. "This morning when you went to the office?" He turned his head slowly to one side and rubbed his neck.

"When were you fired, Rafael?" He still didn't respond. "What time were you fired?" She wanted to know. But more than that, she wanted him to speak.

Rafael shook his head and grimaced, holding onto his neck with one hand. He spoke softly, without looking at Alexa. "This morning. I got in at nine. I was in my office on the phone." As if not wanting to omit what might be an important fact, he added, "The landline. They walked into my office at nine minutes past nine." His voice was lifeless, but at least he was making full sentences now.

"How come you know the exact time?"

"The landline has a clock on it. I was talking to a client."

"Okay. You were on the phone with a client. Who walked in?"

"Bob and Jason. Bob Stamen is the General Manager, and Jason Alandro is my superior."

"Why were you fired?"

He shook his head slowly, his eyes unmoving, then said, "I don't know. They wouldn't tell me." With hands that shook, he took a cigarette out of his pocket and lit it. Alexa didn't have the heart to remind him that her house was a no-smoking zone. She got up and opened the several sets of French doors in the room and hurriedly found him an ashtray tucked deep inside a drawer in the bar, then sat back down on the couch.

"You don't know why you were fired, and they didn't tell you? That doesn't make sense. Did you do something you shouldn't have?"

"No."

Alexa frowned. This sounded weird. Surely, there must have been some reason he was terminated. "Tell me exactly what happened."

Rafael's gaze was fixed somewhere that Alexa sensed existed only in his memory. He spoke without looking at her in an unsteady voice, recounting the scene he found impossible to believe. "I was on the phone with a client – a potential client, a wealthy Argentinian. Bob walked in with Jason and…" he looked at Alexa, shaking his head, "fired me." He paused. Alexa waited.

Rafael sat with his hands thrown carelessly on his thighs, the lit cigarette between two fingers of his right hand, forgotten. Alexa took the cigarette from him and put it out in the ashtray. He looked at Alexa with eyes filled with questions. "I thought it was a joke – but it wasn't." He turned away then and scanned the living room before going on. His jaw tightened. "I asked why. I kept asking Bob why, but he wouldn't tell me. He said I had to leave right away, and I'd find out." His left hand rubbed at his hairline. Suddenly, in a burst of anger, he said, "Alexa, the security guard walked me to my car like I was a criminal. A fucking guard took my key and actually escorted me out of my office and to my car!"

They were both quiet then. Rafael sat hunched over. Alexa sat looking at him, digesting what he'd said. "I'm so sorry," she said. After a breath, she asked, "What will you do?"

Rafael looked over at her. He looked scared. She thought he was about to cry. He held his hands up. "I don't know. I have no idea. What should I do?"

Alexa thought about what to say. He was depending on her to answer the question. "They fired you with no explanation and no warning. You're going to need a lawyer. Did you sign anything?"

"No."

"Did anyone discuss severance pay?"

Rafael looked at her, realizing he'd been double duped, fired, and fired cheaply. "No."

Alexa thought that was strange. From what she knew of these situations, employees who were terminated were asked to sign hold-harmless papers and given severance pay. But perhaps that wasn't always the case; after all, she wasn't all that knowledgeable about employment law.

Rafael's cell phone rang. He looked at the caller ID and silenced it without answering. "You're not going to answer that?" Alexa asked.

"I can't talk to anyone. Anyway, it's a wrong number. It's the second time they've called. It's a New York area code."

Just then, Lupe entered the living room along with the movers. "Excuse me. Alexa, the movers are finished."

"Thanks, Lupe," Alexa said.

The man in charge spoke. "Anything else you need, miss?" When Alexa confirmed they were through, they left.

"My god, you're moving today?" Rafael said. "I'm sorry, Alexa." He sighed, adding this intrusion on her day to his insurmountable problems.

Reggie and Savannah came running into the room, excited. "Mommy, all your stuff is in the garage!" Reggie pronounced it 'gawage.'

Savannah was quick to correct him. "It's not the garage, Reggie! It's the guesthouse."

Their mother corrected her. "It's actually my office. Come say hello to Mr. Lamon. Mr. Lamon, these are my children, Reggie and Savannah."

The twins obediently went to Rafael and smiled shyly. Rafael made an effort to smile back and said, "Hello."

Alexa addressed Lupe. "Please make the twins some lunch. I'm going to the office with Mr. Lamon."

"Very good. Can I bring you and Mr. Lamon anything?" Lupe asked.

"Alexa, I need to take more Aleve," Rafael said, rubbing his neck and stretching it to one side.

Alexa turned to her housekeeper. "Could you please bring Mr. Lamon the bottle of Aleve?"

I have a bottle here," Rafael said, bringing the bottle of Aleve out of his jacket pocket. "I only need water."

Lupe nodded. "Would you prefer a cup of tea or coffee?"

"No, water is fine," he answered, then added, "Thank you."

The children left the room with Lupe. While waiting for water, Alexa asked Rafael about his neck. Rafael shrugged. "It's arthritis. The old man's pain." He said he was going to physical therapy. As an afterthought, he added, "I guess I won't be going any longer. My medical insurance is gone, too."

Alexa had to smile. Rafael was definitely not an old man.

Lupe returned with the glass of water. As he downed two pills, Alexa excused herself and went to the children's room. "Reggie, Savannah, I'm going to go to my office now with Mr. Lamon. I'll be working there. I'll see you when we're finished. Okay?" They nodded.

She returned to the living room and motioned for Rafael to follow her, then headed for the door to the backyard. She led him down the walkway where the air was filled with the fragrance of orange blossoms and ripening fruit that hung heavy on the nearby tree. Kumquats and orange blossoms mixed with the heavy scent of the budding narcissus running along the edge of the garden. Though the rose bushes alongside the wall were still bare, Alexa knew that soon her roses would be blossoming. It seemed too lovely a day for bad news.

On the way, Rafael said, "Your children are beautiful. God bless them."

They entered her new office through the French doors. Daylight made it unnecessary to turn on any lights. The movers had placed her desk facing the garden. That was lucky because it was exactly where she wanted it. Lupe must have orchestrated that. Her chair was set behind the desk, with the two client chairs in front. Boxes were strewn around the room. Those filled with books had been placed closest to the built-in shelves.

Rafael stood just inside the room, his shoulders slumped, his arms hanging at his sides. "Alexa, this is bad. I don't know what I'm going to do."

"Do you have an employment contract?" she asked.

"No. What the hell just happened?" Rafael almost shouted. His hands were at his temples, and Alexa again feared he was on the verge of a meltdown. It was as if the reality of what had happened in the last two hours was hitting him bit by bit, and his shock and realization were hyphenated by these short eruptions of anger.

"We're going to find out, Rafael. How long have you worked at the bank?"

"I don't know," Rafael answered. Oddly, his voice was normal again, and he shrugged. "More than seven years; probably close to eight years."

Alexa nodded. "Okay, so you may have an implied-in-law contract."

He held his breath. "Is that good? What does it mean?"

"Well," Alexa said, "basically, in this state, any employer can fire you just because they want to. They can fire you if they don't like the color of your tie. But there are exceptions. One exception is where you have an employment contract. If you don't actually have a written employment contract, but you've worked long enough, the courts reason that you may as well have a written contract. In both those cases, the employer needs to show good cause to fire you. There are other exceptions as well."

She went over to the boxes and looked down at them. "I'm going to find my old notes in all this and start calling around to find the right lawyer for you." She knelt and began to shuffle through the papers in one box.

Rafael's reaction was instant. "Can't you represent me?"

Alexa shook her head as if it were spasming. "Oh, no. You're going to either need a lawyer who specializes in employment law or one who specializes in banking law. I'm neither. You know that. I know a little about employment law, but I'm not a specialist. I've basically already told you everything I know about employment termination. I have a general practice." She began opening more boxes, searching for her notepads.

"You're the best lawyer there is."

"Don't be silly, Rafael. I'm not the right lawyer for you."

"You don't want to represent me because of our relationship."

She stopped what she was doing and looked up at him. "We don't have a relationship. We haven't had any relationship for a while now. So no, that's not why. It's because I'm not the right attorney for you." She resumed riffling through the boxes, searching.

After some seconds, Rafael said, "How am I going to pay an attorney?"

"You'll figure it out." Then she asked, "Have you told Viviana yet?"

Rafael sighed deeply. "I tried calling, but she didn't pick up. I didn't leave a message."

Alexa found what she was looking for. She stood, holding a spiral notebook somewhat worn by age. "Why don't you go home? Tell Viviana. Try to relax. You should be hearing from someone soon with an explanation." She put the notebook on her desk. "I'll make some calls."

Rafael sounded totally defeated. "I'll call you if I hear from anyone."

8

After Rafael left, Alexa sat at her desk, opened the notebook, and scanned her notes. She came to a page listing the names and contact numbers of attorneys she'd worked with or gotten to know over the years, mostly in L.A., San Francisco, and New York. Then she went through the list of attorney contacts on her phone. She didn't yet know if Rafael needed an employment lawyer or a banking lawyer. She knew several employment attorneys but no banking attorneys, so she began calling the lawyers she knew who might be able to point her to a capable banking attorney. She made a barrage of phone calls, crossing names off her list and scribbling down a few new names and phone numbers as they were recommended.

Two Los Angeles attorneys referred her to Sheri Lee, an attorney said to have substantial experience with the Federal Reserve and who had represented bankers in trouble with the agency. She was about to settle on her when Jerry Weingarten returned her call from New York. Jerry was a partner in a top law firm and married to Jana, one of Alexa's oldest and dearest friends. The two girls had met in their senior year of high school. Then, finding themselves together at UC Berkeley the following year, had done some serious bonding. Jana had gone into fashion and moved to New York, where she met and married Jerry. Their friendship had endured. Strangely, both had married attorneys, and both had two children, but whereas Alexa had divorced, Jana and Jerry remained in what seemed to be a happy marriage.

"Hey, Lex. What's up? Everything okay?"

"Yes, thanks for returning the call, Jerry."

"Sure. I was about to leave when I heard your message. You don't usually call the office. You're certain everything is okay?"

"Yes. I didn't want to disturb you at home," Alexa said.

"You never disturb," Jerry said. "So, how are you? Have you been snatched up yet?"

"I'm fine, and no, I haven't been snatched up yet," Alexa answered. "How's Jana?"

"She's fine. Off to another Paris show."

"Of course, she's fine. How could she not be with a husband like you? Kids are well?"

"Yup."

"Listen, Jerry. I need a referral. I need a banking lawyer in L.A., and since you're in with the big guns I –"

"Larry Bloom's your guy."

"Wow, you didn't even have to think. He's that good?"

"Yup. He's the best."

"Okay, Larry Bloom. Like flowers?"

"Yup. Like flowers. Century City."

"Okay, got it. Give Jana my love. Thanks, Jer."

"Just a sec, Lexie. Is someone in trouble with the Federal Reserve?"

"No, just fired from a bank. Can't figure out why."

"Okay, as long as it's not with the Federal Reserve. That's heavy stuff. Doesn't get much heavier."

"Well, I'll tell him he's lucky, then. Things could be worse. Bye."

9

While Alexa was on the phone with Jerry, Rafael received a third call from the same New York phone number as he was driving the freeways. He didn't answer.

When he got home, he listened to his three messages. His heart stopped. All three calls were from the Federal Reserve. Attorney Gilmore at the Federal Reserve in New York wanted to speak with him, Rafael V. Lamon, and it scared the hell out of him. He couldn't return the call. His fingers couldn't function, and his brain was numb with panic. He sat trembling, realizing that this call had something – and probably, everything – to do with his termination, but he didn't know what. Fear overtook him completely. His heart swooned, and his temperature shot up until he was soon nearly soaked with sweat. He smoked one cigarette, then lit another as he saw his entire life going up in flames. When he could get his fingers to punch the numbers, he called Alexa.

When she heard that he'd received three calls from the Federal Reserve, Alexa recalled Jerry's words and was probably more concerned than Rafael. She masked her concern with the somewhat comforting news that she had already found an excellent banking attorney and was about to call him to schedule an appointment. Hopefully, he could see them the next day. She advised Rafael not to return the call to the Federal Reserve just yet; he may as well wait until he consulted first with Attorney Bloom. In any event, since they were three hours ahead in New York, their offices would close soon. So, Rafael downed two shots of straight vodka then showered, dressed, and accompanied Viviana to his daughter's new in-laws for an early dinner. He told his wife the story of his day as they drove. Viviana kept repeating that she couldn't understand how Rafael could be unaware of the reason for his sudden termination.

Alexa called Larry Bloom's office as soon as Rafael had hung up. With the Federal Reserve involved, there was no longer any doubt that Rafael needed a banking lawyer, and he needed to retain one fast. Despite the fact that Bloom's schedule showed an all-day deposition set for the next day, on the strength of dropping Jerry Weingarten's name, Alexa secured an appointment with him at ten thirty. She called Rafael, and they arranged to meet outside his office building at twenty minutes past ten.

At ten twenty-five Tuesday morning, Alexa and Rafael entered the sparkling lobby of the newly built tower in Century City. No one entering could help but notice that "Larry Bloom, Attorney at Law" was scrawled across the lobby wall in massive letters behind the concierge's desk.

"That's impressive," Alexa said as they made their way to the elevators marked for the upper floors.

"That's expensive," Rafael said under his breath.

When they exited the elevator on the tenth floor, they found themselves in what was the midsection of an office. To their right, they saw cubicles with people bustling about on the other side of a glass door, and offices lining the far wall. To their left was a tasteful façade that pointed to the office entry. They entered, and when Alexa gave their name to the attractive receptionist dressed in black, they were promptly escorted to Attorney Bloom's office. Bloom left his deposition and joined them in minutes.

Larry Bloom was a seasoned Westside attorney in his mid 50s. His office was graced with photos of him on the slopes and on the golf course, some with various B-grade celebrities, others with his wife and child, both of whom were surprisingly young for a man of his age.

"Thank you for seeing us on such short notice," Alexa said.

"Jerry's the password around here," Bloom said, showing a perfect set of pearly whites. He sat in a white leather chair behind a large travertine desk. "So, what do we have?"

Alexa spoke for Rafael. "Let me explain. Mr. Lamon was a Director at TriWorld Bank International's Beverly Hills branch for almost eight years. He was fired yesterday morning without warning or explanation and was immediately escorted off the Bank's property by a security guard. He has no idea at all why he was fired. After he left, he received several calls from the Federal Reserve, which he didn't answer because he wasn't expecting them and didn't recognize the New York phone number. They left messages asking that he call them back. I advised him not to return the call until he consulted with you."

Alexa looked at Rafael, who had been sitting quietly in his chair. He looked miserable. This was not the man Alexa knew. Rafael had always been sophisticated and cool, smooth and confident. Now he looked beaten, small, and miserable.

Bloom picked up his pen, turned to Rafael, and started writing on his legal pad. "Give me some names, Rafael. Who fired you?"

"Bob – Robert Stamen, the General Manager of the Beverly Hills branch." Rafael's voice broke. "He came into my office with Jason Alandro, my supervisor and immediate superior. Alandro is the Executive Director in Charge of New Accounts."

"Okay, and I think TriWorld International's headquarters are in New York?"

Rafael nodded, then rubbed his neck. "That's right. And the Bank's President, Lee Han, lives in Virginia He doesn't like to travel, so his place in Virginia is the unofficial headquarters." He was rubbing his neck.

Bloom didn't look up. "Okay, and you have no idea what the Federal Reserve wants to talk to you about?"

"None." Rafael said.

"Okay," Bloom went on. He looked up at Rafael. "Tell me what you do as a Director. Simply. In terms I can understand."

"I'm – I was – the Director of South American accounts. It's simple. I bring in accounts. I'm from Argentina. I'm well known in the Latin community – I lecture and I have a weekly 30-minute TV show on satellite TV. I interview people and talk about different things, so people in the community hear about me, know my name. I promote the Bank to those who need a loan or require a line of credit, so long as they are not U.S. citizens. There's a little more to it, but in a nutshell, that's it."

"What else?"

"I try to sell bank products to my clients – you know, credit cards, whatever." He stretched his neck towards one shoulder and grimaced, and then towards the other shoulder and grimaced again.

"I see," Bloom said. "And that's it? I mean, you were a Director at TriWorld Bank International. That's pretty impressive."

"TriWorld is a corporation, Mr. Bloom. Director is an almost meaningless title. Executive Director – that at least has some power, but Director? Corporate directors are a dime a dozen, as Americans say. I did whatever I was told to do. I took orders. That's all."

Bloom had stopped taking notes and sat with his elbows poised on his desk, his fingers making a steeple. He looked at

Rafael for a moment, as if appraising him. "Okay, Rafael, I'd be happy to represent you. You seem like an upstanding man. This is probably a little mix-up."

At this, Rafael let out an audible sigh of relief. Bloom smiled. "Why don't we do this: Let me have you sign a retainer. Then I'll call the number they left, and I'll speak with the Federal Reserve on your behalf this afternoon or tomorrow and see what it is they want from you."

Alexa reached for Rafael's arm. "It worked out for the best that you didn't answer the phone. This way, your attorney will speak with them."

Bloom rose and spoke to Rafael, "I'll call you after I've spoken with them. A retainer agreement will be ready for you in a minute if you'll just wait here." He nodded at them both. "Please excuse me. I need to get back to the deposition. They're waiting for me in the conference room."

Rafael got up. "Thank you for helping me. I'm very scared. I didn't sleep at all last night." He started to tear. "I'm extremely nervous."

"I completely understand," Bloom said. He came around his desk and held out his hand. As Rafael took it in his, he added, "The Federal Reserve is pretty intimidating. They make the combined FBI and CIA look like nothing." Rafael started at this, beginning to realize how truly dire his situation was.

Alexa smiled at Bloom from her chair. "Thank you. I'll let Jerry know we met."

Bloom smiled. "Please give him my best. He's quite a guy. Remind him he owes me 18 holes."

Bloom left his office, and Rafael sat down again to wait for his retainer agreement to be drawn up and delivered. Alexa took the opportunity to change the battery in one of her hearing aids.

"Did you hear everything he said?" Rafael asked.

"Yes. It just died this second."

When the secretary brought the retainer agreement to Rafael, he scanned it, then gave it to Alexa, who also scanned it before he signed it and was given a copy.

Exiting Bloom's building, Rafael didn't waste a second lighting up.

"So, what do you think?" Alexa asked him.

"Alexa, he's expensive," Rafael said.

"Well, you need the best."

"$700 an hour and a $20,000 retainer for a phone call?"

"You said you can take it out of your retirement fund."

"I don't know how long I'll have to be living off that fund," Rafael said. "And there's not all that much in it."

"I'm sure Bloom isn't trying to get rich off of your case, Rafael. He's just covering himself. He'll charge you hourly and subtract that from the $20,000 and return the remainder to you."

"Where are you going now?" Rafael asked as they walked through the parking lot.

"I have to get back and do some work and some organizing. The computer guy is coming to set up some things for me."

Rafael followed Alexa to her car. "Alexa. I miss you."

They were steps away from Alexa's BMW. "I'm right here."

"You know what I mean."

"I'm surprised your mind is anywhere but on Larry's phone call to the Federal Reserve," she said.

"I'm a mess. I need you to relax me, to calm me down."

Alexa got into her car. "Go home, Rafael. You need your rest. Call me when you hear from Bloom." And with that, she shut her door.

10

For almost fifteen years Alexa had left home for the office every day, except for the last month of her pregnancy and the first two months after the twins were born. The next day, she was happy to wake up, walk the children to school, then roll into the guesthouse to start her workday with a cup of home-brewed coffee.

Sitting at her desk that Tuesday morning, she hoped to finish organizing the office and get some work done. She had plugged in her computer but was having some problems connecting to the Internet from the new office and hoped that would be resolved today as well. At about nine thirty, after having organized for about an hour, her phone rang. It was Mark Galligher, the buyer of a subdivision one of her clients owned. Mark was acting on behalf of himself and his father. The closing of escrow had been postponed several times over the last two months, so the seller brought Alexa in last Thursday to finally close the deal. Three phone calls later, Mark was still stalling for a reduction in price of $120,000. Recognizing the caller ID, Alexa went to her desk, quickly opened her client's file on her computer, and answered the call.

"Good morning, Mark. What's the status of our escrow?"

"We're wondering if your side is still alive."

Alexa smiled slyly. "Lionel's always been ready to close."

"Listen, Ms. Starr, that's actually why I'm calling. My dad and I really want the property, but we just don't have the cash right now. We can pay that $120,000 after it's developed. How about it?

"How about this, Mark? What if I can persuade my client to accept $60,000 now and another $20,000 a month for the next 3 months? That way, the pressure is off, and you and your dad will have what you want. Every day you wait, you lose on the other side in construction and delivery."

There was a pause. "Well, that might work. Let me talk to Dad."

"Okay. I'll wait to hear. Say by tomorrow, 5 pm? That's really the best we can do. Bear in mind that if we sell to another for less, you may well be found liable for the difference, and you'll have nothing to show for it." After she disconnected, she made some notes on the file. She would have to email a short note to her client, Lionel Loft, letting him know that she'd communicated their new offer to Mark Gallagher and given him the deadline they'd agreed to. She hoped they could close the matter tomorrow. She went back to organizing her law books on the bookshelf and enjoying her coffee. After that, she had a contract to draw up.

The phone rang again. It was Rafael, but it was impossible to understand what he was saying. "Rafael? What's wrong? I can't understand you. Are you okay? What? Speak louder. Are you crying? I can't understand you."

She finally understood him to say, "I'm coming over."

"Okay. Come to the back. I'm in the office."

11

When Alexa saw Rafael, she was appalled. He was in even worse shape than the day he'd been fired. He held his cigarette in a hand that shook badly. His lips were trembling. He looked ashen and his eyes were red. He collapsed onto one of the chairs in front of her desk, and she sat in the other one. He tossed the remains of his cigarette into her almost empty coffee cup. He was biting his upper lip.

"Speak to me," Alexa said. "You heard from Bloom. He called?"

"I went to his office. I'm in shit trouble."

"What happened?"

Rafael put his head in his hands. "They're out to get me."

"Who?"

"The Federal Reserve."

"Tell me exactly what Bloom said."

He looked at Alexa and rubbed his red eyes as if to soothe them. "He said TriWorld gave me to the Federal Reserve with a bow on top. No," Rafael held his head between his palms, "he said, they 'gifted me in a box with a bow on top.'"

Alexa shook her head in disbelief. "You're kidding." Rafael looked at her but said nothing. He obviously wasn't kidding. "Why? What did they say you did?" When Rafael just looked at her with swollen eyes, she asked, "Think. Are you absolutely positive you've done nothing wrong?" He nodded and his head went back onto his hands.

"Well, what else did Bloom say?"

Rafael sniffed and made a face of distaste. "He wants me to write a letter to the Federal Reserve explaining what I do and the process I go through with each new account. He wants it by tomorrow morning."

"Okay," Alexa said. "Start writing."

Rafael looked up and sighed. With every breath he slouched further into his chair. Finally, he said, "Can I write it here?"

Alexa was more than a little concerned for Rafael but tried to maintain an air of normalcy. "Sure, if you won't get distracted by my phone calls and my work." She gave Rafael a pen and a fresh legal pad. "I'll be using the computer. You can write it out. Bloom's secretary will type it up if that's what he wants." Rafael took the pen.

During the next couple of hours, while Alexa made calls relevant to the first draft of an LLC agreement she was drawing up, Rafael said nothing. He wrote down a few words and stopped, then wrote another few words then stopped and wrote nothing more. He lit cigarette after cigarette, looked into space and sulked. He got up and paced.

When she had completed the contract, Alexa walked around her desk to Rafael and confirmed that he'd written only one sentence.

"What's the problem?" She asked.

"I can't do this."

"Ok, let's start off with when you were first employed by the Bank."

"2008."

"Don't tell me. Write it down." He wrote, *I was hired by TriWorld Bank in 2008.* "Good. And you were hired as a Director?" He nodded. "Write it down. He wrote, I *was hired as Director of South America Accounts.* "Who hired you?"

He wrote, *I was hired by the General Manager of the Bank, Robert Stamen.* "Who – I'm sorry, I don't remember his name – who was your immediate supervisor?" He wrote, *My immediate supervisor was Jason Alandro.* Excellent. Now write how often you met with Jason… And what were your duties?... And what was the first step you had to go through with every client you had?... And then?... And then?... Keep going… Is that all the steps?"

There was a pause before he said, "Yes."

"Good. And who gave you the paperwork that you had your clients sign?... The attorneys? Okay, write it… That's it. You're finished." He was done. Rafael thanked her.

"You're welcome. What time are you supposed to see Larry tomorrow?"

"I'll be at his office at 11:30."

She nodded. "Tomorrow is my day for doctors and tests."

Rafael looked as if he'd been jolted by an electricity. "What's wrong with you?"

"Nothing. It's all just checkups."

"Really?"

"Really."

"I don't know what I'd do if anything happened to you." Rafael bit his upper lip. He was about to lose control. "I wouldn't know what to do. I'm a nervous wreck as it is."

"I don't blame you," Alexa said. "But you have to stay calm and clear. Let me know what happens tomorrow."

"Alexa, let's go have a drink somewhere."

"I can't. I'm picking up the kids from school early today and expecting the computer guy to come." She glanced at the time. "In fact, I have to get going right now." She began shuffling papers, closing the windows and doors that she'd opened when

Rafael had lit up, and turning off the computer and lights. "Okay, that does it. Time to leave."

Rafael went to her. "Alexa, you have no idea how much I miss you. I dream of you."

She brushed him off. "Go home to your wife. She's worried about you.

12

Alexa couldn't help but worry that her divorce would affect her young children badly. But in fact, the twins seemed to be doing well.

They had no apparent problems, and their teachers said they were socializing normally. When Alexa decided to divorce, she and Ben had gone to a child psychologist to learn how to best deal with the children, not quite three years old. They were told that the most important thing for children of their age was consistency; knowing that they would be taken care of and that they had not done anything wrong. And so, Alexa and Ben had sat the twins down and explained that Mommy and Daddy still liked each other very much, but they would now be living separately. That meant that Savannah and Reggie would have two houses, one with Mommy and one with Daddy, and both loved them to the stars and back. The advice had proven to be excellent. Recently, while putting Savannah to sleep, Alexa had asked her how she felt about having two houses. To her mother's surprise, Savannah had answered without hesitation. "I like it. I have two bikes and two sets of toys. I have friends here and friends at Daddy's house. It's fun, Mommy."

Today, there was a teacher's meeting, so Alexa picked her children up from school at lunchtime. The two sat, as they always did, in the back seat. On the way to lunch, with the radio on and turned up, Savannah said, "Mommy, Reggie doesn't have his seatbelt on."

Alexa had been thinking about Rafael's case. She looked at her daughter through the rearview mirror. "What?" she asked. "Reggie doesn't like his meatball sauce?"

The children burst into gales of laughter. It was another of their mother's memorable gaffes, courtesy of her poor hearing, and they loved them all. They also liked that when they came very close to her ears, she made a whistling sound.

Alexa had explained that it was feedback from her hearing aids. They didn't understand what that was, but they knew they had the only mother whose ears made that cool sound. Alexa laughed with them. But for the billionth time, she wished she could hear well.

She surprised the twins with a pizza lunch at Mulberry's on Canon Drive. Over lunch, she told her children how much she loved being with them. She told them how happy she was when she spent time with them and that she wished she could be with them all the time. But she had to work to pay for the things they had – although Daddy also helped pay. She told them how proud she was of them for being so grown-up and understanding that she had to work. They asked how Mr. Lamon was and asked if she had helped him. She answered in the affirmative and said he still needed help. After lunch, she took them to Paint a Posy. Savannah painted a special cup for Lupe, and Reggie painted a gargoyle.

Later that night, when the twins were fast asleep, Alexa showered and lounged on her bed wearing silk pajamas, a break from her usual night garb of shorts or sweats and a T-shirt. The lights were out, and she was watching The Crown with the volume turned up. Then Sheyanne called, and she put the TV on mute. Sheyanne was Alexa's best friend and the closest thing she had to a confessor. Sheyanne knew almost everything about Alexa's life. She knew about her past indiscretion with Rafael and that he was back in her life.

"So, you haven't slept with him again, right? Not once since that time?" Sheyanne asked.

"Right!"

"Wow! Lexie, the way you talked about how amazing it was – that's control!"

Alexa reached over to her nightstand and took a swig of water from the sports bottle. "Yeah, well, it's not easy," she said, "He keeps pushing, and I'd like to. But it was a mistake I won't repeat."

"It's just as well. Besides, isn't there some law or something about not sleeping with your client?"

Alexa shifted on her bed. "He wasn't my client then, and he's not my client now. Anyway, it's not going to happen again. Honestly? He's too hot. He's also married. Anyway, he's totally devastated, and I can't blame him. The fucking Federal Reserve! Shit!" She shook her head. "It's heavy. He's so miserable that I just have to stay cool, you know? Act like it's not such a big deal."

"Yeah. And it must be hard for you, too."

"It breaks my heart to see him like this because my guess is he's not guilty. It's really fucked up. He swears he's done nothing wrong, and I believe him. He's way too conservative and too cautious to have done anything wrong. But meanwhile, his entire life is screwed up."

Alexa sighed so deeply that Sheyanne changed the subject. "So, tell me again, what's the plan for tomorrow?"

"A mammogram and hearing test."

"Why a hearing test? Has your hearing gotten worse?"

"No, it's still the same in both ears. I still need to test. It's like you and your glasses –you need to have your vision tested every year, right? Even though my hearing most probably hasn't changed, I still get tested."

"Right," Sheyanne said.

"What did people do before they had aids? I can't hear a thing without them."

"I know, girl. You don't hear so great with them either." They both laughed.

"Can you imagine me with one of those huge cones in my ear like you see in those old pictures?" They laughed again. "So, seriously, girl, what about you? How are things with Joshua? He's a good guy, and he really loves you, Sheyanne."

"Yeah, I know. I love him, too." She paused. "We're now officially living together."

"What? That's terrific! Good for you!"

"Yeah."

"When did that happen?"

"Over the weekend. It's about time, don't you think?"

Alexa chuckled. "Well, it happened."

"Lexie, I don't want to play house. I want to get married! I want to marry Joshua! If he doesn't propose soon, I swear, I'll either leave him or kill him – or both."

They giggled, and then Alexa said, "Give him some time. He's on the right track, he's just moving slowly. I think he needs to ease into the idea. I'll have a talk with him and get him to pop the question. But right now, I need some sleep."

"Sure thing, girlfriend, Night. Love you," Sheyanne answered.

"Love you more," Alexa said. "Give Joshua my love, too."

The next day, Alexa had her annual mammogram and waited in the radiologist's office until she got the results. Hearing that everything was okay, she breathed a sigh of relief, then went for her annual hearing test, the exam Alexa loathed;

the one test she was always certain she'd fail. She'd long gotten used to wearing her hearing aids but had never gotten used to her hearing deficit. There were the obvious nuisances she ran up against several times a day, of either not hearing people at all or hearing them incorrectly. She was the Near-Sighted Mr. Magoo of the hearing world. More often than not, what she misheard made people laugh aloud. Beyond that, she had to give up courtroom litigation, and she'd loved arguing before the judge, tripping up opposing witnesses and addressing the jury.

Her audiologist wanted to fit her with the newest aids. She led Alexa to the soundproof room, closed the door, put a one-sided headphone on her, then went to a console, and the test began. Alexa tried to hear various tones in one ear, then the other, often wondering whether she had really heard them or was second-guessing the audiologist. Next, she had to repeat words spoken at different volumes, both without and with the use of aids. It was beyond frustrating to sit straining her ears to hear tones and words she either couldn't hear or couldn't understand no matter how hard she pinned her ears. It was sheer hell. Finally, it was all over, and the good news was that her hearing loss, though moderately severe, hadn't worsened. After a discussion with the audiologist, she was fitted with the latest aids using the newest available technology. Hopefully, they would allow for more clarity and better overall hearing. She would be notified to pick them up as soon as they arrived.

Gathering her things to leave, Alexa noticed she'd gotten several calls while she was being tested. One call was from Mark Galligher, and three were from Rafael. She knew Rafael was calling after having met with Bloom.

Anxious to call him back, but unable to hear him in a noisy environment, she waited until she was in her car, then dialed his mobile. "Rafael? I know you called, but I was with the doctor and couldn't answer. How did it go?"

"Get me another lawyer."

13

Alexa swerved to avoid hitting the car in front of her.

"What? Why?"

"He can't be my attorney."

She looked in the rear-view mirror, wanting to move off the road and pull over. "You're talking about Larry Bloom? Why?"

"He doesn't believe I'm innocent. And I can't pay him anymore money."

"Hold on a second." She quickly pulled the BMW over and stopped the car. "He wants more money?"

"Half the money I paid him is gone and he wants me to replenish it," Rafael said.

Alexa gasped. "Half the $20,000 retainer?"

"Yes," she heard him say.

"My God!"

"And he doesn't believe me. He thinks I'm guilty," Rafael said.

"Why do you say that?" Alexa asked, confused. "Did he say something?"

"I can tell. I feel it. He barely met with me. He wants to see me back in his office in a few minutes. He says it's important. He probably wants more money. I'm outside in my car right now. I'm about to leave."

"No, don't do that. Meet with him; see what he wants. Don't give him any more money. Ask for an hourly invoice. See if you still feel that way after you meet with him again."

When they hung up, Rafael remained in his Volvo, hunched over the steering wheel. Alexa sat for a moment in her car as well, then sighed, looked at the time, and pulled back into traffic. She returned Mark Galligher's call. Galligher was calling to say his father had agreed to the terms she'd offered yesterday. They had a deal. She told him she would draw up the new contract and send it out within twenty-four hours, then called her client with the news. At least there was some good news in the world.

"That calls for champagne," Lionel said. "Expect it and please accept it with my thanks, Alexa." She hung up and smiled weakly to herself, wishing there was some good news for Rafael. He loved champagne.

When she opened the front door of her house, Alexa was met by Lupe. "Mr. Lamon is here."

Surprised, Alexa looked around. "Where?"

"He's in the guesthouse – sorry, Alexa – your office. I didn't think you'd want him waiting here." And then in a confidential tone, "He was smoking."

"That's fine. But I was just talking to him. When did he get here?"

Lupe shrugged. "Maybe five minutes ago."

"Okay, I'll just put my handbag down and go see him. The children okay?"

"Yes. Mr. Marzi called. He'll be picking them up from school today."

"Right. He switched nights. Thanks, Lupe." She was headed for her bedroom when Lupe called after her.

"Alexa." Alexa turned back. Lupe was shaking her head. She looked concerned. "Mr. Lamon? He doesn't look good."

Though Alexa knew that Rafael was devastated, she was still unprepared for what she saw when she entered her office that day. He hadn't bothered to turn on the lights. He was sitting in a corner of her office with his legs apart, his elbows propped on his thighs, his head down, crying. She hurried to him.

"Rafael, what's happened?" Rafael only shook his head, his mouth set, tears running down his face. "Rafael, speak to me. What did Larry say? Is it the money?"

Rafael pointed lamely to a sheet of paper lying on her desk. Alexa picked up the sheet of paper, glanced at it, noting that the letterhead was from the Federal Reserve Bank. She looked back at Rafael. "You got a letter from the Federal Reserve." Rafael said nothing. She read aloud, her eyes skimming through the document dated April 4, 2016.

The Federal Reserve Board of Governors.... impose assessment of a civil money penalty against you.... fines up to $25,000 a day... and refer you to the Justice Department.... Apparent violations of banking laws.... violations began January 15, 2014.... TriWorld Bank ("TWB") entered into an arrangement with Bank of Taiwan ("BC")... loans to domestic parties related to customers of TWB... secured against deposits at TWB... TWB indemnified BC against losses... TWB began placing money with BC... ultimately used to fund loans made by BC... in violation of Federal banking law... prohibited loan arrangements...

Order to show cause ... submit any and all facts within your knowledge to mitigate the proposed fines and penalties as well as charges to be brought against you... any additional evidence or information that may serve to mitigate... within 10 business days from the date of this letter to me... All should be verified and documented... tax records for the last three years...

If you have any questions…

It was signed, *"Gary Gilmore, Attorney, Federal Reserve."*

"My God. $25,000 a day since 2014 and then referred to the Justice Department?" Alexa slammed the desk. She turned to Rafael. "It's not going to happen!" She marched around the office, turning on the lights, opening the door and windows. "Did you hear me? Rafael! It's not going to happen!"

"I want to die," Rafael said between tears.

She handed him a box of Kleenex. "Stop!" When he didn't take it, she set the box on the chair between his legs.

"I do." He pushed his two palms into his wet eyes.

Alexa spoke impatiently. "Nonsense. What did Larry say?"

Rafael shrugged. "He wants me to write the letter they're asking for."

"They want the proffer by the 13th of April," Alexa said. "That's next Wednesday."

Rafael looked up at her with red, swollen eyes. "What's a proffer?"

"It's just an offer of evidence. It's your defense. It shows why you're innocent. They want you to tell them why you're not guilty."

Rafael digested that. "But, Alexa, how the hell am I going to do that? How can I show them that I haven't done anything illegal? Don't they have to show that I did do something illegal? Isn't that the law in America?"

Alexa shook her head. "In case you haven't yet noticed, this isn't a court of law. This is the Federal Reserve. You have the burden of proof. Now, let's see. Today is Thursday, April 7th. That leaves today and tomorrow; then there's the weekend, and then Monday and Tuesday. It's due on Wednesday. It's far too important for you to write. You need Bloom to help you write it. You need a lawyer who's experienced with the Federal Reserve to do it with you."

"I told you, I don't want him to be my lawyer."

"Why? He's an expert in banking law."

"Now that the letter's come, he wants more money. And he wants me to write it."

Alexa's lower lip disappeared into her mouth, but she couldn't hold back. "If you can't pay Bloom, where do you plan to get $25,000 a day times the number of days the Federal Reserve has you down for?" The look on Rafael's face made her turn away.

"But Alexa! The man doesn't believe I'm innocent." When she looked back, Rafael was pointing to the letter on the desk. "He didn't believe me before that came. And I can't write that letter! That proffer!"

Alexa crossed her arms. She wasn't sure what to do or say, but she had to console him. "Okay. If you're sure you don't want Bloom to represent you, we'll go meet with Sheri Lee. I'll call right now for an appointment.

"Who's Sheri Lee?" Rafael asked.

"She's an attorney with a lot of experience with the Federal Reserve. She'd have been my first choice if Jerry hadn't raved about Bloom like he did." Rafael reverted to his 'head in hands' pose. "I'll tell her it's urgent and see if we can get an appointment for tomorrow since the proffer is due next Wednesday. It'll be a long shot. Friday's a busy day."

Rafael looked up at her, his tears streaming down. "How the hell am I supposed to pay her? My 401K is almost wiped out. I'm out of a job, and Sofia's wedding cleaned me out. I'm borrowing money from my cousin. I can't get another job. No one will hire me. Can't you please represent me? You believe me. And you're a good lawyer."

"I keep telling you, that's absolutely ridiculous! For you to even think about putting your life in my hands when I know dip about banking is ridiculous! Did you read that letter? Come on,

Rafael! Stop it! You flatter me, but absolutely no way would I do that."

"You're better than Bloom."

"I'm less expensive."

"And better. What the hell did he do? He made a call. You and I wrote the letter," Rafael said.

Alexa couldn't argue the point.

14

Alexa was able to get an appointment with Sheri Lee for late Friday afternoon. Rafael came to her house and she drove them, taking the 1-10 freeway downtown. Rafael hadn't been in the United States when Love Story came out and Alexa had not yet been born, but she'd seen the movie and assumed it was filmed in the offices of Sheri Lee. Rich wood paneling was everywhere, red Persian rugs adorned the dark hardwood floors, and a spiral staircase stood in the middle of the reception area.

Alexa and Rafael were shown to a large conference room where Alexa took a seat in the middle of a table that could have easily seated 30. Rafael sat at her left. She opened her attaché, brought out her laptop, and brought up Rafael's file to a page with questions she had prepared to ask Attorney Lee. Wanting to lock that page on the computer, she also brought out a legal pad and pen to jot notes down on. She put the letter from the Federal Reserve on the table. Just as she finished setting up, Attorney Lee walked into the conference room and introduced herself. She was a serious-looking, matronly woman with silver hair styled in a shoulder-length flip. She wore no discernible make-up other than a bright shade of red lipstick that emphasized her blue eyes. Her thick middle showed under the light gray jacket she paired with a loose-fitting gray skirt. Her shoes were as sensible as she probably was. Simple gold-rimmed glasses hung on a black chain.

After Alexa summarized Rafael's plight, Attorney Lee spoke. "I think I understand the picture." She turned to Rafael. "Mr. Lamon, you are certain you've done nothing irregular? It's best if I know anything that may have been done, whether intentional or unintentional. That way, I'm ahead of the game."

Rafael made eye contact with her. "I've done nothing wrong."

"Very well," the attorney said.

Alexa launched into her list of questions, asking one after the other, taking notes as Attorney Lee answered each. When she was through with all her questions, she pushed the letter across the table. "We received this letter from the Federal Reserve yesterday asking for a letter, a proffer explaining why Mr. Lamon is not guilty."

Ms. Lee nodded. "That's standard in a case like this." Alexa was somewhat relieved to hear that.

"But how can he proffer negative evidence? I mean, he didn't do anything wrong. How can he prove that? What's he supposed to write?"

Attorney Lee put on her glasses, glanced over the first page of the letter from the Federal Reserve, flipped to the second page, and read the last paragraph, then flipped back to the first page to check the date. She took her glasses off and addressed Alexa. "They want a response within 10 days. I believe that would be next week."

"Yes," Alexa said. "April 13. That's next Wednesday."

"Oh, my! Well, I'm afraid I just couldn't take this case."

Rafael and Alexa showed their disappointment on their face. "You could ask for a continuance," Alexa said.

To her surprise, Attorney Lee laughed. "A continuance?" She shook her head. "You apparently haven't had much to do with the Federal Reserve. They don't give continuances, my dear."

Alexa didn't get it. "But if you tell them that you are new to the case and that you need time to familiarize yourself with the facts..."

"No, no. No continuances. Period." Attorney Lee set her forearms down on the table and leaned forward. "This is not a court that you're dealing with. The Federal Reserve is in many ways more powerful than the President. No continuances."

Alexa couldn't believe it. "Not even a few days?"

"My dear, you'd be striking gold – making history! – If you got even one day. It never happens."

Alexa's shoulders fell as her hopes deflated. "I'm so disappointed. He really needs you. Is there really no way you could see to representing him, Ms. Lee?"

"No, I am sorry. I should also mention that our fees are quite high. I would require a retainer of at least $25,000 against my hourly rate of $850." There was a squeak as Rafael reacted by pushing his chair away from the table. "But, let me say this," Sheri Lee went on. "And I hope you'll trust that I know what I'm saying. From the questions that you've asked, Ms. Starr," – she motioned to Alexa's laptop – "I'm relatively certain that you would do a fine job of representing Mr. Lamon yourself."

Alexa was stunned. "Me?"

"Yes. All your questions were exactly on point. You seem to have an excellent grasp of the issues. You can certainly research the regulations, the law, and all that. But there's no doubt that you could represent him quite well." With that, Sheri Lee ended the meeting by rising. Rafael also stood up. Flustered, Alexa gathered her legal pad, crammed her laptop into her attaché, and rose as well.

"I wish you luck, Mr. Lamon."

"Thank you," Rafael said, rising.

"And you, Ms. Starr."

"Thank you," said Alexa, not at all sure that Attorney Lee merited her thanks.

15

Alexa and Rafael were stone silent as they left Lee's office, rode the elevator down, exited her building, went out onto the street and got into Alexa's car. Then, no so sooner had they put on their seat belts, than they started a 'he-she' argument that lasted the entire trip home.

He: "You heard her. She said you could do it."

She: "She doesn't know what she's talking about."

He: "She didn't have to say that."

She: "Look, she felt bad that she can't help you. She was flattering me."

He: "But you asked all the right questions. She said so."

She: "I went to law school. I know how to spot issues. That doesn't mean I know anything about the Federal Reserve or anything about banking. My God! They don't even grant continuances!" She looked out the window at the other drivers. "Besides, she probably thinks I've got an army of law clerks or associate attorneys to help me."

He: "No one will care as much as you do."

She: "I hate to see injustice. If you didn't do anything wrong

– and I believe that you didn't – you shouldn't have to go through this. The Bank has apparently scapegoated you. That's despicable. It shouldn't happen. So, I care."

He: "You mean it's not because you love me?" He was actually smiling.

She: Looking at him and squinting. "How come you're in such a good mood? Why aren't you crying? You have a letter to the Federal Reserve due on Wednesday, this is Friday and you don't have a lawyer."

He: "Because now I know that you can do it. You just have to say you will."

She: "Look, this isn't like seducing me into bed. This is your life! Jail! Financial wipeout! Why are you being so goddamn stubborn?"

He: "Because I know how good you are."

She: "You're crazy, stupid."

He: "Alexa?"

She: "What?"

He: "Will you please be my lawyer?"

She: "Stop!"

He: "I can't stop. I need you."

She: "I'm tired of hearing you say you need me."

He: "I do."

She: "Well, I'm tired of you needing me."

They were quiet for a moment. Alexa made an unsafe lane change and after almost side swiping another car caught her breath.

He: "Alexa?"

She: "What?"

He: "I'm not asking you. I'm begging you. Please be my lawyer."

She looked over at him. He was looking at her imploringly. After gritting her teeth, biting her lip and silently cursing, she spoke, daring him. "I'll tell you what, Rafael." They made eye contact. "This is Friday. Go home, talk to Viviana. Tell her what I'm telling you. Tell her I know absolutely nothing about banking or banking law. Tell her I've never spoken to anyone at the Federal Reserve. I didn't even know that they don't grant continuances. You heard Lee. Tell her they don't fuck around. The two of you talk it over. Think about it over the weekend. Seriously. If you both agree that you should put your life in my hands, let me know on Monday and if you're still stupid enough to want me to represent you then yes, I will."

He: "Thank you."

She just shook her head.

16

Alexa's weekend was a welcome break. Saturday, she attended the twins' soccer practice and their classmate's birthday party. On her return home, she took delivery of six bottles of fine champagne. Lionel Loft was as good as his word. The enclosed card simply said, "With thanks to my favorite lawyer."

Saturday night she saw a play with an old law school friend at the Ahmanson. Sunday, she and the twins had brunch at her mother's house. Her mother surprised Savannah with an easel that had a blackboard on the other side, a box of paints, and a box of chalk. She had a Lego spaceship for Reggie. "These aren't just any toys," she said, justifying them to Alexa. "They'll use their hands and they'll need to use their imagination."

Afterwards, Alexa took the twins to the park where the three played Frisbee. When they came home, Alexa put the easel and the Legos in her office nook; they could play with them when she wasn't meeting with a client. The twins took showers and watched television, and Alexa treated herself to a relaxing bath. Afterwards, she called Sheyanne, then finally finished reading a copy of Vanity Fair that was two months old before sitting down with the children to enjoy Lupe's fabulous spaghetti dinner.

Monday morning, dressed in black leggings and a pink surfer T-shirt, gray and pink Nikes, a Dodger cap on her auburn ponytail, a gray hoodie tied around her waist and carrying a bottle of water, Alexa walked the twins to school and was working off the calories she'd collected over Sunday brunch and dinner. As she power walked through her neighborhood, she noted that several homes in her area were either being demolished or under construction. She took that to be a sign that property values in her section of Beverly was once again rising and that, of course, was a good thing. Turning a corner, her cell phone rang. She answered without breaking her stride to look at the caller ID. "Hello?"

Recognizing Viviana's voice, Alexa stopped walking and almost stopped breathing. "Good morning, Viviana. How are you?"

"I'm well, Alexa. How are you?"

"I'm fine, thank you. How's the new bride?"

"Sofia is very happy, thank you."

"I'm glad. And again, congratulations."

"Alexa, thank you for the help you have given Rafael."

"Oh, no problem." What could she say? "I know you're both going through a hard time."

"Yes. It is very hard. He is very upset, as you know." Alexa looked up and watched a crow land on a branch high up, just ahead of her, where a line of crows had already formed. Had she heard that crows foretold bad news? She knew what was coming and cringed. "We would be pleased for you to be his lawyer."

"Viviana. It's up to you. This is an extremely serious situation, and, as I explained to Rafael, it's an area of the law I truly know nothing at all about. I hope you understand that. I imagine he's explained that to you."

"Yes, he told me. But Rafael has faith in you. I think that is important. He believes you are an excellent attorney, and I will support his decision."

Alexa kicked the cement sidewalk. She wanted to tell the woman that she'd slept with her husband; that would change her mind. "Well, Viviana, as I told him, I'm not the best person to represent him, but he does seem determined."

"Yes."

Alexa gritted her teeth. "Okay, well, I told him it's up to you. I appreciate your vote of confidence. Let's hope it's well placed."

"I'm sure it is."

"Okay then, I guess that's that. Give my best to Sofia and to Joe."

"I will. Goodbye, Alexa. Thank you very much."

"Goddamn it!" Alexa screamed when she hung up. Then she kicked the cement again.

She headed home, frustrated as hell. What had she gotten herself into? She didn't calm down until she'd showered, changed into jeans and a T-shirt, and had something to eat, and even then she was upset.

She went into her office. Everything was finally in its place. Her law books were on the shelves, and her plaques and various licenses were hung on the walls along with two of her favorite photographs of the children. Savannah's blackboard and a small basket of Reggie's Lego blocks stood in the nook. Satisfied with what she saw, she sat at her computer punching away.

Twenty minutes later, she was still typing when Rafael appeared at the door. He stood gazing at her before making himself known. "Good morning," he said.

Alexa looked up. "Good morning, Rafael. Perfect timing. I just finished your retainer agreement." The printer spat it out. She picked it up and handed it to him, reading along on the computer.

Rafael cut her off before she started. "Do you have a pen?"

She handed him one. "The first paragraph states that you're retaining me to represent you before the Federal –"

"I signed it," Rafael said.

"What do you mean you signed it?" Alexa said. She sounded insulted. "You haven't read it."

"Alexa, I signed Bloom's retainer. Remember? I have no problem signing anything you put in front of me."

"I'm sorry, but I don't work that way. I need to go through this with you."

"Don't you think you should be calling the Federal Reserve?" he said.

"After we go through this."

"You know they're three hours ahead of us," Rafael reminded her.

"Then we should hurry and go through this, don't you think?"

Rafael surrendered. "Go on."

Alexa proceeded. "So, I know you are worried about your finances. According to this, I'm charging you $250 an hour. You'll pay me $1000 now. Once you pay me more than $5000, if you do – that's 20 hours – then you'll just owe the rest of the money. I'll have a lien."

"Sweetheart, how am I going to pay you the rest? A lien against what?" He started to shake, and Alexa thought he might break down again. He reached for a cigarette.

"Don't worry about that now. It also says I don't have malpractice insurance, and it says that I don't specialize in banking law and, in fact, have not been involved in a case like this before." She paused before adding, "And don't call me sweetheart!"

"You've told me 100 times," Rafael said, "I know: You're not a banking lawyer."

"Right. And now it's in our retainer agreement as well."

"Okay, fine."

"So, the rest of it is pretty run-of-the-mill stuff. There's an arbitration clause, and you'll tell me the truth and cooperate, and I'll try my best, and so on and so forth. Do you want to sign it?" Alexa asked deadpan.

Rafael handed her the already-signed Retainer. She made a copy of it and handed it to him.

"So," Rafael said, "Alexa, I'm going crazy. Are you planning to call the Federal Reserve?"

Alexa took a legal pad and the letter from the Federal Reserve bearing Attorney Gary Gilmore's telephone number. She was poised to dial on the landline.

"I'm calling. I'll put him on speaker," she said.

"My God, Alexa!" Rafael had turned extremely pale. "What will you say?"

"I'm going to tell him that I want an appointment as soon as possible. We're going to see them, hopefully today."

She had dialed the number and was already listening to a recorded greeting when Rafael said, "But they're in New York!"

Having researched the Federal Reserve, Alexa had discovered that there was the Federal Reserve Bank of New York and there was the Federal Reserve Bank of San Francisco. It was impossible for Rafael and her to fly to the East Coast; they had neither the time nor the money. Her plan was to ask Gilmore to allow them to fly to San Francisco as soon as possible and meet with an attorney there. She knew that if she had any chance at getting a continuance, it would be if she asked in person with Rafael at her side.

She was finally connected to Gilmore's office and then to Gilmore himself. She introduced herself, and they passed through some introductory talk, with Rafael literally sitting on the edge of his seat the entire time. He still thought Alexa would ask to make the trip to New York that day, and he looked as scared as Alexa imagined he could. Then he heard her explain to Gilmore that a trip to New York was not feasible, and she was therefore requesting a visit with an attorney at the Federal Reserve Bank of San Francisco. "I'd like someone at the Federal Reserve to meet Mr. Lamon as soon as possible," she said.

They heard Gilmore inhale and exhale loudly, and then he said, "I suppose it's all right." Alexa was beaming. "When do you think you'll be going?" he asked.

Alexa looked at the time. "We'll be catching a flight within two hours," she said.

"I'll contact Jordan Cerise there to let him know to expect you. Ask for him."

17

One hour and fifty-five minutes later, Rafael and Alexa were seated on Southwest Airlines flight 77 to San Francisco. The plane was still in the process of boarding, and Rafael was fidgeting in his seat, longing for a cigarette as he listened to Alexa's one-sided cell phone conversation.

"You don't have to tell me that, Scott. I know you don't take your client to the police. But this is different. My client is not a criminal, and this is not the police, it's the Federal Reserve.... Yes, I know they're worse. But there are exceptions, and this is one... Damn it, they're not going to lock him up, for Christ's sake!" At that, Rafael started biting his lip and hyperventilating. "Well, we have the appointment, and they're expecting him... No, Scott. We're on the plane right now... Yes, I know you think I'm taking him to the lions, and I know Ben would agree with you. I got that loud and clear, but I disagree, and since I'm his lawyer, it's a go."

The airplane doors closed then, and the fasten seat belt lights went on. "I have to go, Scott, the plane's moving. Can't talk. I'll let you know." She disconnected and put her cell away.

Rafael spoke hesitantly in a soft voice. "Whoever Scott is, he doesn't think I should go with you. He thinks it's a mistake."

Alexa saw the look on Rafael's face. "Scott is my husband's law partner, and he's wrong. Let's have a drink."

They arrived at the Federal Reserve Bank of San Francisco on April 11th. Alexa had put fresh batteries in both her hearing aids in the cab as a precaution; she didn't want to miss a word at this meeting. As they got out of the cab and approached the building from the side, both Alexa and Rafael were impressed by the grand seal above the colonnade leading to the entrance. At the Office of Legal Counsel, they were ushered into Attorney Jordan Cerise's office. Cerise was a toothy, long-faced man. Alexa guessed he was in his early 40s. He greeted them, then sat down behind a standard-issue desk in a standard-issue room with a standard-issue U.S. flag and a standard-issue photo of the President.

"I received a brief summary from Attorney Gilmore outlining the facts of the case. I am curious to know why you wanted to meet with me," Attorney Cerise said.

"I felt there was no reason not to. We are all on the same side. That is, we all benefit from getting to the truth. And my client," Alexa extended an arm out towards Rafael. "Mr. Lamon will be talking to the Federal Reserve at some length. We can't afford to go to New York. My client's budget doesn't allow it. So, we thought it would be a good idea to come here to meet you and have you meet Mr. Lamon."

"Well, I'm always glad to meet a fellow attorney. And of course, we've all been anxious to meet Mr. Lamon."

For his part, with every passing minute, Rafael was expecting to be carted off to jail.

"As you know," Alexa said, "I have recently taken over as Mr. Lamon's attorney. In fact, this is my first day representing him."

"He was represented by Attorney" Attorney Cerise looked at

a sheet of paper on his desk. "…Bloom." He looked up at Alexa. "He wasn't pleased with Attorney Bloom?"

"My client didn't agree with Mr. Bloom's strategy of shielding him from you, not allowing him to speak directly with the Federal Reserve. Mr. Lamon wants very much to talk with you himself, and I agree with him on that." This was news to Rafael. Not bad news, but news, nonetheless.

Attorney Cerise was cynical. His cynicism was the result of the last decade he'd spent dealing with bankers who, in his experience, were generally guilty of the crimes they'd been charged with. "I see," he said, his elbows on his desk, fingers interlocked like a steeple. "And what would Mr. Lamon like to tell us?"

Alexa had other priorities. "Before we delve deeper into that subject, Mr. Cerise, I'd like to discuss the proffer you are requesting due by Wednesday."

"Yes?"

"As I said, this is my first day as Mr. Lamon's attorney, and I'm not all that familiar with banking law. I'd like to request a continuance." Attorney Cerise chuckled. "A short one," Alexa hastened to clarify. "It's presently due in two days. I'd like a continuance – a modest continuance of, say, a week." The chuckle became a laugh.

"Ms. Starr, apparently, you're not aware of how the Federal Reserve functions. We don't grant continuances."

"But surely you understand that we need more time. The 13th is the day after tomorrow."

"It's impossible. Out of the question."

Alexa slumped back into her chair. "Okay, you don't grant continuances. Then let me ask you this."

"Yes?" Cerise asked.

Rafael watched Alexa with bated breath as she sat up again and then said, "Can you stop the clock?"

"Stop the clock?" Cerise repeated. He looked at her dumbly. "What do you mean?"

"My client is ready and willing to answer any question you have for him. He is prepared to cooperate fully and completely with the Federal Reserve. Today is Monday. The proffer is due on Wednesday. That's two days away. I'm requesting that you stop the clock. Talk to him. Ask him questions. You and anyone else: the people in New York, the Justice Department… If at any point you feel Mr. Lamon is not being completely forthcoming in his answers or that he is not being completely truthful in any way at all, start the clock again, and from that minute we'll have two days to get you the proffer."

Cerise sat back in his chair and stroked his smooth chin. "Ms. Starr, that's a very interesting concept. Tell you what. I'll discuss your request with my superiors and get back to you."

Cerise stood, then Alexa, and Rafael rose. "Thank you," Alexa said. "We'll head back to Los Angeles. I'll wait for your call. Of course, the time is getting shorter, so I hope the answer is positive."

"I may be able to get an answer for you in a few minutes if you can wait. Or do you have a flight to make?"

"No, no. Certainly. We'll wait."

When Cerise left his office, Alexa and Rafael sat back down and simply looked at one another, too tense to speak. After some time, Attorney Cerise returned, and they held their breaths. He went to stand behind his desk. "Ms. Starr, I've spoken with my superiors, and they've agreed to stop the clock for so long as Mr. Lamon cooperates with us."

Alexa let her breath out. "Thank you! That's wonderful! I assure you he will cooperate. Mr. Lamon is as anxious as you are to make sure you have accurate information so he can clear his name."

Rafael sat motionless. Not only had he not been cuffed and

jailed, but Alexa had also just gotten more time. He couldn't believe it.

Cerise remained somber. "I will tell you that this is the first time that we have been presented with this concept of stopping the clock,'" he said. "Now, I must warn you not to speak with any of the other parties involved; that is, any TriWorld employees."

He looked at Rafael. "All the top bank employees have pointed their fingers at you, Mr. Lamon. I urge you not to contact any of them. If you are contacted by them, refrain from speaking to them."

He turned to Alexa. "Ms. Starr, we have begun questioning the employees and, as one would expect, the Bank has obtained legal representation for all of them. Separate representation for each. Some individuals have two attorneys. I caution you to refrain from communicating with either the employees or any of their attorneys for any reason." He looked from her back to Rafael. "Am I making myself clear here?"

"Absolutely," Alexa said. She looked at Rafael.

"Yes, sir," Rafael said.

Cerise came around his desk to say goodbye to his visitors. Alexa and Rafael stood. "Thank you for meeting with us on such short notice today and for speaking to your superiors on our behalf," Alexa said.

"Expect a call from the New York office at some point," Cerise said. "I expect there will be someone from the Justice Department on the conference calls as well. Justice is very interested in this matter, as you know."

"That's fine. Thanks again. I'm sure you'll find my client completely forthcoming and free of any wrongdoing."

Cerise ushered them to the door. "We'll see. Goodbye."

"Goodbye."

18

Having been eager to continue her research into the Federal Reserve, then wanting to draw up Rafael's retainer agreement before he arrived at her house that morning, then racing to the airport, Alexa hadn't had more than a cup of coffee all day, and she now realized she was starving. As soon as they got to the airport and bought their tickets back to L.A., they went to the coffee shop and sat at a table.

After deciding what she wanted, Alexa put her menu down and noticed that Rafael hadn't yet looked at his. He was looking at her.

"Aren't you hungry?" she asked him.

"My God, Alexa, you are amazing," he said.

She pushed. "Aren't you going to eat something?"

He looked down at the closed menu, pushed it away, and grunted. "You paid for the tickets," he said.

"And? Did that kill your appetite?"

"Alexa, you can't pay for everything."

"Can you?" She asked.

"No."

"So, what do you propose? Are you ready to take the blame and go to jail?" When Rafael looked down and didn't answer, Alexa said, "I take that as a no. Okay then, stop talking about it. Trust me, I'm keeping a tab of everything I pay for. And don't forget I have a lien. When this is over, and you've been cleared, you can pay me back. Now, I'm having the turkey burger with fries. What about you?"

Rafael ordered the same, and both asked for iced tea. Rafael shook his head in wonder. "You were brilliant, Alexa," he repeated for what must have been the twentieth time since they'd left Cerise's office. "Totally brilliant."

Now that she was seated and simply waiting for her food, Alexa could reply to his compliment. "I liked that bit about stopping the clock, too," she said.

"I wanted to kiss you right there. Hell, I wanted to make love to you right there in his office." Alexa gave him a look that said he was hopeless. He grinned. In a lower, sexy voice, he said, "I want to make love to you here." It was the first time in days she'd seen his lips turn up. She was caught off guard by that statement, and he went on in that same low voice. "Remember –"

"Rafael, I'm going to call up Cerise and tell him to start the clock if you don't stop this minute."

"Okay, but you can't blame me, Alexa. What you did today was amazing. We went to the top banking lawyers, supposedly experienced with the Federal Reserve. They charge an arm and a leg, and they told us we couldn't even get a one-day continuance. How did you come up with that 'stop the clock' thing?"

Alexa smiled. "Truth? I have no idea. It just spilled out. I didn't have an inkling what I was going to say until the words came out, so don't think I'm so smart. I was as surprised as you were."

"Alexa, in one single day – and your very first day representing me – you spoke with the Federal Reserve in New York, got an appointment with the Federal Reserve Bank of San Francisco, flew here with me against the advice of that attorney you spoke to, met with Cerise, and got them to stop the clock, which no other attorney we spoke to could do. And you thought you couldn't do this."

Alexa slammed her water glass down. "Rafael, for once and for all, that's all well and good, but I am not a banking lawyer! I don't know the first thing about banking. And if you think that's nothing, you're wrong!"

Rafael was completely unfazed by her outburst. "For someone who's so brilliant, you surprise me. You're forgetting something."

"What?"

"I know about banking. I can teach you whatever you need to know."

"That's very sweet of you. But I doubt that you know the US Codes, what the Feds can and can't do, what your rights are in a case like this and – oh! Never mind! I just need to spend a lot of time in the law library."

"What about your law clerk?"

"No way. I have to do this. I don't even know what to tell him to research, and I won't know until I start. I'll learn the information as I go along."

"I'll go with you. I'll do the legwork."

"We'll see."

19

Rafael Lamon and his family had received US permanent residency in the United States on the strength of family members residing in the United States who were US citizens.

When he immigrated to America with Viviana and their young daughter Sofia, they first resided in the city of Bakersfield in California's Central Valley, which had the greatest concentration of Argentines in the state. But both he and Viviana had been born and raised in the capital city of Buenos Aires, and they missed living in a big city. Added to that, Rafael, who had a background in finance, had hosted a popular weekly television show in Argentina discussing topics like smart credit and how to manage money. Bakersfield presented him neither an opportunity in broadcasting nor a job that he felt held much of a future. Three years after their arrival in America, Rafael bought a modest two-bedroom house in North Hollywood. He paid all cash for it, swore he would never refinance it, and never did. He was soon employed by Bank International, then by TriWorld, and had a weekly television program on Argentine satellite TV discussing topics of popular finance.

Almost two months ago, Sofia, his twenty-one-year-old daughter, got married and moved out of the house. Her bedroom had remained unused. The box Rafael had brought out of the Bank had been sitting untouched in a corner of his bedroom. On his drive home after the trip to San Francisco, he was inspired to make his daughter's bedroom his home base. On arriving home, Rafael went into his bedroom, took the legal-sized box he'd brought home from his office into what had been Sofia's room, and began emptying its contents onto the wrap-around desk he'd bought his daughter when she had started college.

He had already set the photograph of Viviana and Sofia on the desk alongside the miniature Ferrari. He had mentioned to Alexa that his dream car was a Ferrari, and she had presented him with this perfect miniature replica on his birthday, saying he'd never specified the size or color, so she'd bought within her budget and chose red because red suited him. Next, he brought out the newspaper photo he'd kept in his desk drawer and gazed at it. It was a photo of Alexa, once accompanied by an article written about her in a Beverly Hills magazine. He heard Viviana call him to dinner, but he took another moment to meditate on the photo of the woman whom he was depending on to save his life.

There was a knock at the door, then it barely opened. Sofia's pretty head poked in. "Papa?"

Rafael placed the photo of Alexa face down on the desk. "Dulce! Come in."

Sofia saw the photo of her mother and her on the desk and smiled. "Are you making this room into your office?" she asked.

"Yes. Is that okay?"

"Yeah. It's not like I live here anymore. I think it's a great idea."

"I thought so, too," Rafael said. "But if you ever decide to come home, it's yours."

Sofia scoffed. "I don't think Joe would like that." They both smiled.

"Sweetheart, when did you get here? I didn't hear the doorbell," he asked.

Sofia smiled slyly. "I still have the key. We're having dinner with you."

"Good." He gave her an appraising look. "You look beautiful," he said. "Come. I need a hug from my little girl."

After a warm and delicious embrace, Sofia said, "I came to get you. Mama wants us at the dinner table. She's waiting there with Joe. Dinner is on the table."

"Okay, you go on," Rafael said. "I'll wash up and be there in a minute."

When Sofia left the bedroom, Rafael stood looking around at the room his daughter had grown up in – the bed with the pink bedcover, the single poster of Michael Jackson still on the wall, and the few knick-knacks left behind when she'd readied herself for her new life with Joe. He held up the photo of Alexa again, looked at it, and sighed before consigning it to the bottom drawer of his new, empty desk.

Then he went to wash his hands for dinner.

20

As soon as Alexa and Rafael left his office, Attorney Jordan Cerise put through a call to the Federal Reserve Bank in New York and shared the details of their meeting with the Federal Reserve Bank's lead attorney in the TriWorld matter, Attorney Gary Gilmore. Following that briefing, Attorney Gilmore, a large, stocky man with red hair and a short red beard, called Attorneys Stern and Campbell into his office for a pow-wow. Though the weather outside was chilly, it was hot inside the building, and all three men had their jackets off.

Sitting behind his desk, Attorney Gilmore brought up the subject of Cerise's meeting with Lamon. "Lamon's got himself a new attorney, a woman. No one's heard of her. Name's Alexa Starr. I spoke briefly with her." He looked down at the file. "She asked to meet with an attorney in Frisco. She's pretty clever. His proffer was due tomorrow. Couldn't get a continuance, of course," he paused. "So, she got us to stop the clock." He blinked and spoke those last three words very slowly.

The two men looked at him uncomprehendingly. Attorney Campbell, short and mostly bald, sat with his chair balanced on the two back legs. He was always looking for a laugh. He squinted. "Stop the clock? What's that, a game show?"

"Yeah," said Gilmore. "Well, as long as the guy *cooperates*" he stressed 'cooperates' sarcastically, as though it was something Lamon would never do, "we stop the clock. Get it? Time freezes. And then, when we find that he's not *cooperating*," and again he stressed the word, "then the clock starts back and he'll have two days from that point to get us the proffer."

The three men snickered and scoffed. Attorney Campbell said, "Okay, so we win." His statement reflected the general belief that bankers under investigation generally do not fully cooperate with the Federal Reserve.

"So, how come Lamon's got only one attorney?" Attorney Stern asked. Stern was, as usual, chewing gum, a habit that irritated Gilmore, though there was little he could do about it. "Everyone else at the bank's got themselves two. And word is they've even got some ex-Reserve guys on the payroll."

"The General Manager, Stamen, and the guy in charge of new accounts, what's-his-name Alandro, have got themselves attorneys out of Silverman & Gold," said Attorney Campbell.

"Not too much of a surprise," Gilmore said. "The bank's paying for them, and the bank can afford the high-end legal."

"Bank's thinking they can't afford to have the most expensive there is," Stern said.

"They're right about that," Campbell said.

"Yeah. They've got a bunch of lawyers. They've all got criminal lawyers, too. The same guys that represented those CEOs who were popped." Campbell added.

"Guess poor Mr. Lamon can't afford anything but this unknown woman," Gilmore said.

Attorney Stern sighed theatrically, then posed as though he was delivering lines on stage. "Well, there are enough attorneys as it is. I'm suddenly Mr. Popular. My calendar is filled with meetings all this week with the lawyers representing everyone at the TriWorld."

"Me too," said Attorney Campbell, his thumbs in his belt. "And damn, it's a large crew. But only the lawyers."

Attorney Gilmore looked back down at the file on his desk. "Yeah, bet you'd be surprised if any of them bring in their client like Starr did with Lamon."

The men snorted. "I'd shit my pants," said Campbell.

"So," Gilmore said, getting back down to business, "Cerise has warned Lamon and his lady lawyer to stay clear of the others." He leaned back, and the chair squeaked with his weight. "I wish we could isolate all of them like that."

"Right," Stern said. "Like it could happen. Like they wouldn't all compare notes."

"Yeah. They stand to gain by sticking close," said Campbell.

Gilmore sighed as he leaned back in his chair and locked his fingers behind his head. "Well," he said, "they may be right. Either Lamon's our guy, or he's not. If he is, the question is, was he in this alone? If not, who else was involved? If he's not our guy, who is? In that nest, it's going to be hard to pick out the guilty ones." It was quiet then. He abruptly came forward on his chair. "What do we know about Han?"

Campbell answered. "He's been President of TriWorld for the last 10 years. Before that, he was with Bank of Asia, and before that with New York Bank. Always been involved with international clients. Done well for himself, apparently has quite a spread in Virginia. Headquarters for TriWorld is New York, but the entire crew, including the lawyers, fly out to his home to meet with him there; he doesn't like to travel."

"Jesus!" Gilmore said. "And the Bank pays for that?"

"You kidding me?" Stern asked. "They're flying here to meet with us and to Virginia from L.A, the whole bunch."

"Well," Gilmore stroked his short beard. "I suppose Han's gotten the go-ahead from the bank's Board. Meanwhile, while these others will be flying here, Lamon apparently wants us to believe he's got no money and can't afford even a single trip, so maybe we'll assume he's not the bad guy. It's either true, or that lady lawyer he's got is one hell of a sharp cookie." He paused. "Did you say you've heard of her?" They all shook their head.

Gilmore sighed. "This sucks." He slapped his desk. "Okay, gentlemen, let's get back to work. Even though these people are comparing notes, let's put what they're telling us – or rather, what their attorneys are telling us – up on the board alongside one another and compare."

"Sounds good," said Stern.

"We're on it, Chief," said Campbell as the two men left Gilmore's office.

"Yeah," Gilmore grunted.

21

Early Tuesday afternoon, Attorney Gilmore's first call came through to Alexa's office. He called to inform her that he would be contacting her again the following morning at eleven Los Angeles time to officially begin talks with her client.

On the day his proffer had originally been due, Rafael arrived at her door an hour early, looking ashen and smoking nervously as he paced, awaiting the first phone interview with attorneys from the Federal Reserve.

"Good morning," Gilmore started out. "Let's establish some ground rules before we begin." Without waiting for a response, he went on. "These discussions will be between me and Mr. Lamon, Ms. Starr. You have represented that your client wishes to cooperate fully, so I doubt that your participation will be required; that is, unless it's asked for on this end. There's no reason why your client cannot answer my questions himself. Agreed?"

"Yes, agreed," Alexa answered.

"Okay. As you've been told, someone from the Justice

Department will be on the line with us. Our conversations are being taped. Do you consent to that?"

"Yes," said Alexa.

"Mr. Lamon, do you consent to that?"

"Yes," Rafael said. He looked at Alexa and shrugged as if to say he had no choice. She could see he was sweating and didn't blame him a bit. This was scary stuff he was walking into.

"Okay, let's start. Mr. Lamon, how long have you worked at TriWorld?"

Rafael started, then cleared his throat and began again. "Between 7 and 8 years."

"Do you recall the exact date you began work there?"

He thought for a moment before answering. "No. But I can look it up."

"Does May of 2018 sound right?"

"Yes. I think that's right. It was 2018. It could have been May."

"All right. And who hired you?"

"The General Manager, Bob – Robert Stamen."

"You were hired as a Director?"

"Yes. Director of South American affairs."

"You always worked in the Beverly Hills branch?"

"Yes."

"And what were you told were your duties?"

"I was a relationship officer. I was hired to get customers for the Bank, form relationships with them."

"Now, TriWorld is an international bank. As such, it can only deal with non-U.S. citizens. So, as a relationship officer, you were to open accounts for only non-US citizens. Is that right?"

"Yes. That's correct."

"And U.S. citizens were given a power of attorney over most of these accounts at the Beverly Hills branch?"

"Yes."

"Now, let's talk about the security agreement that TriWorld had with Bank of Taiwan. TriWorld created that."

"Yes. That was my understanding."

"Did you create it?"

"Absolutely not," Rafael said.

"Who did?"

"I was told it was TriWorld's attorneys."

"When did you first see this security agreement?"

"I don't recall. But I objected strongly to it when it was handed to me."

There was a moment's pause. Alexa nodded to let Rafael know he was doing well.

"Who gave it to you?"

"Bob Stamen. Jason Alandro was there when he gave it to me."

"And you say you objected to it?"

"Yes, that's right. I objected right away, as soon as I read it."

"Objected to Robert Stamen?"

"I objected to both of them; to both Bob and Jason."

"And you did that separately?"

"No. When I went to Bob's office to object, Jason was there."

"Why did you object?"

"Because it felt wrong."

"It *felt* wrong?"

"Yes. I mean, to me, it meant that if Bank of Taiwan's borrowers who held power of attorney on accounts at TriWorld didn't pay their loans back and defaulted on Bank of Taiwan's loans, TriWorld would pay for them. It seemed wrong. We were using the accounts at TriWorld owned by non-U.S. citizens as security to guarantee loans that Bank of Taiwan was making to U.S. citizens with power of attorney over accounts at TriWorld. There was no consent form signed by the owners of these accounts to use their money that way."

There was an almost imperceptible pause then, but to Rafael, it seemed it lasted forever. Had his answer been okay?

Then Gilmore asked, "And what did Bob Stamen say when you voiced your objection?"

"Bob told me that the bank's attorneys had drawn it up; it had their blessings."

"Who told you that?"

"Bob. Bob Stamen."

Another pause. "Did you ask the bank's attorneys if that was true?"

"No."

"Why not?"

Rafael scoffed. "I couldn't just call them up and question what Bob had said. They weren't my attorneys."

"Mr. Lamon, how can you say they weren't your attorneys? You worked at the Bank, didn't you? These were the Bank's attorneys. What did you think they were there for?"

"I assumed they were there for the President and the General Manager. Maybe for the Executive Directors, but not for me."

"Did anyone tell you that you couldn't call them?"

"No."

"Did you ever ask?"

Rafael paused, and a wave of fever overtook him as he realized what had probably been his naiveté. "No."

"So, you never thought to pick up the telephone and call the attorneys when you saw the security agreement that you so strongly objected to?" Gilmore's tone was sarcastic as hell.

Rafael swallowed. "No. If they were there for me, then I should have called. I guess I didn't know better." He looked at Alexa and shook his head with eyes reflecting doom.

"Okay, Mr. Lamon. We'll get back to you. As always, I warn you not to have any communication with any of the other employees of the bank and Ms. Starr?"

"Yes, I'm here."

"You are likewise reminded not to communicate with them or with any of their legal counsel."

"I understand," Alexa said.

"Okay, you'll be hearing from us tomorrow at the same time. Goodbye."

When they heard the click that ended the call, Rafael looked up at the ceiling. "Why didn't I call the lawyers?" He turned to look at Alexa as he answered his own question. "They made it seem like I didn't need to, like it was a done deal. Was I supposed to call the lawyers and say, 'Stamen's telling me you okayed this. Did you really okay it?" He looked up at the ceiling again. "They think I'm lying."

"Maybe they just think you were stupid," Alexa said. "Better to be stupid than guilty of illegal acts at this point," she added.

Just then, her hearing aids beeped, signaling two dead batteries. Alexa took out both aids. opened the top drawer of her desk, brought out two new batteries, and changed them while Rafael said, "I even showed them to the auditor!"

With her aids out, Alexa didn't hear him.

22

True to his word, Gilmore called the next day again at the same time.

"Good morning. Mr. Lamon, we spoke about the security agreement yesterday. Today, we'll discuss the agreement TriWorld had in place with Bank of Taiwan to fund them. Did TriWorld create that or Bank of Taiwan?"

"TriWorld."

"We were told that you created it. Did you?"

"Absolutely not."

"Who did?"

"I was told that was also created by TriWorld's attorneys."

"Who told you that?"

"Bob Stamen."

"When did you first see the funding agreement?"

"I don't recall. But I also objected very strongly to Bob and to Jason when I read it."

"Separately?"

"Yes. I first spoke to Jason about it, and he told me to talk to Bob."

"What specifically was it that you objected to?"

"Sir, I'm not an attorney, but from what I understood, it seemed pretty strange to me. It didn't make sense." There was a silent pause that stretched out until Rafael added, "But again, sir, I was told that the attorneys had written both the security agreement and the agreement to fund."

"Well, good for you." Rafael and Alexa heard what sounded like a chuckle on the line and realized it must have been the person at Justice. "Tell me, Mr. Lamon, why did it seem strange?" Gilmore asked.

"Because it seemed that TriWorld was funding Bank of Taiwan the money that Taiwan lent to the powers of attorney who came to them for loans."

There was a pause. And then Gilmore said, "Well, let me ask you this, sir." He sounded surly. "If the attorneys had written these documents, yet they both had what you as a layman saw was a problem – namely, the indemnity issue and the agreement to fund Bank of Taiwan with these amounts that it was loaning out – how could you trust that the attorneys had, in fact, created them?" Rafael looked at Alexa and shook his head. He bit his lip and said nothing.

"Mr. Lamon?"

"I'm not sure," Rafael said softly. "I guess I believed Bob."

"You believed Bob?" Gilmore asked sarcastically. "And maybe when you participated in the illegal funding, you just believed Bob."

"Mr. Gilmore, I did not participate in the illegal funding. I swear to you. I had nothing to do with any funding."

Gilmore clicked his tongue. "Okay, then, tell us why your signature is on all these agreements."

"I was told to sign them."

"Of course, you were," Gilmore said, sounding sarcastic. "And who directed you to do that?"

"Bob. Bob Stamen. The General Manager."

Gilmore sighed. "Of course. Okay, Mr. Lamon. That's all for now. We'll get back to you. And Ms. Starr?"

"Yes, Mr. Gilmore?"

"You'll be hearing from me. Please make sure that both you and your client refrain from any communication with anyone from the bank."

"Yes, sir."

"Good day." Click.

Rafael was upset. "Alexa, he ended so abruptly. He doesn't believe a word I'm saying. I'm cooperating, and they're making a fool out of me."

"They have to do that," Alexa said. "They need to grill you. They need to put you through the wringer. The clock is still stopped, so I'm not concerned."

Contrary to her words, Alexa was feeling insecure. Having listened to these preliminary conversations, she heard Rafael and the Feds talk about the security agreement and the funding agreement.

Rafael had talked to her about basis points, matching funds, and the intra-bank cost of funds. They would soon be tossing those and other terms around, and she had no idea what they meant. She recognized the impossibility of being ignorant of terms vital to the case. She knew absolutely zip about banking and had shared her lack of confidence about her naiveté of these banking issues with Rafael for what must have been the twentieth time. She didn't appreciate the fact that he took her feelings of insecurity so lightly. Even more frustrating was the fact that he'd laughed at her as if she were cute when she complained.

"Damn it, Rafael! I feel like a blind person leading a tour. And you put me in this position!" She stormed out of the office and was pacing in the backyard.

"Okay, okay, Alexa. It's not the science of rockets." Every

once in a while, Rafael would make a slight blunder that gave away the fact that English was not his first language. Alexa found these mistakes endearing and, despite herself, would have smiled if she hadn't been so frustrated.

"Come inside. I'll draw it out for you," Rafael said.

23

Alexa followed Rafael back into the office. Rafael positioned Savannah's small blackboard in the center of her office and began drawing with a piece of chalk. He drew a stick figure with long curly hair and what was supposed to be a skirt, at the bottom center of the board. He pointed to her.

"This woman is Anita. Anita is in South America. Anita has been to America only once, and she is not a U.S. Citizen. She has money." He drew a box with a dollar sign above the Anita. On her right, he made a rectangle and labeled it 'TW.' "This is TriWorld Bank. Anita, who is in South America, has a business, so she takes out a line of credit with TriWorld for, say, 5 million dollars. Are you with me?"

"Yes. Of course," Alexa said.

"Okay." He drew a dotted line connecting Anita in South America to TriWorld Bank. Then he drew another stick figure at the top of the blackboard with very short hair and a bowtie. "Now, this is Bob. Bob is Anita's cousin. He lives in California with his family. He is a U.S. Citizen. Because Anita is not here, she gives her cousin Bob, power of attorney over her account at TriWorld.

"Bob wants a loan. He wants to borrow one million dollars. TriWorld can't lend Bob the money because Bob is a U.S. citizen and TriWorld is an international bank. We can't work with U.S. citizens. Bob has to borrow from a domestic bank like California Federal, Bank of America, or Bank of Taiwan. What TriWorld did was set up a relationship with Bank of Taiwan." Rafael drew a triangle on the left side of the blackboard, opposite TriWorld, and in it wrote BT. "Are you with me?"

Alexa nodded. "The Bank of Taiwan is not an international bank," she said.

"That's right. It's a domestic bank. That means it can loan money to U.S. citizens. So TriWorld sets up this relationship with Bank of Taiwan and tells Bob to go there to ask for a loan." Rafael put down the chalk. "TriWorld has an international relationship with Bank of Taiwan. We loan them money."

Alexa put her palm up. "Whoa, Stop! TriWorld lends the Bank of Taiwan money?" Rafael nodded. "Is that legal?" she asked.

He nodded again. "Yes. Banks make short-term loans to other banks at what's called the interbank cost of funds."

"Okay, slow down. What determines the interbank cost of funds?" Alexa asked.

"It's not important. Just all a matter of basis points over whatever index is used."

Alexa was rubbing her forehead. She sighed in exasperation. "What are basis points?"

"It's not a big deal, Alexa. Each basis point is just one-tenth of a point. A point is one percent, so a basis point is one-tenth of a percent. It's not a big deal. So, when a bank lends another bank money, they talk in terms of basis points charged, like you talk about interest rates."

"Okay. Go on."

Rafael turned back to his drawing and picked up the chalk. He drew a dotted line from the rectangle representing TriWorld to the triangle representing the Bank of Taiwan. "Now, Anita's cousin secures a loan from Bank of Taiwan. So far, it's all legal." He put the chalk down again. "The problem is that the loan Bank of Taiwan gave Bob was secured in effect by Anita's account at TriWorld. That's what TriWorld indemnified or guaranteed Bank of Taiwan full payment with. That was the security agreement."

"Is that what the Federal Reserve letter meant by 'matching funds?'"

"In essence. Bob would have me call Bank of Taiwan to ask how much they were lending to people who had a power of attorney on our accounts, and then TriWorld lent them that amount. Did you get that? TriWorld matched the amount it lent to Bank of Taiwan with the amount Bank of Taiwan lent to these people. And then, TriWorld indemnified these loans to Bank of Taiwan. By agreement, TriWorld promised that if a U.S. borrower defaulted on their loan, we would pay it back with money that belonged to our non-U.S. citizen customers. So, the Federal Reserve is saying that TriWorld actually made the loans to the clients of Bank of Taiwan who were U.S. citizens – and they're not supposed to do that."

"I get it," Alexa said. "Bank of Taiwan was a straw bank."

"What's that?" Rafael asked.

"It means that TriWorld was using Bank of Taiwan as a dummy conduit." Rafael nodded. "So, what was your part in this?" Alexa asked.

Rafael threw his arms up. "I had no part in it at all, Alexa. I swear. I just got new business for the bank. That's all."

"You had nothing to do with the loans?" she asked.

"No. I had no authority to place loans, none at all. I was a relationship officer."

"Right. We've told the Federal Reserve that already. I would think they're grilling Stamen about that."

"That's why this is all so crazy," Rafael said. "When I first saw what they're calling the security agreements, I screamed. I highlighted language in it and went to both Jason and Bob. They told me it was no problem."

"Well," Alexa said, folding her arms. "Apparently, they were wrong."

24

With a new understanding of the situation as the Feds saw it, Alexa couldn't help but wonder about Rafael's role in the alleged illegal activity at the bank. She wanted to believe he was innocent, but she didn't want to be naïve. She would represent him to the best of her ability in either event. But she wondered if he was, in fact, innocent. Gilmore had said his signature was on every agreement made with Bank of Taiwan.

She wasn't the first woman Rafael had been unfaithful to his wife with; she knew that. Her logic told her that if he could be duplicitous in his marriage, he could be duplicitous in his business dealings. *Why not?*

But what was in it for him? What did he have to gain by putting himself at such risk? He was obviously short on cash, so he hadn't done it for the money. Maybe he was told to do things he knew were illegal and did them for fear of losing his job. That made more sense because she saw Rafael as someone who would hold on to his job at almost any cost. Yet, being that he was very conservative and cautious and took few risks, did it make sense that he would risk being busted by the Feds for illegal acts? Probably not. Her gut told her he was innocent, and she would go with her gut until and unless something changed her mind. She prayed her gut was right.

Friday morning, as she walked up the steps of the Hugh & Hazel Darling Law Library at UCLA, she was once again transported back to her law school days, when she spent hours studying there. And along with the memories of books and exams came memories of law students and lawyers who hit on her as she studied.

Alexa was unlike the girls she'd known who had entered law school looking for husbands or wanted to be attorneys so they could join the club whose members they respected. In fact, Alexa had never liked lawyers. She found them to be generally pompous, arrogant, small-minded, not at all well-rounded, and boring as hell. As a law student, she had welcomed being asked out by a fellow law student and, later, as an attorney, had welcomed being hit on by attorneys, only to relish the opportunity to reject them.

She realized the irony in having married a lawyer. But Ben had been different. They'd met when Ben, who was a criminal litigator, had needed some help with a client whose green card might have been in jeopardy if Ben pleaded him guilty to a charge of cocaine possession. He needed help from an attorney who knew the immigration laws.

From their first meeting, Ben had her smiling. His humor was self-deprecating, and he did not seem to share the narcissism so prevalent in their profession. It helped that their practices were so different. Yet they had commonalities. They had both been born in Canada. Both enjoyed skiing, and both loved to dance; they couldn't dance enough. Their sex was good too – at least Alexa had thought so. Though her married life was her first experience with monogamy, she had no problem with it, but, surprise, surprise! Apparently, it proved to be harder for Ben. And that was the end of that.

She entered the library, showed her ID for admittance, and set about discovering the secrets of banking law tucked away in the U.S. Codes, the FDIC, the OCC, and a myriad of laws going back from the National Bank Act of 1864 through the Patriot Act to current legislation. She took one coffee break and another short break to enjoy munching on an apple in the fresh air.

At three o'clock, she left the library for home, knowing she would be returning to the library for more research. For now, she wanted to be home when the gardener got there so she could have him prepare for the landscaper's project. She left the library and started for home.

Alexa loved her house, and enhancing it was her never-ending hobby. She would see something in a random magazine, at a restaurant, hotel, or at someone's home, and she'd be inspired.

She had bought her house when she and Ben divorced and had been attracted to it because it was a three-bedroom within walking distance to El Rodeo, an excellent elementary school in the Beverly Hills school district. Its backyard was enclosed, which she thought was safe for her then not-quite-three- year-old children to play in.

When she first saw it, the house she and Ben had shared for the length of their marriage was due to close escrow, and it had been sold to a couple who had asked for a substantial amount of money off the agreed purchase price because of a crack in the chimney. The broker was holding an open house to secure a backup offer in case their escrow didn't go through. Alexa didn't care about the crack. She offered the owner the full asking price. Without time to secure a loan before escrow closed on her house, Alexa offered to pay all cash; she would refinance it afterward. The seller couldn't refuse. He rejected the discounted offer, and Alexa had herself a house.

The day the key to the front door was in her hand, she removed the double drapes covering the entire house, which had been hung by the orthodox rabbi who had been renting the house, and had the cypress trees that covered the large living room windows uprooted and taken away. Removing the wall-to-wall carpets, the light immediately shone on the beautiful dark peg-and-groove floors.

She was jubilant the day she found a lovely oversized silk Chinese rug for the living room that mirrored the pastel colors on the painted stenciled antique beamed ceilings. Persian rugs found their way onto the floors here and there throughout the house, and recessed lights were set behind the overhead beams.

Alexa kept all the old charm of the house built in the late 1920s intact and decorated the house with a mix of antiques, glass, and mirrors, some ultra-modern pieces, artwork, and lots of plants. She added a bedroom for Lupe and converted the garage into the guesthouse that was now her office.

Though there were many things about the house that she loved, she most enjoyed the many French doors. She counted sixteen. The French doors in her bedroom opened to a lovely Mexican-tiled courtyard where she often entertained friends around a large table. Sometimes she sat there alone, meditating on the tall, serene statue of the woman surrounded by night-blooming jasmine. In the summer, the sweet scent, mixed with the scents of roses and gardenia bushes, wafted into her room.

Alexa was on an eco-kick and had spoken with a landscaper months ago about changing her front yard over to foliage that required less water. She had decided to transition in stages and went home to speak with her gardener and discuss the next stage. When they were done, Jose left, his white pick-up driving away as Ben's black Mercedes with the vanity license plate CRIMLAW pulled up in front of the house.

Ben had come to pick up the twins for his weekend with them. In a suit and tie, it was obvious he'd come straight from court. He greeted Alexa, and they went inside the house. He kissed the children who were, as always, overexcited when they were about to visit with the man Alexa had sometimes referred to as "Disneyland Dad." The children's time with Ben was all fun and games, whereas time at home with Mom meant schedules, discipline, time-out for bad behavior, and routine. Ben planned to take the children to Knott's Berry Farm that weekend, their favorite amusement park. While Reggie and Savannah ran to gather their weekend bags, Ben, still standing at the threshold to the living room, spoke to Alexa.

He turned his attention to his ex-wife. "So, how did it go?"

"Scott told you."

"We are partners."

Alexa noticed a leaf on the nearby ficus tree had turned brown. She walked over to it and picked off the dead leaf before speaking. "Well, they didn't arrest him. Actually, it went rather well."

Ben smirked, nodding. "Why should that surprise me?"

She smiled back at him. "I don't know, Ben."

Ben shook his head. "You've done things no lawyer I know would ever do and yet," he paused, looked up at the beamed ceiling, and shrugged, "you keep coming out fine."

"I guess I'm just lucky that way."

The children came into the living room ready to go. "Daddy, will we have time to see the science museum this weekend, too?" Reggie asked.

"I don't know, son. Maybe. Are you ready, Savannah?"

She nodded and went to Alexa. "Bye, Mommy. I hope you have a nice weekend."

Alexa answered, "You too, baby"

As Reggie approached her, Savannah whispered in her mother's ear. "Do you have a date with a boy?" Alexa nodded, and Savannah smiled widely. "Good. Mommy."

Reggie gave her a tight hug and a quick kiss. On their way to the door, Ben said, "Let me know what happens. Good luck."

Alexa followed them. "I will. Thanks. Have fun, guys." She closed the door behind her family. It was time for her to bathe and think about what she would wear.

Alexa was getting ready for a second date with Steve Chado, a dermatologist she'd met some time ago at Sheyanne's dinner party right after Valentine's Day. Every time February 14th rolled by, Alexa was temporarily reminded of her single-again-and-alone status and vowed that by the following year at that time, she'd be in a loving relationship. Then came the Fourth of July, and the same thing happened. Thanksgiving passed, as did the Christmas holidays and New Year's Eve. With every one of them, she'd make the same vow: when the next one came, she wouldn't be alone. But then the next one came, and there she was again, still alone, repeating the same vow. She really meant to make a greater effort to meet someone. It was just so hard! There was her practice, the kids, and taking care of herself and the house, and she wondered: if she didn't have time to meet the perfect man, would she have time for a relationship if she met him? Would she have the energy to devote to making a new relationship work?

In the far corner of her mind, behind the daily morass of thoughts, lay the idea that perhaps she should try therapy for a while, just to get some help prioritizing her life and making sense of a few things. She'd like her private life to be more complete than it was. Maybe soon she'd try that. Yes, that sounded like a good idea. In fact, it was a great idea, and she would do it. She'd go into therapy.

On her first date with Steve, they'd gone to Chaya in Venice, where the food was great, and the place was fun. But the acoustics were hell on Alexa's hearing aids. It was a noisy restaurant, and their table wasn't by a wall, so she had noise coming at her from all sides and had trouble keeping up a coherent conversation. Now, as she dressed, she thought again of how eager she was for her new hearing aids to arrive. Hopefully, they would make a substantial difference in her ability to hear and to hear clearly.

In any event, it turned out that she didn't need to participate much that first evening with Steve. It had been a warm night, and after dinner, they took a walk on the beach, just a block from the restaurant. That had been lovely. The stars were out, and Steve told her all about himself and his life, how he had planned to go to law school but then realized it really wasn't for him and entered medical school. How he'd landed on dermatology because, as the body's largest organ, the skin fascinated him. Alexa had never before thought much about the practice of dermatology beyond an attempt to deal with moles or acne. He told her how he enjoyed flying and how he was about to get his pilot's license. How he used to be far more into sports until his knee required surgery. How he had married his ex-wife after knowing her for only four months, and how she'd changed so much as soon as they'd married. He spoke of his partner and how their partnership had dissolved over financial issues. At some point, Alexa realized Steve talked ad nauseam about himself and only learned about Alexa via an occasional interjection she'd almost fought to make. She sensed that Steve's one-way conversational mode was a sign that he was prone to deal with relationships in a one-way mode as well. If so, Alexa had no interest in pursuing anything further with him. Tonight, she was on a mission to see if, in fact, her first impression proved valid; maybe he'd just been nervous that first night. If tonight proved to be a replay of their first date, she'd take a Lyft home after suggesting he buy himself a pocket-sized mirror to save his breath, his money, and gas.

Tonight, they'd be going to the Comedy Store on Sunset after dinner at a restaurant close to the venue. She bathed and shampooed her hair, then looked over her options and decided to wear all black. She chose tight-fitting black pants and a soft, cashmere black sweater that plunged a bit low at the neckline. Her first choice for shoes was her black Guess platform heels, but she took them off and wore more comfortable Stuart Weitzman black boots that boasted a touch of silver. Deciding to play up the silver, she wore a simple silver necklace and silver hoop earrings.

She grabbed her black leather jacket by Armani, put her keys, credit card, cell phone, and some cash in her pocket, and was ready to go when Steve rang her doorbell.

25

Saturday morning the house was quiet. Lupe had decided to spend the weekend with her daughter in La Mirada and return Sunday in time to make dinner. She sometimes visited her daughter when the twins were with Ben for the weekend. Alexa sat at the round table in the courtyard enjoying a tall mug of freshly brewed coffee and her second piece of toast with cream cheese and lox. It was a clear day, fresh and warm and at that time of day, not yet too hot. The strips of lox shone in the sun. She planned to take a long power walk after breakfast.

Her date with Steven the night before would be her last. She had confirmed a definite lack of balance in their relationship. She had refrained from suggesting he buy a mirror, but when they'd gotten to her house and he moved in for a kiss, she'd smiled and given him a hug instead. She'd thanked him for the evening and said that though she thought he was a great guy, she didn't think the chemistry was there.

Finished with breakfast, she did a minimal job of organizing her papers in the office, then drove to the Santa Monica beach and took a long power walk along the shore. Afterward, she lay down on the sand and rested, then enjoyed a salad at a café on the Venice boardwalk. She was leisurely walking back to her car about two miles away when her cell phone rang. It was her mother.

Hearing her tight voice, Alexa was immediately worried. "Hi, Mom. How are you?"

"I'm fine. Where are you?"She didn't sound fine to Alexa. She sounded upset.

"I'm at the beach. What's wrong?" Alexa asked.

"Nothing's wrong," Giselle said impatiently. "Does something have to be wrong for me to call you?"

"Okay, but you just sound-"

"Alexa, can you come here?"

"Sure. But Mom, is everything okay?"

"Yes. Just come," she said and hung up.

Alexa was baffled. Though her mother had insisted that everything was okay, she had never been so curt. And she had hung up without saying goodbye; she never did that. Alexa got into her car and sped to her mother's house.

Alexa's father had died four years ago. Richard had suffered an unforeseen and massive heart attack while the couple was attending a dinner party at a friend's home. The paramedics were called but arrived too late. Theirs had been a fairytale marriage, and they had recently celebrated their forty-sixth wedding anniversary. His death had left Giselle devastated. It had taken some time for her to re-engage with life, so Alexa was delighted when her mother went on a cruise to Alaska with three of her girlfriends. That was two months ago. While on board, she had met Buddy, a widower, also from Los Angeles. Since then, the two had been spending time together and seemed to be getting along well. Alexa knew they'd recently gone to see Romeo and Juliet performed by the American Ballet Theater. Alexa was happy for her mother and even envied the compatible relationship she'd found.

Ringing Giselle's doorbell, Alexa couldn't imagine what awaited her. When the door opened, and Alexa hugged her mother, she noted Giselle was still in her pajamas. Yesterday's makeup hadn't been washed off, and her hair hadn't been combed. Her mother was a woman who prided herself on her grooming and general appearance. She would not normally allow herself to be seen like this.

"What's wrong, Mom?" Alexa asked.

Giselle brushed her daughter away. "Stop asking me that! I told you, I'm fine."

"Okay, sorry."

Her mother's next words to Alexa were telling. Her voice was filled with tension. "You don't know what I've been going through," Giselle said, then turned and walked away.

Something *was* wrong. "Tell me, Mom." Alexa was concerned and ready to hear the worst. As she followed behind her mother, she scoped the living room and dining room. Everything seemed to be in order.

They entered the kitchen and then the breakfast room. Giselle pointed to something. "Look at this," she said. But Alexa was looking at the sink where only a half-empty cup of tea sat, the teabag still inside. "Have you eaten, Mom?"

"I had coffee," Giselle said curtly.

Alexa didn't point out the cup of tea. There was obviously something her mother wanted urgently to show her. Giselle stopped at the small desk in the corner of the large breakfast room. Her fists were clenched at her sides, her face drawn tight. She was obviously stressed.

"What is it, Mom?"

"You don't know what I've been through. Everything has been going wrong!" She emphasized 'everything', pushing it out as if giving birth to the devil. She pointed to the archaic answering machine that sat in the corner of the desk. "This isn't working," she said with obvious frustration. She sat on the green chair by the desk. "I can't get my messages." Her voice was filled with equal parts frustration, bitterness, sadness, anger, and hopelessness.

Alexa looked at the answering machine her mother had used for more than 20 years. She doubted that they even made these machines anymore. Did they even still sell answering machines? Weren't they all built into phones now?

"I've spent hours trying to fix it." Then in a panic, Giselle wailed, "I can't fix it! Everything is going wrong!"

Alexa noticed that the machine was dark; there were no lights on. Shouldn't there be a light on somewhere on the machine? She bent down, followed the wire to the wall socket, and confirmed it was plugged in. She stood and moved closer to the machine so she could read the markings on it, all almost completely worn out.

"Be careful with it! Don't break it!" Her mother's anxiety scared Alexa. She gently placed her hand on her mother's forearm to try to calm her. "Mom, relax. If it's not already broken, I promise I won't break it. I just want to look at it."

Giselle's knuckles went to her mouth. Alexa pried her baffled eyes away from her mother and forced herself to look at the answering machine. She saw the "On/Off" button. She clicked it and saw her mother flinch. The small red light went on. The machine had been turned off.

"There, Mom. It's working. It was just turned off."

"That no-good-bitch! Motherfucker!" Giselle said. "She did this!"

Alexa was in shock. She couldn't believe her ears. She had never ever heard her mother curse or speak so vindictively.

"Who?" She asked.

"That Carla! She did this. I'm going to raise hell with that cunt!"

Something was wrong with her mother. Carla had been cleaning Giselle's house every week for years. She was family.

Carla loved Giselle, and Giselle loved Carla. She was as much a part of the family as Lupe. She had cleaned Giselle's home the day before; she did every Friday. Alexa couldn't let her mother accuse Carla of wrongdoing. At worst, Carla may have inadvertently pushed the 'off' button while dusting. But her mother said she had spent her entire day trying to fix it when all she had to do was click it on.

Giselle pushed a button on the machine, and a voice came on. "You have four messages." Alexa watched her mother's face relax into a smile as the machine began to play back the messages she'd missed. While her mother listened, Alexa sat down at the breakfast table and watched as Giselle's face registered her emotion about each caller: a smile for the first, a sneer for the second, a look of happy surprise for the third, and disdainful boredom for the fourth.

Alexa realized that her mother had apparently done nothing since waking up other than trying in vain to fix a machine that had simply not been turned on, had finally called Alexa to fix it, and then cursed a woman she loved for pushing a button while dusting. What did it mean? Was she having mini strokes? What was wrong with her? Add to that, her mother had not yet eaten that day. It was past two o'clock, and she'd had no more than a cup of tea and had said she'd had coffee.

"Mom, let's go out. I'll treat you to lunch. I'll wait while you take a shower and get dressed."

"I won't go anywhere with you dressed like that. Why are you dressed like that?"

"Like what?" Alexa asked.

"Like a vagabond. A beatnik. You don't look chic."

Alexa laughed and took her cap off. "I was taking a power walk at the beach. You expect me to wear Chanel?" Her mother didn't look all that chic just then either, but Alexa didn't mention it.

She continued. "Okay, listen, Mom. You take a shower and

get dressed, then we'll go to my house. It won't take me more than five minutes to change. And you haven't even seen my new home office yet." Thankfully, Giselle smiled.

While her mother showered, Alexa quickly called Steve Chado and left him a message asking him to return her call.

Dressed to her mother's satisfaction, Alexa and Giselle lunched at The Grill. Alexa made sure that Giselle ate a full lunch and insisted on ordering a dessert to share. Afterward, they took a walk down Wilshire Boulevard and up Rodeo Drive window-shopping before Alexa took her mother home. The entire time they were out together, Giselle had seemed perfectly normal, but when Giselle was getting into Alexa's car, she again shocked her daughter. Alexa had leased her BMW almost two years ago, and her mother had been in it innumerable times. Yet before she got into it that afternoon, she'd eyed it approvingly and asked, "Alexa, a new car? It's nice."

Alexa was uncomfortable leaving her mother alone and would have stayed with her. But her mother had said that Buddy would pick her up in about two hours for a reunion with friends from the cruise. So, the two women hugged at her door and said goodbye.

That night in bed, Alexa thought about her mother. The episode with her answering machine and then her car had definitely not been normal. And then there was the cup of tea. Alexa couldn't explain her mother's behavior. It wasn't like her at all. Giselle had been dependent on her husband for many things. But in the four years that she'd been without him, she had proven herself to be a trooper and had managed to take over her finances and every other aspect of her life with only occasional help from Alexa.

Her behavior today had been so over the top, so unlike her, and – Alexa had to admit – clearly, abnormal. She'd almost had a complete breakdown over the answering machine!

Alexa wished her older brother were home, back from his

trip. Mike was a doctor and would know whether this was serious. But Mike was somewhere in Africa with Doctors Without Borders. Alexa had no idea exactly where on that continent he was and had no clue when he'd be home. Thank God, he did have sporadic access to email. She would email him to let him know what had happened. She owed it to him to let him know. Meanwhile, Alexa would make sure her mother was checked out by a doctor.

Alexa's thoughts then traveled to Rafael as they often did recently and, more often, when she was in bed. Not his case, but him. Just thinking of him made her entire body tingle. She closed her eyes and relived the feelings of ecstasy that came over her when they had been locked together that one time. Only one time. And yet, even now as she lay there, her breathing became slow and deep, and her heart yearned to burst.

But even alone in bed under the cover of darkness, she couldn't allow herself to dwell in that paradise. She told herself she had to be more careful not to conjure him up. Because whenever she did, she'd imagine their union, his silken lips on hers, and then she'd be under a spell she'd have to pull herself out of and away from. Her guilt would not allow her to luxuriate in that bliss. She would inevitably feel as though she were betraying someone, but who? Was it Viviana, his unsuspecting wife? Was it Rafael, whose passion and lust she insisted on rejecting? Or was it herself, for refusing to honor the emotions he conjured up in her?

She fell asleep in the midst of these unsettling thoughts into dreams she would not recall.

26

The black Lincoln limousine pulled up in front of the home on Cielo Drive in Beverly Hills at twenty minutes past six on that same Saturday evening. Douglas, on this cell with his sweetheart, killed the engine. "Baby, they'll need me until at least nine thirty or so. If they go home right after, I'll be at your place by ten thirty, latest. If not, you'll see me when you wake up." He listened to her response, then laughed. "Okay, if that's what you want, Sugar," he said, "That's what it's gonna be."

He hung up, exited the car, put his cap on the hood, and lit a cigarette. Exhaling, he eyed the French country-style house facing him at the end of the short cul-de-sac. Douglas knew about the atrocity that took place in that house in August of 1969, the infamous Charles Manson murders. It had been a bloody crime, grotesque, and had held onto the headline for months. Douglas wondered if the adjacent homes had lost value because of their proximity to that house of horrors. Who would want to live across from a constant reminder of the depths of man's ability to commit heinous acts? He shivered at the thought. As he took another drag off his cigarette, he saw his ride walking down the path. Robert Stamen was putting on a black coat over his black suit as he walked. With him was a young girl Douglas took to be his daughter. The driver quickly threw his cigarette on the ground, stepped on it, and hurriedly took his cap off the hood and donned it. Then he went around the limo to tip his cap and open the back door for his passengers. "Good evening," he said.

Seeing the pair up close, Douglas was no longer sure they were related. The girl didn't resemble Stamen in the least. He was a tall, blond-haired man. She looked Hispanic. Whereas Stamen had the sort of face that was expressive and constantly in motion, the girl's face was devoid of expression. Whoever she was, she was decked out in diamonds and mink.

When Douglas was seated, Stamen addressed him. "We're going to pick up another couple."

"Yessir," Douglas said.

"They're on Doheny Drive. Up in Birdland."

"Yessir."

"And then we need to hustle over to the Ahmanson."

"Yessir."

Douglas had picked up Stamen before. He remembered the house, and the man. He'd taken him to the Philharmonic on a Sunday afternoon. Stamen had been alone then, wearing a business suit. Stamen apparently didn't recognize Douglas; if he did, he didn't acknowledge it.

His passengers were silent on the drive to Doheny. "Good, they're outside and waiting," Stamen said when they approached the address.

Like Stamen, Alandro was dressed in a black suit. A brown coat was folded over his arm. With him was a redhead, whom Douglas guessed was in her mid-thirties and not bad looking. Also formally dressed in fur and wearing jewelry, Douglas marked the total worth hanging on her as a fraction of what the woman with Stamen wore. He got out of the car and again tipped his cap, opening the car door for them. Then off they went, headed for downtown.

"We have dinner reservations at Patina in the Disney Concert Hall," Stamen said to Douglas.

"Yessir," Douglas said.

"That's Caruso's account," Alandro said.

Stamen nodded. "Ten mil,"

"Isn't that how much the Board is giving the New York Philharmonic?"

Stamen nodded again. "For the Children's Orchestra. And another ten mil for the London Phil."

Alandro laughed. "We're everywhere you go," he said.

Stamen slapped his thigh. "Yup! And that's just the way I like it."

"So, tell me again, Bob. What's the name of this Congressman we're meeting?"

Stamen shook his head in frustration. "Jason, come on, man! Get with it! The name's Bukoski."

"Bukoski," Alandro repeated the name as if trying it on. "What kind of a name is that? Russian?"

Stamen shrugged. "How the fuck should I know? Just be nice."

The redhead said, "It's Polish." Alandro and Stamen looked at her. "I'm part Polish," she explained with a smile that displayed her overbite.

Alandro smiled in fascination. "No kidding," he said. He put his arm around her then, as though to claim her wealth of knowledge.

Stamen, in turn, put his arm around the still-mute girl sitting at his side. He hugged her to him so tightly she almost disappeared inside his bulk. Ignoring the redhead's comment, he said, "This little lady has seen more opera, more plays," he waved his free arm in circles at his side, "more ballets and concerts in the past year than she ever thought she'd see in a lifetime, right Baby?" He looked at the sullen-faced girl whose expression didn't change at all. He kissed the crown of her head. She said nothing and did nothing.

The redhead spoke up, advising the little lady. "Honey, I hope you're out buying new dresses for every one of these things and jewels to match."

Alandro laughed. Stamen only smirked and said, "Watch out for this one, Jason."

Emboldened, the redhead addressed Stamen. "A hell of a thing at the bank," she said.

Stamen said nothing. He tore his eyes away from her and glared at Jason. He could not believe Jason had been so fucking stupid that he had told this bimbo about their business with the Feds! Was he really that fucking dumb? He saw Jason elbow her ribs.

She flinched and then looked at Stamen and said, "Oh, sorry." Stamen would deal with the moron later. For now, he just looked at his Rolex and spoke to Douglas.

"Driver, speed it up," he said.

Douglas nodded. "Yessir."

Stamen decided to ignore Alandro and his bimbo for the duration of the ride. He stroked his lady's cheek. "We'll be sitting in a special section just for the Donor's Circle tonight," he said to her. "That's a very special honor on opening night. It's reserved for people who donate lots of money." Of course, she didn't know that the donated money came from TriWorld and not Stamen's personal generosity, and neither Stamen nor Alandro saw fit to educate either woman on that point.

Douglas drove them to the Walt Disney Concert Hall and helped them alight from the limousine. Before Stamen walked away, he said, "Driver, don't go far. When we're done eating, we'll come out front. Be here. We need to get to the Ahmanson on time. There'll be people waiting for us."

"Yessir."

Stamen nodded and walked off, leaving a very happy Douglas standing at the Lincoln. After the valet agreed that Douglas could leave the limo parked where it was, the driver brought out his pack of cigarettes and lit one. Once he'd deposited those four people at the Ahmanson, he'd get himself a nice dinner, maybe some Mexican food or a sandwich. If they were eating now, they probably would go straight home right after the play so he could boogie right over to his honey's house.

He took a drag, exhaled, and smiled.

27

Days and weeks passed with phone calls from Attorney Gilmore, grilling Rafael on every aspect of TriWorld's business protocol with their non-U.S. clients and every aspect of TriWorld's relationship with Bank of Taiwan. They asked hundreds of questions about Rafael's relationship with all the other directors at the bank, with Alandro, Stamen and TriWorld President Han. They asked about his tax records for the last three years and how he was compensated for his media activity and lectures.

When three days passed without a call from Gilmore, Alexa wondered why they were suddenly quiet. She had no illusion that they were through with her client.

Rafael called daily to see if she'd heard from them. When she said she hadn't, he wanted to know if he could come to her office anyway. He was nervous; he was worried; he couldn't just sit at home. When she told him that she would be at the library, he wanted to join her there. "I can help you," he said. She demurred. He asked to meet her for lunch or to have dinner with her. Alexa avoided him. She had enough on her mind. She didn't have the energy to fend him off and had more than a premonition that continuing to spend huge amounts of time with him would make it harder for her to do so.

Though she had heard nothing from the Federal Reserve, she had received the call she'd been expecting from the audiologist letting her know that her new aids were in. Excited, she went in to have them fine-tuned and begin her trial period, testing them to see if they improved her hearing and clarity.

Except for that single appointment, Alexa camped out at the library daily. She studied everything she could about the Federal Reserve Board, the Federal Reserve Bank of New York and again went through Title 12 of the US Codes then through the regulations controlling cease and desist proceedings initiated by the Federal banks in detail. By the end of that week, she had studied the various types of cease and desist orders, the violations that result in their issuance, the affirmative acts that could correct the underlying violations, the possibility of a hearing in the appropriate Federal jurisdiction, the enforcement of civil money penalties for said violations, and the imposition of criminal penalties – which seriously unnerved her and signaled the true danger Rafael faced if justice failed. There was good news too. Alexa had asked the librarian where to find something and had actually heard and understood every word of the hushed answer.

Despite Rafael's blackboard presentation and her research, Alexa's basic lack of banking knowledge was still causing her feelings of insecurity. Because she lacked the experience of dealing with the Federal Reserve, she didn't know what direction Rafael's case would take. And there were all those high-powered attorneys representing Stamen and Alandro and the other employees of TriWorld who were huddled together and conspiring, concocting theories to explain Rafael's guilt.

In fact, from what she'd learned from her research, Alexa felt like she'd just awakened anew to the humongous nature of the charges hanging over Rafael. She simply had to rescue him from the Bank's treatment of him. They were like a posse that was preparing to lynch him on the tall tree of the Federal Reserve. She knew she had to save him; but she had to figure out how to do that. It was absurd to think that TriWorld could persuade the Federal Reserve that a relationship officer could have had any power over funding, yet that seemed to be exactly what TriWorld employees were doing. Why would the Federal Reserve believe that?

The question went 'round and 'round in her mind. Unable to come up with answer, she changed her line of thinking. What if TriWorld hadn't in fact told the Federal Reserve what Gilmore was saying they had? What if Gilmore was baiting Rafael? After all, she had nothing more than Gilmore's representation that TriWorld had in fact accused Rafael. She had no independent proof that the bank had pointed the finger at him. He was terminated, yes. But to this day, TriWorld had never actually given Rafael a reason for his termination. In a flash, she realized she needed TriWorld's stated reason for his termination. The next step became clear. She knew what she had to do, or rather, what Rafael had to do.

The following Monday, she met with Rafael. They were ending another call from Gilmore that morning. The call didn't go well. Gilmore had pounced on Rafael, expecting him to explain why all the others at TriWorld were pointing their finger accusingly at him. It seemed that Gilmore couldn't fathom that a lot of people could lie to protect the few and save their own jobs.

After the call, Rafael lit a cigarette with shaking hands and Alexa's heart went out to him. But she had to be stern. "Rafael, you really have to cut down on your smoking," she said. He looked at her as if she was being sarcastic. "I'm serious. I've noticed."

He stretched his neck. "I'm trying hard," he said. "It's hard. I'm too nervous."

"Well, you have to do better. By the way, is your neck better?" she asked. "It looks like it is."

"It's as good as it can be for an old man," Rafael said stretching to the opposite side. Alexa turned her head away and smiled. "The therapist had said it would take at least a few months. It's been a lot longer and I'm still doing the exercises he showed me when I was going." He shrugged. "I guess it's better. I have bigger problems."

"Glad it's better. And did you find a job?"

"I'm still looking. I really want a job. I need one. I can't sit at home and worry, and we need the money. Viviana's never worked and she never will." He sighed. "It has to be an evening job, so I'm available for these tete-a-tetes with Mr. Gilmore and friends. Part-time jobs are not easy to find."

She nodded. "I know," she said. "But you need to keep looking. When we sue the Bank, we need to show that you tried to find a job."

He scoffed. "Sue the bank? Right. Anyway, I am trying. I'm keeping track of every job I apply for, just like you said; date, time, and I keep the ads in a file."

He got up and took a few steps then turned to her. "Alexa, they don't believe I'm innocent."

"I don't know about that," she said. "They have to grill you. It's their job. But they're not stupid. The more they talk to you the more they'll see that it makes no sense to blame you. You need to relax. Look at the big picture, not the little conversations where he tries to catch you or tries to make you feel stupid, but the big picture where he finds you innocent. And remember, the clock is still stopped so they believe you're cooperating. That means they believe you're telling the truth."

Rafael laughed. "So, they think I'm stupid but innocent."

Alexa ignored the comment. "How are you doing with the psychologist?" Rafael shifted in his seat as though he was uncomfortable with the question. She had touched a nerve. "Rafael?"

"It's...interesting. I'm learning a lot about myself and my life." Alexa immediately envied him. This was why she wanted to start therapy. "I decided to really use the time with her to straighten some things out in my mind." She didn't have the time to ask him to expand on that just them. She needed to talk about something else.

"Rafael, I want you to file for unemployment benefits," she said.

"Alexa, I was fired," Rafael said, as if she didn't know. "I can't collect unemployment."

"That's not the issue. I want you to go down to the EDD. I know most things with EDD can be done online but I want you to actually go there in person and file," she repeated. "Immediately."

"Alexa -"

"Rafael, I'm instructing you to go and file for unemployment insurance today."

"Why?"

"I want to know what TriWorld has actually stated as the reason you were fired. You're probably right. You probably won't get any benefits, but I want to see what's on the record."

"Okay. I'll go today."

"Go now. If there's a line, wait."

When Rafael left, Alexa called Steven Chado again and left another message. If he didn't return her call within hours to give her a referral, she would find a doctor on her own. She called her mother to check on her. Giselle was eating when Alexa called and sounded completely normal.

Rafael called to let her know the outcome of his trip to the Employment Development Department. "I'm disqualified. No unemployment benefits. I have the statement TriWorld made on the record. I'm home, scanning it and emailing it to you." He sounded angry.

Alexa was temporarily distracted from her anxiety about her mother as she read the statement TriWorld had given to the Employment Development Department. To quote, TriWorld Bank had fired Rafael V. Lamon "due to misconduct in that he acted illegally while at his job, having approved and funded illegal loans." The statement was absurd but importantly, she now had clear, uncontroverted evidence that TriWorld had pinned itself into having clearly accused Rafael, a relationship officer, with having committed crimes relating to funding loans and then passed him to the Federal Reserve. Though she thought the accusation was immeasurably ridiculous, the danger Rafael faced if the Federal Reserve believed it, was huge.

Rafael called to make sure she'd received it. "It's insane!" he said. "They can't do this! I was told to sign the papers but Alexa, you have to believe me; I had no power to make loans."

"Okay, okay! I believe you," Alexa said, trying to calm him down. "We had to know what they wrote down. Of course, it's crazy. I'll call you back." And she did mean to call him back but didn't because just then Steve Chado finally returned her call and she was again preoccupied with her mother.

"Sorry I didn't call earlier," Steve said. "I was really glad to get your messages. I'm hoping you called because you had a change of heart," he said.

Alexa answered with a smile in her voice. "No, I still think you're a great guy. Actually, I called to ask about my mother."

"Ahh, she needs a dermatologist."

"I wish she did but actually, I'm not sure what she needs," Alexa said. She'd proceeded to describe the events of that morning at her mother's house to him.

Steven advised a neurological exam. "I doubt that she's got a serious problem. She was probably tired, or whatever, but if you're concerned it will put your mind at ease. Meanwhile, Dr.

Mindox is the best neurologist around. Your mother will be in good hands with him. He's also a great geriatric doctor." Alexa thanked him. Just before they ended the call, Steven said, "Alexa?"

"Yes?"

"Listen. I really enjoy spending time with you and I really like you. If you change your mind and you'd like to hang, give me a call."

"Sure. Thanks. And thanks again for my mom. I'll let you know what he says."

As soon as they'd hung up, she called and made an appointment with Dr. Mindox. She couldn't concentrate on Rafael's case or on anything else until she knew that her mother was all right. There was an opening in his schedule for that very day at three o'clock. Alexa had an appointment at twelve thirty but she would be able to make that three o'clock appointment, so she took it. Then she called her mother to see if she was free. She was. Alexa would be picking her up after her twelve thirty appointment.

At noon Alexa went into the kitchen, ate some cold chicken she found with and an orange, then returned to her office.

28

Preoccupied with thoughts of her mother's upcoming doctor appointment, Alexa had to force herself to focus on her meeting with Melody Landau, a new client.

Alexa had met Melody at a charity luncheon she had attended with Giselle. She was the daughter of one of Giselle's friends. She and Alexa had been introduced briefly, but they had not spoken beyond obligatory greetings. She remembered that Melody was naturally pretty. She was young, probably in her late twenties, and Alexa could see she took great care of her appearance. Giselle had mentioned to Alexa that Melody was married to a man substantially older; this was his second marriage. He had two children in their late teens and, according to Giselle, was fabulously wealthy. When Melody had called to make the appointment, she hadn't said what she wanted to talk about, only that it was "personal."

Melody arrived right on time, wearing a scarlet red dress to die for with fabulous heels and a silk scarf as light as the breeze. Alexa guessed the dress was a Valentino, the shoes Jimmy Choo, the scarf – she hadn't a clue. Her ombre-shaded hair shone, and her makeup was perfect. And yet, Alexa noted that her face bore an expression that clearly said, "I am not a happy woman."

After asking about her mother and offering tea, coffee, and water, all of which Melody refused, Alexa asked how she might help.

"Charlie's divorcing me. I need a lawyer."

"Oh, I'm so sorry." That explained the sad face. "But I'm not a divorce attorney, Melody."

Melody looked like she'd been punched in the stomach. She looked at Alexa dumbly, then, no longer able to hold back, she began to cry. She was hunched over, her hands covering her face, sobbing. Alexa passed the box of tissues across the desk. "Please. You have to help me," the young woman said between sobs. "Really. I don't know what to do. My mother said you could help me."

Alexa got up and went around her desk to sit beside the younger woman. "I'll help you as much as I can." She took another tissue out of the box and put it in Melody's hand. "I'll help you find the right attorney." She put her hand on Melody's shoulder and rubbed it gently as she might when comforting one of the twins. She sighed. "I'm sorry. Divorce is always tough. I think you know that I divorced." Melody looked up at her with red, watering eyes. "But Melody, you – you're still so young."

"I'm twenty-nine," Melody volunteered.

"You're young. You can marry again and have a family." The tears continued, shoulders shaking. "Melody, I promise you, you'll be fine. If divorce was in the cards, you are so lucky that it happened now, while you're still young and not ten or twenty years from now, when your options are fewer. If he's not right for you, isn't it better to find out sooner rather than later?"

Melody looked up at her. "But I don't know what to do."

"Your attorney will know." Back in her chair, Alexa opened her contacts and found what she was looking for. She wrote down the names and phone numbers of two divorce attorneys on her legal pad, tore off the page, then walked back around her desk to Melody and handed her the paper.

"These two attorneys are both excellent. You can see, one's female and one's male. Again, they're both excellent. All they do is divorce. They are used to big boys like Charlie. I urge you to make appointments with both and see which you like. If you don't like either one, call me. If you decide on one, and you'd like to keep in touch with me, let me know. I'm here."

Melody took the sheet of paper from Alexa, picked up her tote, and stood. She reached for the box of Kleenex and took two more tissues. "Thank you, Alexa. I appreciate this."

"It's no problem at all. I'm glad to help. Sorry I couldn't do more."

Melody hesitated. "How... how much do I owe you?"

"Owe me? Don't be silly! I didn't do anything."

"But I took your time."

"When this is over, or at least when the initial shock has worn off, and you feel better, we can have lunch. I'd like that."

"I'd like that, too," Melody said, attempting to smile. And with that, she left. Alexa stood with her arms crossed, watching the pretty, young girl whose future was presently a long, unknown walk away, and sighed. She knew the heartache Melody was experiencing. She herself had thought she'd had a wonderful marriage with Ben until the time she'd discovered his affair. The hurt she'd felt then was immeasurable. Her family had become divided, and for that – as well as for her shattered dream of living happily forever after – she could not forgive Ben, though she managed a cordial friendship after the divorce was final for the sake of their children. At least Melody and Charlie had no children. Melody really could start over again.

Relationships! They were all so imperfect. And even if you were lucky enough to have a good marriage, you would eventually outlive the one you loved like Giselle had outlived Alexa's father, only to wind up alone again and.... Alexa's mind had anchored on Giselle again. She looked at the clock, closed up the office, and went into the house and to the children's room where the twins were playing. With the few minutes left before she had to leave, Alexa sat on the floor and watched as Savannah filled up one half of a bumblebee in her coloring book with orange and told her mother all about Skye, her classmate, who'd just gotten a new kitten she'd named Cat.

"That's a silly name," Savannah said. "If I had a kitten, I'd name her Cookie." She'd started to color the bee's wing purple, then dropped the crayon and looked up at Alexa. "Mommy, can I have a kitten?"

Reggie, whom Alexa would have sworn had been totally focused on the television show he was watching, suddenly got up, turned around, and jumped. "No, Mommy! We have to get a dog!"

"Reggie, I asked first."

Reggie looked heartbroken. "Mommy, I weally, weally want a dog." Alexa wondered if he'd heard himself say, "weely, weely."

"Chickies, you can stop arguing because we won't be getting a kitten or a dog – at least not for a while." Alexa always felt bad when she denied her children. Not because she felt guilty; quite the contrary. She certainly didn't want to spoil them. She was enormously empathetic because children were powerless and could only have what the adults in their lives provided.

Then it was time to pick up her mother and go to her three o'clock appointment with Dr. Mindox. Alexa kissed the children goodbye and told Lupe she'd be home before dinner.

29

Afraid Giselle might refuse to see a doctor, Alexa hadn't told her mother where they were going until they were both seated in the car. Now, as they drove west on Wilshire Boulevard, Giselle was resistant. "Please, Alexa! There's absolutely nothing wrong with me. I'm healthier than you are."

"I didn't say there is anything wrong with you, Mom. I just want you to meet this doctor. I told you he's supposed to be really good."

Giselle's droll sense of humor showed itself. "All doctors are supposed to be really good."

"Very funny. I've heard he's the best of the good," Alexa said. "It won't hurt you to meet him. And I want to meet him, too."

In fact, Alexa's concern was growing. Before getting into her BMW, Giselle had again congratulated her daughter on her new car.

Dr. Mindox was a jovial looking senior citizen, tall and handsome with a full head of shining silver hair and turquoise eyes behind gold-rimmed glasses. His white doctor's jacket was spotless as were his hands, nails, and shoes. When he ushered them into his office, and all three were seated, Alexa was tickled to notice her mother actually acting coquettish for the doctor's benefit.

The doctor asked preliminary questions about the medications Giselle was currently taking, any present health problems she had, and her prior medical history. Alexa took her mother's cell phone and found the contact information for her other doctors as he requested. She was impressed when Dr. Mindox took her mother's weight, temperature, and blood pressure rather than leaving them to a medical assistant. He shone a light in her mother's eyes. He laughed when Giselle told him what she'd said to Alexa. "Dr., there's nothing wrong with me. I'm healthier than you are."

Eventually, the doctor gave his patient a piece of paper and a pen and asked her to draw a clock. Giselle laughed. "Can I have some crayons?" The doctor joined her, laughing along.

Alexa loved Dr. Mindox. She would thank Steve for referring him. She knew her mother would be happy she'd met him. When the meeting had ended, the doctor said, "I'll have my office call you to set up your next appointment." Then, he tactfully asked for Alexa's contact information, which she provided.

Doctor Mindox called the next morning. Knowing Alexa's father was deceased, he asked if Alexa had siblings. She told him that she had an older brother, presently abroad serving with Doctors Without Borders.

"I see. Then you will be the family member I will be in touch with about your mother."

"Yes, doctor, at least for the time being. And thank you for calling. It was a pleasure meeting you, and I'm so glad my mother apparently liked you. I look forward to seeing you again." Alexa was ready to hear the doctor say goodbye and hang up.

"Do you live with your mother?" The question surprised

Alexa. "No, my mother lives alone. I live about one mile away from her."

"And do you see her daily?" It seemed to her that the doctor's questions were oddly pointed.

"No, as much as I would like to, it's not possible. I'm divorced with two young children and a law practice."

"You may want to think about placing a caregiver with your mother," the doctor said.

Alexa felt her heart drop. "Why?" She asked, not wanting to know.

"I'm sorry to tell you that your mother is in the beginning stages of Alzheimer's. You may have guessed as much when you made the appointment. Now, we don't know everything about the disease. With some, it takes years to progress, and with others, it progresses faster. But you'd be doing your mother – and yourself – a great favor if you can find someone she can bond with now. And I'd like to put her on medication."

"I see."

"I'm sorry to have to give you this news."

Her response was automatic. "Yes. Of course." Her mind was numb. "Doctor, I haven't yet told you why I brought her to see you, and I'm wondering if these were the signs of Alzheimer's. She has repeatedly congratulated me on my new car when she's been in it for two years."

"Yes, it is. Anything else?"

"Yes. She's far more irritable at times than she's ever been and has accused the cleaning woman she's had for years of acting maliciously."

"Yes, that too. We think it's because she senses or realizes she has these memory lapses, and she becomes hostile–paranoid; she doesn't trust herself or those around her."

Alexa's heart cracked anew. "I see. Well, thank you for all the information. I suppose I'll be seeing you again."

"Yes, we'll be in touch. Goodbye, now."

"Goodbye."

"Oh, wait! Dr. Mindox?"

"Yes?"

"Does my mother know?"

"I haven't yet told her. But, as I said, she surely suspects something. I will be telling her at her next appointment and prescribing medication. You may want to be here with her."

"Yes, of course. I'll be there. Thank you."

She hung up, her life as she knew it forever changed. She emailed her brother with the sorry news.

Alexa tried to concentrate on her work, but it was impossible. She couldn't get her mother off her mind. Alexa thought back to the way her mother flipped out over the answering machine. This was the woman who had always been Alexa's rock. When she had discovered Ben's infidelity and decided to leave him, Giselle had been – as always – her safe harbor, her best friend. Now, Dr. Mindox would tell her she had Alzheimers. Her heart pined with empathy for her dear, dear mother. She was such a good person. Why her? It wasn't fair. Alexa wondered how Giselle would take the news.

She was jarred out of her reverie with a message on her phone from Gilmore's office letting her know that Attorney Gilmore would be contacting her the following morning at eleven o'clock Los Angeles time to speak with Rafael. She called Rafael to inform him, then decided to cancel her plans tomorrow after Gilmore's call. She wanted to spend as much time as possible with her mother. She called Giselle, and they planned a day together.

The next day, mother and daughter had lunch at the restaurant inside Neiman-Marcus on Wilshire Boulevard, then browsed the shop. They had apparently run into a sale. Alexa found a jacket she'd wanted, now reduced in price. Unfortunately, they didn't have it in her size, so she took the jacket to the cashier with her mother and asked if she could order it in her size from another store.

"I'll be glad to see," said the pretty, dark-haired, dark-eyed, young girl. She looked up the item in her computer. "Yes, we can order it for you. If you give me your Neiman's card, we can have it shipped directly to your home."

"Great." Alexa brought out the black credit card and handed it to the cashier. When the girl looked at the card, her mouth fell open, and her eyes widened. She ran around the counter and hugged Alexa tightly. "Oh, my god, it's you!"

Startled, Alexa and her mother looked at one another. When the girl came away, Alexa was startled to see her wipe away a tear. "You are famous in my family! When I saw your name… I can't believe it! I never met you, but my parents talk about you, and we bless you every Friday night at our Shabbat dinner." Alexa had no idea what she was talking about. "You helped us stay in America when we were going to be deported. You changed our lives. You saved us!"

Alexa smiled. "Oh," she said, understanding the girl's reaction. She smiled. "Hi, I'm happy to meet you. What's your family name?"

Alexa recalled the name. She had filed an asylum application for the girl's family when they had been ordered to leave the country. Her father had been in dental school at the time. The application was based on the fact that his country of origin was in the aftermath of a revolution, and Alexa had documentation that his family's return would almost certainly put their lives in jeopardy.

"And what's your name?" she asked the young girl.

"Nila."

Almost 85,000 immigrants had been granted U.S. asylum from Nila's mother country.

Curious, Alexa asked, "How are your parents?"

"They're fine. My father is a dentist. His office is on Bedford

Drive in Beverly Hills, and my mother is a branch manager of a bank in Sherman Oaks."

"That's wonderful," Alexa said. "And what do you do besides work here?"

"I'm going to college. I'm majoring in Women's Studies with a minor in Communication."

"That's wonderful!" Alexa said. And she meant it. The knowledge that this family was thriving and that this young woman was leading a life that would have been unavailable to her in her homeland – had she been able to survive there at all – was the best kind of satisfaction. It made her proud to be an attorney.

After the jacket was ordered, Giselle said she wanted to go home and rest before Buddy picked her up. They would be going to dinner and the movies. Alexa couldn't point to a single thing that her mother had done all day that had seemed abnormal. Giselle had acted perfectly normal the entire day. Relieved to know that Buddy would be with her and dinner would be seen to, Alexa dropped her mother off at home, kissed her, and headed home to join the twins and Lupe for dinner.

After dinner, Alexa played Candyland with the children, then bathed them and put them to bed. Tired, she took a shower and fell into bed, turned off the light, and began looking back on the day. A lot had happened in the last two days. Most importantly, she had been told that her mother has Alzheimer's.

That piece of news would change her mother's life forever. Then today, she had coincidentally run into the daughter of past clients. That chance meeting had been a most fortunate stroke of serendipity, for it had empowered Alexa anew. The girl's story was proof of the difference Alexa could make in a life – and had made in many lives. Alexa felt confident again. She felt powerful. Lying in the dark, she made two resolutions. First, she would find someone to live with her mother, a live-in caregiver. Second, she would see to it that Rafael was totally exonerated.

She turned on her bedside light and found a pen and paper. She made a list of requirements for a caregiver. Of course, it would have to be a woman. Her mother spoke both French, Spanish, and Italian fluently, but would be most comfortable speaking English. She wondered if, in time, the effects of her disease might even erase her knowledge of a language. Also, she would have to be a licensed driver, have some experience with Alzheimer's, and have letters of reference. Next, she thought about how to find the perfect person. She made a list of people to call. She would ask Lupe if she knew of anyone. Maybe Giselle's cleaning woman, Clara, would know of someone. Maybe Rafael might know someone. She would also ask Sheyanne, everyone at her old office, all her friends, and go through her phone book. There were agencies as well. She would soon have to open up the subject of a roommate with her mother.

She turned the light off and thought about Rafael's case. She was determined to turn Rafael's case around. She had his innocence to work with, and that was all she needed. She was an attorney representing a man who had been wronged. It was her responsibility to set the record straight, rectify the wrong done to him, and make him whole. The feeling of righteousness made her feel she could conquer anything.

She fell asleep feeling invincible.

30

"Rafael, after you speak to Gilmore this morning, I want you to go right back to the EDD and ask for a hearing."

"A hearing?"

"Yes. You're entitled to one. Go back."

"But they denied my request for unemployment because the bank must have forged my name! They're saying I –"

"I know what they're saying. Trust me. Go back. Ask for a hearing."

"Don't you need to be there with me? Don't I need a lawyer?"

"No. When they ask, just say you did nothing illegal."

At precisely eleven a.m. Gilmore called. By now, Rafael and Alexa expected him to be sarcastic and unfriendly, even though he may have started out pleasantly.

"Good morning. Let's review the relationship between TriWorld and Bank of Taiwan, Mr. Lamon. When did you become aware that TriWorld was funding Bank of Taiwan?"

"Let's see," Rafael thought for a minute. "As I told you, sir, I had seen the agreement on paper when Bob showed it to me, and I objected to it. But I learned we were actually funding them at the time of a rollover. Favio Melo at the Bank of Taiwan told me we had started funding them sometime in early 2021. Before that, I would call him when I was asked to by Jason – Mr. Alandro – to ask what interest rate they'd be charging the people who held power of attorney on our accounts."

"I see." It sounded almost like a growl. "And beyond that, it is your position that you had no part in funding Bank of Taiwan?"

"That's right, sir."

"And why did you think Mr. Alandro asked that question?"

"Well, I knew they were one of the banks we were funding. I thought he was asking so we could decide what to charge on the loans we funded them. We funded lots of banks. But I didn't know that we were matching the amount we loaned them to the amount of the loans they were making to their borrowers with the power of attorney over an account at TriWorld."

Gilmore grunted. "And when *did* you first become aware that the banks were illegally matching funds?" Gilmore sounded patronizing.

"I was never actually aware of it. I didn't know for certain."

Gilmore chuckled. "Mr. Lamon, is it your position that you were not aware of the fact that TriWorld was illegally loaning money to Bank of Taiwan in the same amounts as the loans Bank of Taiwan made to those holding power of attorney on TriWorld accounts?"

"That's right. I had no idea. I didn't know either amount."

"Well, let me ask you this, Mr. Lamon. You say Mr. Stamen asked you to transmit TransWorld's funding rates to Bank of Taiwan. Did you do so?"

"Yes, I did as he told me to."

"And how did you do that?"

"I contacted Favio Melo at the Bank of Taiwan and gave him TransWorld's funding rates."

"Favio Melo at Bank of Taiwan."

"Yes," Rafael said. "That's right."

"And why do you think you were asked to do that?"

"They were borrowing money from us. I assumed it was so that they could charge additional basis points on loans to their customers."

"How did TransWorld know how much money to fund Bank of Taiwan?"

"I don't know."

"You don't know, Mr. Lamon? Didn't you call Bank of Taiwan every quarter to ask the total amount of their loans to your people for that quarter?"

"Bob Stamen and Jason Alandro had me call Melo every quarter when there was a rollover to ask the aggregate amount secured for that quarter. But I honestly didn't know they were matching funds. I had no idea. I didn't know how much TriWorld was lending them."

"So, it is your position that when you first learned TriWorld was funding Bank of Taiwan in – let's see, you said that was at a roll- over at the beginning of 2021 – you didn't know that they were matching funds?"

"No. I mean, that's right, I didn't know."

Gilmore sighed audibly as if to signal to them that he was deeply perplexed. "Well, we'll be getting back with you. It will be in a day or two. Meanwhile, remember you're under instructions not to talk to any of the other parties."

"Yes, sir."

"And you, Ms. Starr."

"Of course, Mr. Gilmore," Alexa said.

"One more thing, Mr. Lamon," Gilmore said and paused for a moment. "Between now and the next time we speak, think about what you've told us and let me know if there's anything you've told us that you want to modify."

Rafael and Alexa looked at one another. Then Rafael said, "Mr. Gilmore, I have told you nothing but the absolute truth. I swear it on anything holy."

Gilmore sounded tired. "Okay, Mr. Lamon. Goodbye."

When they hung up, Alexa reminded Rafael, "Okay, go. Remember to ask for a hearing and just say you did nothing illegal."

About two hours later, Rafael called her from the EDD to say there could be no hearing that day. He was told that TriWorld would first have to be given notice, so the hearing would take place the following day.

31

Rafael slept fitfully that night. Alexa had told him that the Feds and Justice had probably listened to his taped telephone interviews multiple times and held them up against what Stamen, Alandro, and all the others at TriWorld had been telling them.

Rafael was sure that after dozens of conversations, Gilmore and whoever else had been on the line still didn't believe he was innocent. And then he had seen the document at the EDD with TriWorld's statement that he, Rafael, had made illegal loans. Alexa had tried to calm him down, but even with all the faith he had in Alexa, he felt it was almost impossible to persuade the Federal Reserve to believe he was innocent when so many others, more powerful and with more resources, were telling them he was guilty.

As terrible as Rafael felt about what was happening to him, his loss of a job, loss of his reputation, loss of his savings, and to some extent his health, Rafael also felt bad that Viviana had to go through this. His wife was a relatively simple woman, and he wondered if she truly understood what he was being accused of despite his explanation. And he wasn't certain if, regardless of whether she understood all the facts or not, Viviana truly believed he was innocent.

Alexa was the only person he was certain believed in his innocence, and he had to wonder if she was biased because of her feelings for him – though she denied having any. He knew he was in love with her. He was crazy about her. She was everything he could ever want. In fact, as far as he was concerned, Alexa Starr was everything any man could want in a woman, and her husband had been a major fool to stray and to let her go, especially when she had mothered two children with him.

Rafael had felt a strong attraction to her the first time he'd seen her at that Rotary meeting two years ago. After a brief episode that was the equivalent of owning a timeshare in Paradise for a few hours, she had cut him out of her life. Since then, it had been hell for Rafael. He still shared his days and nights with her. He spent hours rhapsodizing about her essence even as a memory. She had continued to exist in his mind, in his heart, and in his memory, but never again in his arms. Then he was fired. Since then, he was around her more than ever, but couldn't have her. Could the Justice Department think up a worse punishment?

The next day, he returned to the Employment Development Department. At the hearing, he swore under oath that he had done nothing illegal. The burden of discrediting and thereby disqualifying him from receiving unemployment benefits then switched to the Bank. As no one from the Bank was present at the hearing to prove that Rafael had in fact "approved and funded these illegal loans," that left only hearsay evidence contradicting his sworn statement of innocence. As a result, Rafael was delighted to learn that his benefits were restored and he would be receiving the small monthly income; at this point, every dollar helped.

"Alexa, you're a genius! They're giving me unemployment."

She nodded. He was on a momentary high. "Can we sue the Bank for discrimination?" he asked. "They're discriminating against me, aren't they?"

Alexa laughed. "Yeah, they're discriminating against you. But it's not because of your race, age, sex, handicap, nationality, or any other protected trait."

"It's not because I'm Argentine?"

"Rafael, you got the job because you're Argentinian. Right? I mean, they have Directors from all over the world forming relationships for the Bank, don't they?"

His anger showed itself again like a flash of lightning. "But they're only doing this to me!"

"It's called scapegoating. You know what scapegoating means? It's from the Bible. Killing you for the sins of others, like they used to do with goats."

"I'm their goddamned goat."

"Actually, you're a bull." Rafael looked at her. "You're a Taurus, aren't you? That's the sign of the bull, and you are stubborn." He didn't even break a smile. Her tone changed then. "Rafael, once the Feds are finished with you, you can think about taking TriWorld to court. Their communication to the EDD clearly shows that they fired you because they alleged that you made illegal loans; they can't deny that. And they must have known you were innocent."

Rafael broke out into a smile almost despite himself, and that warmed Alexa's heart. He said, "And you wonder why I love you." When he saw the sour look on Alexa's face, he changed gears. "By the way, I need the paperwork for the therapist's lien."

"Okay, I'll get you a form. Now you need to get a job."

"I can't find one."

"Work anyplace you can. Don't forget to keep all the information." He was silent. "You'll need it for trial."

Rafael rolled his eyes and shook his head "Trial? You're

really something, Alexa." The light in his eyes dimmed. "So, are you dating a lot these days?"

"Excuse me? What brought that on?"

"It's a friendly question, from client to attorney. Are you?"

"Enough," she said and immediately realized her mistake; she'd left an opening, and he pursued it.

"Anyone special?"

Alexa sighed with impatience. "I'll tell you what. When I'm done representing you, and I'm no longer your attorney, we can talk about my dating life."

"Alexa," he said, "you break my heart every day."

Later that evening, when Alexa was with the twins, Steve Chado called. "Hi. Just wondering how your mom's doing. Did she ever go to see Mindox?"

Alexa was embarrassed. "I can't believe I've forgotten to thank you for that referral. I'm so sorry," she apologized. "I meant to. Dr. Mindox is wonderful. My mother really likes him."

"I'm glad," Steve said. Then, "Can I ask what he said? I mean, I don't want to pry, but you were pretty concerned. I hope all's well?"

Alexa hesitated. It was hard for her to admit to someone that her mother was ill. She had not yet told strangers. Her brother knew, Sheyanne knew, Ben knew, Lupe knew, and Rafael knew. Now she would have to use another hand to count on her fingers. She realized it was a question of time before others would have to know. "Actually, she has Alzheimer's," she said.

Alexa heard Steve's intake of breath before he spoke. "Oh, Alexa, I'm so very sorry! I was hoping his diagnosis would be far less dramatic."

"Oh, well," she said. She was actually going to try to make this sound light. "It is what it is," she said, knowing full well that she sounded like an idiot. She quickly tried to change the subject and redeem herself. "I really am sorry for not calling to thank you for referring Dr. Mindox. I know I meant to. He really is an excellent doctor."

"Well, I'm glad that she's in good hands. You can be sure she's getting the best possible care with him."

"Yes, he seems to be on top of things and very caring. She has a live-in caregiver now, thanks to his suggestion."

"That's good. My aunt has Alzheimer's. She's had it for some time now, and I've watched it progress. That's actually how I know how good a doctor Mindox is. I don't know if you know anyone who has it, but if you ever feel you want to talk to someone about it, you can call me."

"Thank you."

"I mean that. Don't hesitate."

"I won't. I mean it, too. Thank you, Steven. That's sweet of you."

"Yeah. And take care of yourself, Alexa."

"I will," she said. "Thanks. And again, I apologize for not calling."

"Sure. Give me a call sometime," he said before hanging up.

Thinking of her mother, Alexa grew sad. She was thankful she had found Madlynn, a caregiver her mother liked and was even willing to have as a live-in, while Carla would continue to clean once a week. When she spoke to her mother, Giselle would always say things like, "We just got home from Bloomingdale's," or "Madlynn sings for me all the time." Alexa liked Madlyn, too. She had been referred by an attorney friend whose mother had used Madlynn's help for four months due to a broken hip and had praised her.

Giselle had become moody and sometimes difficult to deal with because of bouts of paranoia, and Madlynn seemed to instinctively know how to get along with her. She owned a small Honda but drove Giselle's more solid Mercedes when driving with her. She was even able and willing to help Giselle with her bookkeeping and other day-to-day tasks.

Alexa knew that Madlynn's intelligence would be extremely beneficial and that she would become increasingly valuable when speaking with doctors and pharmacists as her mother's condition deteriorated further. Most importantly, she was delighted to learn during their interview that Madlynn had actually worked at a facility for Alzheimer's patients and knew what to expect as Giselle's disease progressed. She had spent two years working in a home for those with Alzheimer's and had finally left the job because she was unhappy bearing the major responsibility of care for twenty patients. When Alexa called the director of the home, she confirmed everything Madlynn had said and added that they were sorry to have lost such an excellent employee.

Ben had run a background check; she had no criminal record. She seemed to be physically strong enough to handle her mother if the need arose. Within hours, the room adjacent to Giselle's master bedroom, which had served as an office for Alexa's father, was converted into Madlynn's bedroom with a television and a computer installed. For the time being, Madlynn had Fridays off – the day that when Carla was there. Alexa only prayed Madlynn would stay.

Knowing she was there to care for her mother enabled Alexa to focus on her children and her work.

32

Rafael found a job working five evenings a week in the lady's shoe department at Nordstrom's.

The calls from Gilmore continued. There was a sudden flurry of calls all about Favio Melo and the Bank of Taiwan, basis points and matching funds then more personal questions about Rafael's background, education and past experience. As always, they were told the calls were recorded; they knew that someone from Justice was listening in.

Despite the fact that the Federal Reserve kept hammering away at him, often covering the same subjects and asking the same questions, Rafael began to feel some degree of relief for as the weeks and then the months went by the clock had still not yet started running again. That was a good sign.

Alexa listened to Gilmore's conversations with Rafael on speakerphone like a hawk but kept her participation minimal, only adding the legal formalities as required. Rafael answered all questions honestly and to the best of his ability. True, they may believe he was stupid or naïve, but they must have seen that he wasn't a criminal. She told Rafael as much and he prayed she was right.

"This is stupid," Alexa said after another phone call that was a rehash of the same subjects.

"You don't think they're starting to believe me?" he asked.

"Maybe, but this could go on forever. They're going around in circles."

Rafael rubbed his forehead. "What can we do?"

"We have to end it."

"How can we?"

"I don't know. Let me think."

And think she did. She refused to be disheartened though she realized that her client was fighting the odds in pure numbers. What could she do to have the Federal Reserve believe Rafael was innocent for once and for all? It would have to be something bolder than answering their questions over and over. He had been doing that and it obviously wasn't enough. A written letter or proffer to them wouldn't do it either; that would only transform his oral testimony into written form. They had to finally realize he wasn't lying.

When Ben came to visit the twins that week, she asked him a casual question. "Do you know if the Federal Reserve gives lie detector tests?"

"Polygraphs?" He shook his head vigorously. "The Feds in general won't touch them." Then he looked at her with an edge of suspicion. "Do I need to ask why?"

"I'm thinking about having my client take one."

The way he simply gazed at her then, his expression frozen in amazement, said it all. But he went on anyway, making it obvious that he thought it was a stupid idea.

"Alexa, don't. You're playing with fire. It'll only hurt your client; polygraphs never come up as truthful, even if the guy tells the truth."

Alexa tossed it off, thanking her ex. "It was only a thought."

The next morning, she emailed both Larry Bloom and Sheri Lee separately, asking if they would be kind enough to help her on a point she had no experience with: Based on their experience, did the Federal Reserve administer polygraphs? Both attorneys answered that the Reserve did not. Attorney Lee added that, in her opinion, this was because polygraphs had not yet been proven reliable.

The next time Rafael met with Alexa, she approached the subject. "Rafael, you think Gilmore doesn't believe you. I think there's only one way to show him you're telling the truth, and that's to tell him that you're willing to take a lie detector test."

Rafael almost fell off his chair. With a shaking arm and trembling hand, he slowly reached for his pack of Marlboros and took out a cigarette. He set the pack on Alexa's desk and, as he lit one, he eyed Alexa. "Are you crazy?" he asked.

Alexa shot up, opened the French doors and both windows in the guesthouse, then sat back down in her chair. "Don't worry. Please. Rafael, I've researched it. They'll definitely say no. I'm sure. The Federal Reserve doesn't use polygraphs. I just want them to know that we're offering. It's just our way of letting them know you have nothing to hide."

When he'd calmed down as much as he was going to, she called Attorney Gilmore's office and was told he would call her back shortly. He called back within minutes. Alexa put him on speakerphone. Smiling at Rafael, she told him that her client was there with her and wanted to submit to a polygraph examination to prove his truthfulness. Someone on the line chuckled, and it clearly wasn't Gilmore. Gilmore simply exhaled and said, "Really."

"Yes," Alexa said.

There was a pause. A long pause during which Alexa looked out the open French doors to the flowers now in bloom, a mix of colors. The fragrance of jasmine wafted in as she wondered why it was taking so long for Gilmore to tell her that the Federal Reserve didn't believe in polygraphs.

Then Gilmore was back on the line. "Well, Ms. Starr, we usually don't like polygraphs." Another pause, an awkward pause, and Alexa could tell that Gilmore had covered his mouthpiece with his hand. She looked at Rafael, her smile replaced with a blank look. She shrugged. Rafael was staring at the telephone now, holding on to the arms of his chair as though for dear life. Gilmore came back on the line. "As I said, we usually don't like polygraphs, but… uh… I think in this case…" Alexa saw Rafael's eyes travel to her face. Then he squeezed his eyes shut. His lips were trembling as Gilmore finished. "I think it might be a good idea."

"Excellent!" Alexa said. "We're glad to hear that." Her heart had fallen into her belly.

"But, Ms. Starr," Gilmore was quick to add, "Hold on. There are certain caveats. He must go to the polygrapher we choose and no one else. Is that understood?"

"Yes."

"We'll send you a name. And we will prepare the questions for the polygrapher to ask. He must ask only those questions. Is that clear?"

"Absolutely. Thank you." Her head was spinning.

"All right then. We will compose the questions and email them to you with the name and contact information of the polygrapher."

"Excellent. Thank you so much, Mr. Gilmore." She felt weak.

"Good day, Ms. Starr."

"Goodbye." She hung up the phone and stood stunned.

Rafael opened his eyes and found Alexa's. "What have you done?"

33

It was a night filled with terror for Rafael. He tossed and turned, his heart hammering, hours later still refusing to calm down.

What had Alexa done?

His body throbbed as his temperature rose in waves, then went cold. He couldn't withstand a test with wires on him! *What had she been thinking?* Alexa had said she'd researched and was sure that the Federal Reserve never used lie detector tests. So why are they going ahead with one for him? He was being victimized by Gilmore! And what were all those long pauses Gilmore kept taking on the phone when he heard Rafael wanted to take one? He was unquestionably monumentally screwed. He could never pass a polygraph. He was far too nervous a person. The stakes were too high, and he was too emotional.

Sometime after two in the morning, Viviana cajoled him into taking a strong sedative. Only after he was finally asleep did Viviana close her eyes to the world.

Alexa lay in bed that night, wide-eyed, filled with self-recrimination. She scolded herself for her arrogance. This time, she had gone too far. Ben had told her not to do it, but, as usual, she'd thought she knew better. As a result, she'd completely sabotaged Rafael's case. How could she have done that? There was no way in hell that Rafael could pass a polygraph! The man trembled with the slightest hint of anxiety. He'd been visibly stressed throughout every conversation he had with Gilmore – and he was speaking over the phone! How could someone as nervous as Rafael come up as anything but 'deceptive' despite his honesty when his bodily reactions were being measured? She had really screwed up, and Rafael would be the one to pay for it. *Damn! Damn! Goddamn!* They'd all said the Federal Reserve doesn't accept polygraphs! Still, she shouldn't have been so cocky! She had to come up with a reason to call it off. Resolved that she would call Gilmore and abort the polygraph, so that Rafael would never have to go through with it, she managed to get a few hours of rest.

In the morning, she drank two mugs of strong coffee and left the house with the twins. She walked them to school and kissed them each goodbye, then continued on, taking a power walk to clear her head. She had no experience with a polygraph examination and had never had a client take one. She wondered what it would be like and, as she walked, her curiosity grew. Slowly, the germ of an idea began to grow. She assumed that she would have at least a couple of days before Gilmore provided her with the name of a polygrapher and a list of questions he wanted asked. That time was her friend. But she had no time to lose.

On her way home, she called Rafael on her cell and asked when he could meet at her office. He said he'd be there in an hour and a half. She arrived home, showered, and dressed.

She met Rafael at the door. He looked gray and nervous.

"I know you're worried about the polygraph, and I'm sorry. But I have a plan."

"Another one?"

She ignored the sarcasm and took his hand. "Come on out to the backyard. Let's talk."

"Alexa, how will you stop this? I can't do it." He bit his lip.

Alexa walked to the blossoming roses. She followed their trail from the dark red to the deep pink, followed by soft pastel pink. She finally came to the vine of tiny white roses that grew up and around the trellis behind the swing made for two in the corner of the yard. She was calm and focused as she sat on the swing.

"This is what we'll do," she said, looking up at Rafael. "Sit."

"I can't. I'm too nervous. Go on."

"Okay, listen. We have at least a day or two before Gilmore gives us the name of his polygrapher and the questions. I'm going to Google polygraphers this morning. I'll find one today. We'll go see him immediately. We'll pay him. I'll tell him the background and the general outline of the case and compose some questions similar to what I think the Federal Reserve will put together. You take a polygraph, like a test run, a rehearsal, so you won't be surprised for the first time if and when you take it with their polygrapher. You'll see what it's all about. Okay?"

Two conflicted Rafaels stood listening to Alexa. One just wanted to do nothing more than gaze down at her. She was so lovely to look at. He wanted to tell her how beautiful she looked just then, sitting on the swing with the roses around her, smiling, her face so radiant in the morning sun. Captured in its glow, she truly looked angelic as she told him her plan. He longed to simply bask in her beauty. The other Rafael needed to be rational and responsive. He shook his head. "I'm not taking it. I can't, Alexa."

"Okay," she said without hesitation, "if you don't like it, if you're not comfortable, you won't. That's the point. This is a way for you to experience what it's like, so you're more comfortable with the mechanics of it, and you can see if you want to take it or not." Rafael was still not sold. "If you don't like it, I'll call it off. Promise."

He put his hands in his pants pockets, and his torso swayed as he bent back to the sky, then put his hand to his neck and rubbed. "I don't know what to say, Alexa. I don't know what God or whoever is up there wants from me." He threw his arms up. "I guess I'll put myself in your hands."

Alexa sprang up and headed to her office. "You can help with the questions – or not. Either way. I'm going to do some googling so we can make an appointment as soon as possible." Despite her lack of sleep, she felt a surge of energy, excited by the adventure that would be a new experience for Rafael… and for her.

Rafael followed her inside. Online, she found several polygraphers in Los Angeles. The second one on the list caught her eye. He was in the Hancock Park area. "Listen to this. This guy was in the Secret Service. He served under two Presidents. He also belongs to the California Polygraphers' Association. He sounds like the kind of person the Federal Reserve would like. I'll call him." She called and scheduled the first morning appointment the day after next. "Okay," she said, hanging up the phone. "Let's come up with some questions to ask."

For the rest of the day, they perused the information the Federal Reserve had gathered during its interviews and reduced it to the major subjects. They both came up with questions, and Alexa noted each on her legal pad to refine. At four thirty, Viviana called to remind Rafael that they were expected at their daughter's new in-laws that night for dinner. He left to battle the afternoon freeway traffic back to North Hollywood.

Alexa's priority the next morning was to finalize the six relevant questions the polygrapher had explained he would need to ask Rafael at their appointment the next day. The questions had to be on point, direct, and concise, leaving no wiggle room.

By evening's end, she was as content as she knew she'd be with the relevant questions she had drawn up and closed up the office.

34

Bright and early the next morning, Rafael was at Alexa's front door. He waited for her to gather her things before they took off in her car, heading east on Wilshire to the polygrapher's office.

Brett Skeet was obviously no longer in the Secret Service. Still handsome with a shock of white hair, his tall stature, which Alexa and Rafael assumed was once lean and muscular, was now on the heavy side and soft; his stomach was large enough to prevent his suit jacket from closing. He was a pleasant man who listened attentively as Alexa outlined Rafael's situation. Then he explained that as Rafael would answer each question, the machine would be measuring his heart and pulse responses, his upper and lower respiration, his blood volume, and electrodermal skin conductance tracings to determine if he had answered truthfully. And then they were ready to start.

Skeet first asked Rafael one or two control questions to set markers. He gave Rafael a box of coins and instructed him to answer "No" to any questions about the coins, regardless of the actual answer. He explained that when Rafael answered "No" to the question, and it was the correct answer, he would have a truthful response on his chart. When Rafael answered "No" to the question, and it was a false answer, that too was significant because his bodily response would set a mark to signal deceptive answers on his chart, allowing Skeet to measure future deception. The questions began. Alexa waited for the relevant questions to be asked.

"Did you ever knowingly participate in making illegal placements at Bank of Taiwan?"

"No."

Standing behind Rafael and a few steps away, Alexa distinctly heard his responses, something that would not have been possible with her old hearing aids. She was again able to confirm that these new aids were excellent.

The questions continued. Alexa felt she was taking the test along with her client. Alexa didn't know how Rafael was faring, but chances were, given his nervous temperament and his extreme stress under the circumstances, his galvanic skin response would be off the charts, his blood pressure through the roof, and his heartbeat too rapid to measure. She was so anxious as she listened to the questions that she was pretty sure her responses weren't far behind. She had no doubt that her client was being completely truthful, but according to Ben, no one ever passed a polygraph; even innocent people reacted badly under test conditions, which was why lawyers never allowed their clients to take one – except for her. Perhaps, like Rafael, they were just nervous, but she was sure that few were as nervous as her client. The exam ended, and Skeet removed Rafael's attachments from the machine.

"How are you feeling?" Alexa asked him.

"I'd love a cigarette," Rafael said, looking at Skeet.

"Go right ahead," Skeet said. "You deserve one after that."

"How did he do?" Alexa tried to sound light.

"I don't know yet. I'll have an initial idea in a few hours.

After that, I'll have my girl type up an official report and get it to you. Would you like an email or a hard copy?" Skeet asked.

"Both, if you don't mind," Alexa said. "Guess that's it. I'll wait to hear from you. Thanks so much. I'll be referring you to all my lawyer friends."

As they were walking out, Skeet called to them. "Mr. Lamon. You seem like a nice man, and you were probably telling the truth, but I'd hate for you to get your hopes up. You've got to know that almost no one ever passes a polygraph. Doesn't mean you're lying, but these test conditions invite a showing of deception. So, like I said, don't get your hopes up."

Rafael thanked him as well, and they left with his head hung down. In the car, he asked, "How much did that cost? I didn't even ask."

"Six hundred dollars," Alexa answered. "I have it all written down with the invoice. But don't you think it was worth it? You know what to expect now."

"Sure. It was hell, and I get to do it again with questions from the Federal Reserve with the guy they chose – and they'll probably have one of their agents there."

"Only maybe," Alexa said. Then she bit her lip.

35

Alexa received a phone call from Brett Skeet late that afternoon,

"Ms. Starr? Brett Skeet here."

"Hi. Thanks for calling. Please call me Alexa."

"Okay. Well, Alexa, I have some good news."

Alexa shot up in her chair. "You do?"

"Yup. Your client showed 'non-deceptive' all the way."

She sat up even straighter. "He did?"

"Yes, he did and it's almost unheard of."

"Oh, my god! That's wonderful!"

"Yes, it is. Your client showed 'truthful' on every one of the relevant six questions."

"Mr. Skeet, that's absolutely terrific!" She was on her feet now, so excited that with her right hand clutching the phone to her ear she was pumping her left arm up and down as she almost ran out of her office and into the backyard. "Thank you!"

"You're welcome."

Her heart was thumping. "When can I have the written report?"

"I can email it to you and mail out the hard copy both by the end of the day tomorrow. Is that okay?"

"That's wonderful. Thank you so much!"

"My pleasure. I just wanted to call and let you know. Bye now."

Alexa hung up and spread her arms out to the sun. "Thank you!" she said to the universe. So, he was innocent after all! She was doubly thrilled; her gut instinct had been right. Rafael had done nothing illegal.

Rafael had wanted to stay with her until she heard back from Skeet, but she had insisted he leave and let her do her work. Now she dialed his cell number. When she told him what Skeet had just told her, they congratulated one another. Then, Rafael landed back on Earth. "What's the big deal? I have to take another one."

She suddenly felt the glow fade. "I have to go. My mom's coming over. We'll talk tomorrow."

That evening, when Giselle and Madlynn joined Alexa, the twins, and Lupe for dinner, Alexa noticed that throughout her entire stay, her mother never let go of her handbag, clinging to it as if afraid that if she put it down for a second, it would be gone. When Alexa tried to insist that she put it down during dinner, Madlynn gave her the high sign and later took her aside and explained that Giselle had lately slept with it by her side as well. She noted that she had seen the phenomenon with other Alzheimer patients who were apparently afraid it would be stolen if left out of sight, and advised Alexa that it was best to humor her. Remembering what Dr. Mindox had said, Alexa nodded and said nothing more about it.

Early the next morning, Friday, Alexa was in the backyard cutting some roses to put in a vase on her office desk. She was thinking about the fact that Rafael had tested 'not deceptive' on the polygraph. What a shame that the Federal Reserve would never know! It would be so helpful if Gilmore could see those results. She stopped cutting and stood up. Why couldn't he see the results? She knew what she had to do. She threw the garden shears down on the grass and ran to the office phone. She dialed Brett Skeet's number. When he answered, she said, "Good morning, Mr. Skeet. This is Alexa Starr."

"Good morning, Ms. Starr."

"Please, call me Alexa. I wonder if you would do me a big favor."

"Certainly, Alexa. And please call me Brett."

"Thanks. When you email me the results of Mr. Lamon's polygraph today, could you possibly copy someone else on that same email?"

"Certainly. That's no trouble at all. Let me get a pen, and I'll jot down the email."

Alexa waited for him to get pen and paper ready, then she gave him Attorney Gilmore's email at the Federal Reserve.

"Will do," Skeet said.

"You'll send it as an attachment?" "Yes."

"That's great, thanks so much."

Then she called Rafael. Viviana answered his cell phone. "Good morning, Alexa. Rafael is in bed with strep throat. He can't talk, but he can hear you. Thank you for all you've already done for Rafael. We're so appreciative."

"It's nothing, Viviana," Alexa said. "I'm sorry he's sick. He sounded fine yesterday afternoon."

"Yes. It started last night. It was a bad night for him."

"If he has strep throat, he really should see a doctor. He'll need antibiotics."

There was a pause. "That's what I told him," Viviana said. "But he won't go." There was an awkward pause, then, "He says he can do without it since we no longer have insurance."

Financial paranoia was typical of Rafael. "Okay, if you can hear me, Rafael, as I told you yesterday, the results of the polygraph were excellent. That's really unusual. You told the truth, and that's what the test results show. Skeet is going to email the results this afternoon, and I asked him to copy Gilmore on the email. I'm also going to scan Skeet's brochure showing his background and his credentials and email that to Gilmore, too. The report shows the questions asked and your answers, and that your answers to each were 'non-deceptive.'"

"Alexa, he heard you, but he wants to say something. Please wait." After a few seconds, Viviana came back. "Rafael wants to know why you want to do that. He says they said not to do what the two of you did."

"I know," Alexa said, "but it can't hurt. Even if they delete it, it would be too tempting not to look at first."

Viviana laughed softly. "He's smiling, Alexa."

Alexa said, "I'll keep in touch. Go to a doctor, Rafael. Bye, Viviana."

Her next call was to Ben. She wanted to know what he thought about her idea of sending the results of the polygraph to the Federal Reserve. Afraid to tell him she had already done it, she told him she was thinking about it. Ben was short and emphatic. "Don't do it."

"Why not? They show he was truthful."

"Alexa, they told you to go to their polygrapher, right?"

"Right."

"And you said that they told you to ask only the questions they gave you, right?"

"Right."

"And you went to some guy you found on the web. You made up the questions to ask?"

"That's right."

He shook his head. "Alexa, do not fuck around with the Federal Reserve. They're bigger than the goddamned President. If they tell you not to do something, don't do it. They'll come down on your client."

"Okay, thanks."

"Are you going to do it?"

"I don't know."

Ben sighed and shook his head as if his ex was just too dense to understand the potential for disaster. "I'll be there to pick up the kids tonight."

She called one other attorney, Stan Hastings. As far as she knew, Stan had no dealings with the Federal Reserve, but he had been involved with dozens of Federal trials and appeals. She posed the same question to him and got pretty much the same answer.

When she hung up, she scanned Skeet's brochure and forwarded it to Gilmore at the Federal Reserve in New York with an accompanying note that read:

Please review the underlined credentials of Brett Skeet, a former Secret Service agent under two Presidents. The questions Mr. Skeet asked during my client's polygraph and the polygraph results have been emailed to you directly from his office. All of Rafael V. Lamon's answers were found to be truthful and non-deceptive.

If your agency has any problem with either Mr. Skeet or the questions asked, my client stands ready and willing to submit to a second polygraph exam. Respectfully

When Ben came over that afternoon to pick up the twins for his weekend, he asked Alexa if she'd made a decision about the polygraph results. "I sent them over," she said.

Ben's reaction seemed excessive. It was so sudden, his voice so cutting, that both children were startled. He boomed. "Why, Alexa? Why would you do that when they've specifically told you not to?" He seemed to take it personally, and he sounded as though he were admonishing a misbehaved child or a delinquent secretary.

Alexa answered calmly. "Put yourself in their place. You get a polygraph result from an attorney under these same circumstances. You know she's done what you've told her not to, so you're ready to discount it, toss it, or delete it. But wouldn't you be tempted to look at it before you do? Look at the questions that were asked? The questions he answered truthfully? Just out of curiosity?"

Ben just shook his head, exasperated. "Come on, kids, let's go."

Both Reggie and Savannah went to Alexa and hugged her extra hard to show how much they loved her, even though she'd upset Daddy. They almost whispered their goodbyes.

After they left, she found that while she was talking with Ben, Brett Skeet had called and left a message. His secretary had suddenly felt very ill and had left for home. As a consequence, the emails and hard copies had not gone out on Friday. He apologized and promised he would make sure they would go out over the weekend and that they would arrive well before Monday morning if he had to type up the final report himself.

36

Early Monday morning Alexa got a call from Gilmore. It was so early in Los Angeles that she had not yet entered her office.

"Good morning, Ms. Starr. I received your email. I see you had your client take a polygraph." Alexa noted the hint of sarcasm in his voice.

"Yes, Mr. Gilmore. I came across Mr. Skeet and I was impressed with his credentials." She had to assume Gilmore hadn't bothered to look at Skeet's brochure. "He was in the Secret Service under two Presidents," she said.

"Yes," Gilmore mused. He sounded as though he was reading through the brochure as he spoke. "I see that." She waited. "Well, he sounds fine." There was a pause. "But you were told that we would compose the questions your client would be asked," he said.

"Yes," she agreed.

"Well, let's take a look and see what you asked." She took a breath and waited. "Question 1. Well, that was a control question. Question 2. Another control question.

"Question 3. Here we are. *Did you ever knowingly participate in making illegal placements at Bank of Taiwan?*

"Question 4. *Did you ever knowingly participate in matching funds?* Alexa heard Gilmore click his tongue in thought. "Well, those are good questions. We'd have asked them." She let her breath out in relief.

"Okay. Question 5. *Did you complain to Jason Alandro and Bob Stamen when you saw the so-called security agreement and indemnity agreement between TriWorld Bank and the Bank of Taiwan?"* After only a second Gilmore said, "Yes, that question is germane. We would have asked that question." Alexa took a deep breath and tried to exhale quietly.

Gilmore continued. "Question 6. *In your position at TriWorld Bank, did you have any power, make loans, or authorize funding?"* Okay. That's good." Alexa could hardly believe the run of luck she was having. She kept her mouth shut, closed her eyes, and kept breathing.

Gilmore was on Question 7, the fifth of the relevant questions. *"Did you have any knowledge of matching funds before the third roll-over of 2021.* Okay, we would have asked that question." With each question, Alexa lived a lifetime as Gilmore repeated it, paused to think, then decided it was one they would have asked, and moved on to the next torturous interlude. Gilmore actually snorted, then said, "Okay, we'd have asked that question.

Let's see," She waited. "Question number 8." This was the final question. *"Did you have any part in funding loans to the U.S. powers of attorney on the TriWorld accounts through Bank of Taiwan?* Okay! Well, that is the question, isn't it?"

Suddenly, Gilmore and some unnamed person were laughing hysterically. Alexa almost fainted. They shouldn't be laughing! *What were they laughing at?* She hurriedly turned on her computer and brought up the email she had not yet seen from Skeet, so she could see what Gilmore was looking at.

Before she could bring it up, Gilmore spoke. "Ms. Starr, are you aware that your client responded Yes to this question?"

"What?" Alexa jumped out of her chair. "No! That's impossible. It's a mistake! He answered NO!"

Gilmore's voice was calm, even sweet. "The report shows it was YES."

"Attorney Gilmore, I'm bringing it up on my screen right now." She opened Skeet's email, opened the attachment, and scrolled down to the last question. And there it was. *How could she have had Skeet send it to Gilmore without checking it first?* Sure enough, Rafael's response to question 8 showed YES. She panicked. "Mr. Gilmore, I assure you, this must be a typographical mistake. If you allow me, I would like you to speak directly with Mr. Brett Skeet, who administered the test and has the actual report. I'm certain he will tell you that he answered No."

"I'd be interested in hearing that," Gilmore said.

"Just one minute, please," Alexa said, her heart racing. "Do you want me to give you his phone number or shall I conference him in? Or do you want to email him?"

"Why don't you conference him in?" Gilmore said, his tone even sweeter. He was obviously enjoying Alexa's quandary and sudden agitation.

"Okay. Please hold a minute while I find his number."

"It's on his brochure," Gilmore offered helpfully.

"Yes. I have it here," Alexa said. "I'm dialing now. Please hold."

She managed to dial the number with fingers that trembled at least as badly as she had ever seen Rafael's fingers tremble. *What if it wasn't a typo?* But it was. Of course, it was! And it had to be corrected – immediately! Once Skeet's number was dialed, she reconnected Gilmore so he could hear it ring and her entire conversation with Skeet. She thanked God when Skeet answered despite the early hour.

"Mr. Skeet, it's Alexa Starr. Good morning. I'm talking to you with Attorney Gilmore of the Federal Reserve Bank on the line with us. Thank you for forwarding the email to both him and me. I'd like you to look at the last question you asked Mr. Lamon during his polygraph examination. Could you please look at your raw report and tell Mr. Gilmore how Mr. Lamon responded to the last question?"

Brett Skeet said, "Certainly. I know that he was non-deceptive in all his answers. Now, let me locate the test results." He was back on the line in seconds. "You're asking about the last question?"

"Yes, that's right. Question 8. *Did you have any role in funding loans to U.S. powers of attorney on the TriWorld accounts through the Bank of Taiwan?* Your email says he answered YES."

"Oh, is that what it says? Well, that is a typo! I'm looking at the raw results. He did not say that. He answered NO. I do apologize to you, Ms. Starr. My secretary was gone, so I typed it up myself. Fortunately, I do not often make mistakes like that."

"Mr. Gilmore," Alexa said, more than relieved, "do you have anything else you'd like to ask Mr. Skeet?"

"No," Gilmore said, unenthusiastically.

"Thank you for your time, Mr. Skeet," Alexa said. "Goodbye." She disconnected Skeet, then said, "Mr. Gilmore, are you there?"

"Yes, we're here. Okay, Ms. Starr. Hold on."

She waited. She didn't know what to think or what to expect. She guessed they were conferencing on his end. Maybe they would accept this polygraph and cut Rafael loose after this. On the other hand, it was equally possible that the Federal Reserve was about to place her under some sort of contempt order for disobeying their instructions. She had not only done what they had expressly told her not to do, she'd flaunted the result in their faces via email, and all she'd heard from everyone was that the agency was more powerful than God.

Maybe she'd taken too many risks. Maybe Ben had been

right. She could be confronting contempt charges from the Justice Department within the hour, and she would have to call him to get her out of jail. Her mouth went dry at the thought. She wanted water, but she couldn't move; she was frozen to the spot. Her heart was in her throat and beating hard.

Eventually, Gilmore came back on the line. "Okay, Ms. Starr. We're going to accept this polygraph in lieu of our own. The administrator meets our standards, and the questions are excellent. There's no need to double our efforts."

"I'll let my client know." Her heart had taken over her entire being, and she was going for a colorless answer, nothing immodest or cheeky, just trying to breathe quietly.

"Ms. Starr," Gilmore said.

"Yes, Mr. Gilmore?" She knew what was coming.

"This is an exception. You understand that. I don't expect you to disobey our instructions in the future."

"I understand, Mr. Gilmore. Thank you."

"Ms. Starr, there's one more thing."

"Yes, Mr. Gilmore?"

"Back in February, Mr. Lamon received a letter from us requesting a proffer. It was due in two days from that date. You arranged with Attorney Cerise that the clock be stopped. Many months have passed now, and we would now like to request the proffer."

Alexa was stumped. "Are you saying that Mr. Lamon has been uncooperative?" Before he could answer, she went on. "Mr. Gilmore, if this is because of the fact that I disobeyed your orders, Mr. Lamon had nothing to do –"

Gilmore interrupted her. "That's not the reason for our request at this time. I won't be divulging our reason. But you will have more than two days. We'll expect a hard copy of the proffer in our offices in seven days. Good day, Ms. Starr."

Gilmore hung up.

37

Alexa sat bewildered. It took her a minute to catch her breath. Gilmore had accepted her polygraph and had acknowledged that her client had answered truthfully, yet he wanted a proffer under threat of humongous fines and jail time. It didn't make sense. *How could she explain this to Rafael?* As she sat pondering all this, her cell phone rang Rafael's distinctive ring.

"I just had an accident. I'm fine. But the ambulance is coming to get me."

"My God! What happened?"

"I was driving to your place in case Gilmore called. I was in the mountains when I was suddenly rammed by a big silver SUV."

"Are you okay?"

"Yes. But I was up on Mulholland Drive and could have easily gone down the mountainside."

"Are they okay?" Alexa asked.

"I don't know. They took off."

"What?"

"They hit me really hard and then took off. They were behind me and then at my side, and they just crashed into me and then took off. Thank God I was alone in the car."

Alexa heard the sirens. "Are you saying they purposely rammed into you?"

"I think so. I mean, it looked like that."

"And they didn't stop? Did you see who it was?"

"I was busy trying not to fall over the side."

The sirens were growing louder. "Okay, it's a good thing you're going to be checked out. Call me when you can."

When she got off the phone, she sat absorbing the possibility that the 'accident' had not, in fact, been an accident. Maybe someone wanted to eliminate Rafael. *But why? And who?* Maybe someone had realized that the Feds were no longer accepting the story that it was all Rafael's fault. It would have to have been someone who had a lot to lose if Rafael could no longer be scapegoated. From what she knew of the people at TriWorld and the consequences of being found out by the Feds, she wouldn't put it past someone at the bank to have caused the accident. Maybe they paid someone to do it. But what good would it do to kill him?

She waited anxiously for Rafael's call. When she finally did hear from him, she was relieved to hear that he'd been discharged from the Emergency Room with a clean bill of health. "I don't know how I'm going to pay for the ambulance and the hospital," he said. "I have no insurance, and my car is going to a body shop to see about the damage."

"Well, you're okay, and that's all that's important," she said. "In other news- ."

"Alexa, I can't take any more bad news."

"Well, there's good news and bad news," she told him, falling back on the classic cliché. "Which do you want first?"

"The good news," he said.

"They loved the polygraph and their accepting it. They loved

Skeet, they loved the questions, and they loved your answers. You don't have to take another polygraph."

"Alexa, that's great news! My God, you're amazing! No one comes close to you."

"I'm glad you're happy. By the way, I see you have your voice back."

"Yes. What's the bad news?"

"They want a proffer in seven days. The one they wanted to begin with."

"Why is that bad? We've had way over a year! And now, they're giving us seven days, not two."

"But it makes no sense! They've gotten everything they want from you. You've shed light on all the others. You've been their greatest source of information. From where I sit, I don't see why they're asking for it if they know you're innocent."

Rafael surprised her then. He responded rationally, with uncharacteristic calm. "They must want it for their files. So far, they have only their notes and recordings of our calls. A letter – a 'proffer' as you lawyers call it – would be something in writing that they can use to check what everyone else is saying against what we give them. And they can put it in my file and close it."

"Okay, that makes sense," Alexa said. "Whatever their reason, we need to get on it. I'll start on it. When you're up to it, you can come and help. Please, do not come here until your throat is better. I don't want to get sick, and I don't want my kids or Lupe to get sick. As for the car," she hesitated a few seconds, "if you need me to advance you the money to fix it, it's not a problem. We're pretty close to suing TriWorld."

The next day, Rafael took care of his car insurance and repairs and rented a car without Alexa's help. The day after that, he joined Alexa, who had made headway in composing the proffer, and three days after that, on the fifth day, Alexa mailed out a 28-page proffer to the attention of Attorney Gilmore at the

Federal Reserve, laying out why Rafael V. Lamon could not be held responsible for the illegal activity at TriWorld. She received a short email confirming receipt, but no other comment about the content of the proffer.

The next conversation Rafael had with the Federal Reserve took place a week after the agency had received the proffer. During that conversation, Rafael was the most relaxed he'd been while speaking with Gilmore, believing the positive results of his polygraph had bolstered his credibility with the agency and relieved that the proffer had been filed. He felt like he had been heard at last. Alexa noted that the Justice Department, an ever-present tentacle during these conference calls, seemed to be absent for the first time – at least she didn't hear their presence – and that was an excellent sign.

Days after Rafael's last conversation with Gilmore, Bob Steman was fired. Friday afternoon at two forty-five, Federal agents entered the Beverly Hills branch of TriWorld Bank. Computers and files were confiscated, and all employees were sent home. The next day, the branch was permanently shut down.

Curious, Alexa ventured to call Attorney Gilmore to ask if any of the other people employed at the Bank had offered to take polygraphs. He said they hadn't. She pushed. "Now that Mr. Lamon has submitted to one, have you suggested that they take one?"

Gilmore sounded as though he was stifling a laugh before answering. "We have suggested that they might want to, Ms. Starr. Their attorneys all tell us that their clients want very much to take polygraphs, but that they have all advised them against it."

"I see," said Alexa.

Serena, Rafael's assistant, called Rafael that same day. When he saw the call was from her, he didn't answer. She left a message. "Rafael, this is Serena. I'm so sorry about all you went through. I wanted to call you before, but things were crazy, and we were told not to contact you. I don't know if you've heard. TriWorld's been ordered to pay civil penalties for every day that the illegal activity went on – it's huge. The branch is closed due to quote, managerial deficiencies, and branch improprieties, end quote, and they received a cease-and-desist order. I was really concerned about you, but as I said, we were told not to contact you. Please call me. I would just like to know how you're doing."

Rafael did not return the call.

When Rafael and Alexa next spoke, Alexa told him she had more good news.

"What is it?" Rafael asked.

"I want to tell you in person."

"OK. I'll come to your office."

"No, let's meet at the Polo Lounge."

"Only if I can take you to lunch."

"Rafael, how can you afford it?"

"I'll put it on a card. And if you say no, I won't come."

"Okay, your treat. We do have something to celebrate."

"Celebrate what?"

"I'll tell you at lunch. I'll call and make reservations. Noon?"

Rafael was smiling when he answered. "I can't wait. I miss you."

On his way to meet Alexa, Rafael made a point to drive by TriWorld's now-closed premises. He wanted to see the ghost of what had been. The walkway was still pristine, the grass and flowerbeds still manicured. But it was deathly quiet in and around the bank.

He recalled how Ed Monroe had ushered him to his car in shame that last morning. He wondered where the security guard had been moved to now that he was no longer needed there.

38

The Polo Lounge located in the flamingo pink Beverly Hills Hotel on Sunset Boulevard has long been the meeting spot for the powerful and wealthy in a city of untold power and wealth. The bar lounge opens onto an extensive restaurant and continues into the large outdoor area. On any given day, celebrities are seated in booths with their agents, managers, or interviewers, recorders on, taping their every word.

Alexa and Rafael were seated outside at a table alongside a bed of flowers. It was another beautiful Los Angeles day in late spring, and both were relaxed and in good spirits. Waiters moved from table to table, refilling glasses with iced tea, Arnold Palmers, or bubbly water, replenishing coffee cups, and serving fresh Martinis, champagne, and Cosmos.

As soon as they were seated, Rafael said, "I can't wait any longer. What are we celebrating?"

"Well, Mr. Lamon, it's time to discuss your lawsuit against the Bank."

"Have you heard from Gilmore? Did he say I'm innocent?"

"I doubt that the Federal Reserve ever tells you you're innocent. But you'd know by now if they still thought you were guilty. They'd have served you with various orders and subpoenas to appear. You know what's happened to the others at the bank."

Rafael realized the nightmare was truly, finally over. He was finally freed from the debilitating burden of shame and undeserved guilt he had been carrying around for well over a year. His family's life had been almost completely ruined. A huge smile took over his face. "Ha-ha! Hallelujah!" He rapped the table with both hands and called the waiter over to order champagne. When the waiter had poured the bubbly into their flutes, he raised his. With tears in his eyes, he toasted. "To you, Alexa. Thank you from the bottom of my heart."

Their glasses touched. "You're welcome, Rafael. From the bottom of my heart."

They both took a sip, enjoying the sensation of the tiny bubbles hitting against their palates.

"This is good," Alexa said.

"Yes. You could tell it's good just from all the bubbles." When Alexa looked at him with her head tilted, he continued. "Ahh, something you don't know, smart lady? The more bubbles, the better the champagne."

"Okay, I'll buy that."

"Now, can we celebrate?" Rafael asked.

Alexa saw the look in his eyes. The light had reappeared there, and a smile washed over his face. The old Rafael was back. He was treading on dangerous ground. "We are celebrating." She lifted her tall flute and took another sip of champagne.

"You know what I mean."

"Rafael…"

"I'm dying, Alexa. Let's enjoy."

"Don't die." She moved away from the table. "Look, if this is what you're going to talk about, I'm leaving."

Rafael pursed his lips and sighed. He shook his head. "I've behaved. I've left you alone since you said no more. But I can't anymore. Have a heart, Alexa. I want you way too much."

"I'm right here," she said, pointing at herself. "I would think you're sick of me by now. You've seen me almost every day for months and months."

"I can't get sick of you. I'll never get sick of you. And you know that's not what I mean. Making love to you was more than incredible. I lost myself in you. I want that again, a second time; even if it's just one more time. *Please!* I just want to hold you again, kiss you, make love to you. I miss… touching your skin and," he looked heartbroken. "I miss looking at your body, kissing your lovely breasts, and caressing your thighs."

Alexa sat very still. *What the hell was it about this man?* She couldn't believe the power he had over her. She hated him for the way he could melt her and render her helpless. Alexa Starr, this supposedly strong, independent woman, became helpless when Rafael went after her like this. She tried hard to repel his spell.

"It was just one time, Rafael. It was a mistake, and it's over." She spoke with her eyes on her champagne flute. She sounded resolute to herself, and with her heart fluttering and her body almost limp, she didn't trust herself to say more just then. Even her teeth felt weak.

Rafael reacted as if she were just too stupid. "When will you get that we will never be over? We've barely begun! One time, and look at me. It changed my life." He leaned forward and took her hand. "You told me to leave you alone, and I did. I miss you so much, I'm going crazy. You're the first thing I think of every morning and the last thing on my mind when I fall asleep. But I've left you alone."

Alexa sat mute. Though her mouth had gone dry, she was afraid she'd topple her glass if she attempted to pick it up.

"And when I was fired, and I saw you almost every day, you

think it was easy being around you like that? Seeing your gorgeousness all the time? Seeing that beautiful rear end and your beautiful face, and not being able to kiss you? And on top of my desire for you, my gratitude and my trust...knowing my life was in your hands. Alexa, I'm madly in love with you."

Alexa was weak. That was the problem with Rafael. His hold on her was way too strong. *Who the fuck spoke like that?* She could feel herself actually moistening as she sat across the table from him, just listening to him. She had to stop him. She gathered her strength, braced herself, and spoke.

"Rafael, you're married! You go on and on, and I have to stop you, stop us. I'm the cop. Why don't you get it? You have a wife. Why are you so stubborn? So selfish? So childish? Don't you realize it was a mistake?"

"It wasn't a mistake. I can't help myself."

The waiter came to take their order. Rafael said nothing. Alexa spoke for them. She snapped. "We're not ready." She picked up the menu, then slapped it down in frustration. "I thought we were here to celebrate and discuss your lawsuit against the bank over a nice lunch. That's what I'm here for. If you're here for anything else, then there's a misunderstanding. If that's the case, I should just leave." She moved to pick up her purse.

He reacted as if she'd slapped his face. Contrite, he immediately tried to stop her, putting his hand on hers, already on the purse sitting on the table. "Alexa, don't go. I'll do anything you want. I'm sorry. I'll stop. I'll just keep it inside me as I've been doing, and I'll smile. Let's have a nice lunch and talk about the lawsuit. We have a lot to celebrate."

"Okay then." Mollified, Alexa opened the menu and eventually decided on a salad. Rafael ordered salmon. Before she finished her glass of champagne, Rafael was quick to refill it.

As they ate, they relived various moments during their confrontation with the Federal Reserve. At one point, Alexa told him how afraid she'd been of finding herself in big trouble for not having followed Gilmore's instructions. "I really got a taste of what you were going through," she said.

She shared the terror she felt when she realized that the wrong answer had been submitted to the Feds. Rafael hadn't known about that until then, and he was aghast to think what she must have gone through as she hurriedly dialed Skeet's number with Gilmore on the other line, not knowing if he'd answer the phone or what he'd say. Now they could laugh about it.

For his part, Rafael shared gossip about TriWorld characters whose names Alexa had heard for months as they drank more champagne, their lunch barely touched.

He described Han's idiosyncrasies as the President of TriWorld. "Let me put it this way. The first time I went to his house in Virginia after I'd been employed, I had no idea what to expect. We landed at the airport, and there were three black limousines waiting there to drive us all to his home. It's quite a mansion, with a private road, a huge gate, columns and statues on the grounds, and servants, mostly Asian. But we didn't go into the main house. We were ushered into another building on the grounds. I think it was his office. It was bigger than your house. The main room was set up with a conference table. It was huge. We all sat around this gigantic table. It reminded me of something I'd seen in one of the James Bond movies when all the bad guys get together. You know which movie I mean?"

Alexa laughed, "Yes, I think so. The one where the baddest guy gets them all in one room and kills them all."

"Yes, that one. Anyway, since I'd never met him before, I introduced myself and put my hand out. He said, 'Good to meet you,' or something, 'I don't shake hands.' He's totally afraid of germs. What do you call that? Like Michael Jackson."

"Germophobic."

"Germophobic. That's why he doesn't travel. He's not afraid

of planes or of flying; he's afraid of germs. He uses a bathroom that has a special key. And listen to this. I used the guest bathroom. Of course, cause he's germophobic, there are no towels, only paper towels that are disposable." Alexa nodded. "So, after I washed my hands and dried them with a paper towel, I tossed it into the wastepaper basket. I noticed there was nothing else in the basket, even though people had been in and out of that bathroom before me, and I thought it was strange that none of them had washed their hands. Then I noticed that as soon as I left the bathroom, a maid went in with a plastic trash bag and apparently emptied the waste basket of my single paper towel."

"Weird," Alexa said.

"Yeah. And when our lunch was served on trays, Han never touched anything. His staff served him separately, and they all wore white gloves."

Rafael went on to share that Stamen was on his fourth marriage. Rafael had met wives three and four. Number three was a young girl from Ecuador who said little, hung on to Stamen's arm, and seemed to have a wide smile painted on her face. Number four was an even younger girl, even quieter, with very full lips and a sullen face, also from some Asian country. He'd heard that Stamen had children, but no one seemed to know how many. As for Jason Allandro, he was famous for the myths tying him and his brother to the Mafia.

They were midway through their second bottle of champagne, and Alexa had relaxed. Looking across the table, she looked at the Rafael that had now reverted back to himself. He was still thinner, his face still gaunt, but he was relaxed and in command, confident and sexy as hell. She couldn't deny that she'd missed him. Or the major attraction she had to him.

"Do you really think someone was trying to kill you on Mulholland?"

"I've thought about that, obviously. I don't know. I can't

figure out why anyone would want me dead. I never told Vivian what happened. She just knows I had an accident."

Eventually, they finished the second bottle of champagne and were left with two choices. They could order a third or leave.

Alexa laughed. "I think two bottles of champagne are enough for one lunch. In fact," she said. "I need the ladies' Room."

"And I need the men's room," Rafael said.

Rafael was out first and was waiting for Alexa by the door to the ladies' room. When she exited, he took her by one arm, then both. Before she knew what was happening, his arms wrapped around her, and his lips were on hers. His kiss was warm and soft and sweet. She couldn't pull away. Truth be told, she was in heaven.

His lips gently pushed at her hair as he whispered in her ear. His voice was throaty. "I want you, Alexa." She wanted him as much. She had denied herself as much as she could in the face of such desire.

"Yes," was all she said before turning to find his lips.

"Can we go to your house?"

She nodded and sealed it with another kiss.

They left her car at the hotel, drove his car to her house, and parked it several houses away from hers. They entered her house quietly through the courtyard's French doors into her bedroom. The children were still in school, but Alexa assumed Lupe was somewhere in the house. She quickly found her and told her that she was home and would be in her room, not to be disturbed under any condition. When she returned to her bedroom, Rafael was in her bed. Alexa locked her door, pulled down the shades on her French doors, and went to Rafael's side of the bed to undress. The entire time, she refused to think. She let her rational mind go and allowed herself to be pulled into the effects of the champagne and Rafael. She would think about it later.

Rafael got out of bed, already erect. He undressed Alexa and ran his hands down her body. With closed eyes, he held her as one would hold a beloved child and inhaled deeply. Then he kissed her again.

Alexa's entire body was tingling. She felt his erection move against her abdomen and his silken tongue in her mouth. She felt his desire for her. He drew her to the bed.

Sometime later, she heard the twins, home from school, and got up. "We need to go," she said. Rafael didn't argue. They dressed and quietly left the house through her bedroom door. He drove her back to the hotel, where she retrieved her car from the valet. When they said goodbye in his car, Rafael touched her shoulder, and she turned to him. "Thank you," he said.

Alexa nodded. "We will not do this again."

39

She told herself it had been the champagne; she'd certainly had enough. She must have finished off a bottle all by herself, and she was not a drinker. She told herself it was the alcohol and the mood of celebration, the relief of having Rafael's ordeal with the Federal Reserve behind her. The huge win, the huge relief. It was the champagne and the celebration and Rafael's insistence. Except that Rafael hadn't insisted any more than usual during the meal, and in fact, at the end, he could probably have been thwarted after the kiss. She was only human. She had wanted it as much as he had.

For the love of heaven, what could anyone expect? She was only human. Rafael had said it was hard for him to be with her on an almost daily basis and not want to sleep with her. What made him think it had been any easier for her? Her choice had come down to either continuing to see him and feeling horrible for what she was doing to his marriage or never sleeping with him again, and so she had told him she was through. But still, she was only human.

The next morning was a Saturday. Alexa was anxious to

spend time with her children. Rafael's legal situation had been all-consuming, and she was craving quality time with the twins. After breakfast, Lupe received a phone call and told Alexa she would be spending the day with her daughter, Graciella. She was concerned as Graciella was having a difficult time with her husband. Alexa wished Lupe the best, and they went their separate ways. She took the twins to the La Brea Tar Pits and Page Museum on Wilshire Boulevard's Miracle Mile. It was their first trip there.

The La Brea Tar Pits captured Los Angeles as it was 10,000 years ago. Though the children couldn't comprehend that span of years, the plants and animals they saw awed them. Alexa explained that they had gotten trapped in the seeping black tar during the Ice Age. The twins ran around the park-like grounds, gawked at the saber-toothed cats and mammoths, and shuddered at the huge bones and fossils. After lunch at Marie Callender's, we enjoyed one of their famous pies. The children wanted to take some home for Lupe, so Alexa bought two whole pies to take home, one apple and one cherry. Afterward, Alexa took them shopping at the Century City mall for new summer clothes, including swimsuits, since both had outgrown most of their clothes.

Back in the car, the twins took their usual places in the back seat. The radio was on, and an Amy Winehouse song came on. "Mommy, don't you like that song?" Reggie asked.

"Yes, I do."

"But you don't, you tuwn it up. Don't you want to heaw it?"

Alexa smiled. "I have new hearing aids, Chickie. Now I can hear it really well without doing that."

Reggie clapped his hands. "Wow, that's gweat, Mommy. Sav, Mommy's new heawing aids wowk."

"I know," Savannah said. "She can even hear the television, too."

Once home, Alexa was putting away the pie when Lupe

called to ask if she could spend the night at Graciella's and return Sunday afternoon. "Of course," Alexa answered. "I hope she's okay."

The children were watching television when Sheyanne called.

"Hey, girl. How's the banking world's newest, best lawyer?"

Alexa laughed. "Sheyanne, you've always been my best fan. How are you?"

"Are you sitting down? I'm engaged!"

"Oh, my God! Sheyanne! Congratulations!"

"Thanks," Sheyanne said.

"That's fantastic."

"Yeah."

"Are you going to make me pull it out of you?" Alexa asked. "Tell me what happened."

"The usual. He proposed, and I said yes."

"I'm so happy for you!" Alexa gushed.

"I know. You apparently spoke to my Joshua. Thank you, thank you a thousand times. You're the best friend ever."

"Actually, I haven't had the chance to talk to him," Alexa said. "He did it on his own, and I'm completely thrilled for you."

"Really? That's so cool! I know you're happy for me, Lexie. I think only my mother is happier than we are." The two laughed, knowing it could be true.

"Well, spill it. When did he propose?" Alexa asked.

"Last night."

"How? Where?"

"Guess."

"Restaurant?"

"Uh uh."

"Bed?"

"Uh uh."

"Not text," Alexa ventured.

"God no!"

"Beach?"

"Nope."

"I give up. Tell me."

"Shower."

"Shower?" Alexa repeated.

"Shower," Sheyanne confirmed. "He brought the ring inside."

Alexa laughed. "Oh, my God! Good thing it didn't go down the drain! Seriously, girlfriend, that's wonderful news. I'm so happy for you. And for Joshua."

"Okay, so much for me. Tell me."

"No, I want to hear all about it. Every detail, Sheyanne. What did he say, exactly?"

"I'll tell you all that later. What's new with you?" Alexa said nothing. "Lexie? Are you there?" Still silence. "Alexa?"

"Yeah, I'm here." "What's happening?"

Alexa sighed. "I don't know."

"What does that mean?"

"I slept with him."

It was Sheyanne's turn to be quiet for several seconds before speaking. Then she asked, "Him as in Rafael?"

"Yes," answered Alexa

"Wow. So, you are human after all." Sheyanne said.

"Yeah."

"How was it?" Sheyanne asked.

"Incredible," Alexa said.

"Hmm," Sheyanne said.

"Yeah," Alexa said.

"Shit. What are you going to do?" Sheyanne asked.

"Stay away from him. Now that his case with the Federal Reserve is over, I don't need to represent him anymore, so there's no reason to see him."

Sheyanne mumbled, "Um."

"What do you mean, 'Um?'" Alexa asked.

"Nothing," her friend said.

"Okay, so I'll help find him the right lawyer. But then I'm gone."

"Okay, Lexie. Whatever you say."

Sunday morning, Savannah and Reggie were playing in the backyard. Every once in a while, they would ask Alexa to join them in what they were doing or ask her to watch them as they showed off. Reggie jumped over invisible hurdles and tumbled. Savannah did almost perfect cartwheels. Then they busied themselves looking for ladybugs.

Alexa sat back in the swing, thinking about Rafael. She wondered if another man could ever compare to the way he loved her – or made love to her. She was confused and didn't really know which it was. She had been loved by men besides him and had always enjoyed sex. She couldn't figure out what made having sex with him so far above par. Her musings always led to the question: did she love him? And that's where she stopped, reaching a dead end and giving up.

"Who wants to go to the beach?" she asked.

As expected, both children stopped what they were doing and answered excitedly. "Me! Oh, Mommy, can we go?"

Alexa thought about asking her mother and Madlynn to join them, but decided against it. She wanted to devote the day to spending undivided time with her children. She called to check in with Giselle, then packed their two backpacks with towels and their new swimsuits. She stocked the small cooler with fruit and water, and they took off for the Santa Monica beach.

The ocean fog was just burning off when they set up their blanket. After dousing the twins and herself with sun protectant, Alexa was ready to lie in the sun. Not so the kids. "Come on, Mommy, let's go in the water."

In between the many forays into the ocean, they built sandcastles, dug for sand crabs, buried their mother in sand, and ate.

Hours later, feeling both exhilarated and exhausted, Alexa packed up, and they headed home. Reggie bathed, and then Savannah bathed, and while Alexa was combing out Savannah's long auburn hair, Lupe returned.

The twins babbled on and on, telling Lupe about their weekend. Alexa found it interesting that they left almost nothing out, telling her about their Saturday trip to the La Brea Tar Pits and Page Museum, even including the ladybugs and insects they'd found in the backyard, and then all about their Sunday adventures at the beach.

Lupe hugged them and said she was going to make them one of their favorites for dinner. At six thirty, they all sat down to enjoy a delicious dinner of Spanish rice and chicken.

40

Relieved, Viviana and Rafael decided to finally celebrate Sofia's marriage and Rafael's freedom from the binds of the Federal Reserve and Justice Department. The gathering was held at the home of Rafael's wealthy cousin who had loaned him money when he'd needed cash.

Alexa hadn't wanted to go but didn't feel she could graciously refuse the invitation.On entering, she saw Viviana moving slowly through the room, mingling with guests. She was wearing a modest dark silk dress with long sleeves that fell at her knees and held a glass of red wine in her hand when Alexa approached her.

"This is lovely, Viviana, and you look wonderful," Alexa said with a smile. Viviana complimented Alexa, whom she thought looked lovely as usual, dressed in a black suit, even Viviana recognized as Chanel. It was definitely understated, but Alexa looked elegant with pearls at her neck and a second necklace with a single diamond pendant.

"I just saw Sofia. Congratulations. She looks gorgeous and so happy."

"Thank you." Viviana matched her smile. "I'm so glad you could come." She looked around the room, looking for Rafael, and was surprised that he wasn't already at Alexa's side. "Have you seen Rafael?"

"No, I just got here. Sofia and Joe greeted me at the door, and here I am."

"Well, let me get you a drink," Viviana said. Now she looked around for one of the two waiters carrying a tray of drinks.

"It's okay," Alexa said. "I can get one."

Just then, Rafael strode over to the two. He looked excited. "Alexa! Where have you been?" He held her by her shoulders and kissed her two cheeks.

Alexa shook her head. "I just arrived. I was just telling Viviana how lovely this is."

Rafael's excitement showed even in his stance. He rocked back and forth on the balls of his feet, as if preparing to take off. "Thank you, thank you." He noticed that Alexa wasn't holding a drink. "Let me get you a drink," he said and hurried away.

Alexa chuckled. "He's certainly excited," she said.

"Yes," Viviana agreed. She could have added that it was apparent that her husband's level of excitement had escalated considerably since he'd seen Alexa, but said nothing.

Alexa looked around the banquet hall. "This looks like a great turnout. Is it what you expected?"

Viviana followed Alexa's gaze as she looked at the many guests. "Oh, yes." She sighed. "Apparently, my husband is not thought of as a criminal any longer." She smiled. "And people are curious, too. Thank you so much, Alexa."

"Thank your husband. I had nothing to do with the fact that he was innocent, and the truth was bound to come out. The idea that he could be blamed for what went on there was ludicrous."

"Don't be so modest. You did a wonderful job. And we owe you a great deal as well as a fee."

Before Alexa could answer, Rafael was back with two drinks.

"It's champagne," he said, handing one to her. "If I can't drink champagne at a celebration like this, when can I?" He laughed, and Alexa joined him, both apparently oblivious to the fact that the glass Viviana held did not hold champagne.

"A toast to you and Viviana," Alexa said, "and of course, the newlyweds."

Rafael said, "And to you." The three touched their glasses together and drank. "You look wonderful," Rafael said to Alexa.

"Thank you," Alexa said.

Viviana hoped her face wasn't flushed. Her husband had not said a word to her about how she looked in her new dress. She wished she could hate Alexa.

Alexa took another sip and said, "Excuse me. I think I should walk around and meet some of your friends."

Rafael was drinking his champagne and slurped when she moved to go. "Wait! I'll come with you. I want to introduce you to someone." He took her by the elbow and steered her away from Viviana and across the room, past several tables. Viviana stood, watching them as they moved away. She'd recently lost her daughter and feared she was losing her husband as well.

After some time, Viviana saw Rafael and Alexa on the dance floor. It was a cha-cha. They looked so comfortable together, so naturally in synch with one another. When the song ended, she saw Alexa turn away from Rafael and start walking away, then saw Rafael grab her wrist. She turned back around to face him. They spoke some words. He dropped her wrist, and they began to dance to an oldie-but-goodie selection. Viviana hadn't seen Rafael dance like that for a very long time. He was obviously having a good time. Then he found her where she sat, bowed low, and asked her to dance. She refused, pleading painful feet, and urged him to continue dancing with Alexa. He did. Watching them, she wondered why she'd sentenced herself to this special torment. She wished the night were over. It was all too painful. She vowed that tomorrow she would figure this out.

She would resolve her dilemma and find a solution. She didn't want to lose her husband.

Meanwhile, Rafael was enjoying himself tremendously. Guests had shown up. His reputation was restored. The Federal Reserve was off his back. The branch was closed. And Alexa was here. And, they were dancing together for the first time. Rafael loved to dance but was never really able to let loose with Viviana. Alexa proved to be a good dancer. *Was there anything this woman couldn't do well?*

They only stopped dancing when dinner was served. Alexa thought it rude that Rafael had virtually ignored his wife – but was that her problem? Several times she'd suggested they stop dancing, but Rafael had refused, and she was enjoying herself, too. It wasn't often she got on a dance floor these days.

During dinner, Alexa took in the people around her. She had nothing in common with them. She would have bet that few – if any – of these women were professionals or even held a job. They were traditional Latin women attached to traditional Latin men. *Were all these men having affairs?*

She looked over at Viviana and Rafael. They sat together, but Rafael hardly seemed to interact with his wife. He was having a conversation with the man across the table from him, then suddenly looked up, caught Alexa's eye, and smiled. She felt guilty. This was embarrassing. It was definitely uncomfortable. She wanted to leave. If she told Rafael – or even Viviana – that she was leaving, they'd insist she stay.

After some time, Rafael and Viviana got up and began to circle the room, going to each table, thanking everyone for coming, as the bride and groom had already done, and posing with the entire table for a photograph. They came to her table. When they moved on, Alexa recognized her chance.

She got up, moved towards the doors, and walked out.

41

The following Monday, Alexa sat in her office thinking. When she last spoke with Gilmore she had asked him if they were finally convinced her client was innocent. As expected, he'd refrained from giving her a definitive answer.

But the newspapers confirmed what he wouldn't say. The Beverly Hills branch of TriWorld had been closed down and the bank had received severe civil penalties. That had to mean that the blame had finally been allocated and Rafael had come away clean. They ought to issue a Certificate of Exoneration to him after the hell they'd put him through for such an incredibly long period of time, she thought.

In any event, Alexa knew it was safe to proceed against the bank now. Rafael would file a wrongful termination suit alleging that TriWorld had fired him, knowing he was innocent, in an effort to scapegoat him. And this time, she wouldn't let Rafael talk her into representing him; there were too many things pointing against it.

She had kept her distance from courtroom work since she'd suffered a hearing loss. Wrongful termination gave rise to civil litigation, and she'd always stayed away from trying civil cases. She'd been fine with criminal procedure, but since law school, she'd harbored a dislike and near phobia of being blown up in the minefield of procedural requirements, whether picayune or arcane, that comprised civil litigation. Alexa had always referred out cases requiring civil litigation to experienced civil litigators who were comfortable with the hornet's nest of procedural have-tos.

Also, though she certainly knew more about employment law than she'd known about banking law, she was by no means an expert in wrongful termination.

Aside from those factors, TriWorld would prove a formidable opponent with an international presence and immense power. It was, as its slogan advertised, 'everywhere you went.'

Its presence on the world stage translated into endless resources and power available to TriWorld's legal defense. The sheer volume of required discovery would be backbreaking. Rafael would have to focus on any number of individuals, potential witnesses, in both TriWorld and the Bank of Taiwan, whereas TriWorld's attorneys would pound away exclusively on Rafael.

No doubt, the number of discovery motions and requests propounded by TriWorld that would require responses would be monumental. Whereas Rafael's attorney would be paid on a contingency basis, taking a percentage of any amounts he might be awarded, the attorneys representing TriWorld would be paid by the hour. That meant their lawyers would benefit by dragging the lawsuit out, making every motion imaginable, making every objection possible to Rafael's motions, and generally creating a nightmare of paperwork. In theory, it wouldn't matter whether they won or lost on the individual motions, so long as they dragged out the lawsuit and generated billable hours. For a myriad of reasons, it was beyond what Alexa's practice could handle. Rafael needed an attorney from a large, well-heeled law firm with a large support staff specializing in wrongful termination.

Rafael came to see her at the appointed time that morning, as she was about to have breakfast. "I'm craving some apple pie and tea. Would you like some?" she asked. Never ready to willingly let her out of his sight if he didn't have to, Rafael followed her out of the office through the backyard and into the house.

"If I win the case against the bank – I said if – how much do you think I would get?" Rafael asked.

"Before you pay costs and attorneys' fees? The bank has to make you whole. They pay what you've lost in salary and future earnings. Probably also the costs of medical insurance premiums if you had to get a medical insurance policy on your own-"

"I didn't. You know we have no medical insurance since they fired me."

"We'll also ask that they pay the psychologist."

"What about Viviana?"

"The cause of action is called lack of consortium and the emotional pain –"

Rafael cut her off. "There's no amount that can pay for that. But what about discrimination?"

"What discrimination, Rafael?"

"Can't we sue the bank for discriminating against me?"

Alexa, about to enter the house, stopped and looked at him. "Rafael, we talked about this before. They didn't discriminate against you."

"But, I don't understand, Alexa. They did more than just fire me without a reason. They fired me for a terrible reason. They were doing something illegal and blamed me for it! They'd have been happy to see me go to jail!"

She headed for the kitchen, Rafael following. "You're right. But the law acknowledges only certain situations to be so heinous that they're what they call, 'against public policy.' If one of those situations exists, you can ask for punitive damages as well as compensatory damages. That's where the real money is. Courts want to make an example of the defendant so others don't do the same thing because what they've done is so heinous; it's against public policy. Firing someone because you discriminated against them is against public policy, but we'll have a hell of a time proving discrimination; you got your job because of your nationality."

"So, what do you call what they did to me?"

"Unethical bullshit." She brought out two plates and set them on the counter. "There's also whistleblowing."

"What's that?" he asked.

She put two napkins alongside the plates, then opened the cutlery drawer and took out two forks. "Exactly what it sounds like. Blowing the whistle. Firing someone because they told the authorities on you."

"Damn it. Isn't that what I did?"

She pivoted around to face Rafael. "No! Telling Stamen and Alandro that you had issues with the security agreement and the indemnity agreement doesn't cut it. They were the ones involved in the illegal act. Whistleblowing is when you tell someone else, like a regulatory agency or the government."

"What about when I told the auditor?"

Alexa froze. Rafael's last words were potentially earth-shattering. "What auditor?" she asked.

"The one who came to the bank and audited us," Rafael said.

"You told the auditor about the agreements?" she was breathless.

"Yes. I told you." There was an edge of impatience in his voice.

"You told me that?" In that moment, Alexa knew what it would feel like to lose her mind. She leaned against the counter, her heart beating loudly, clutching the forks in her hand. "When did you tell me?"

"That day in your office. You were at your desk. I think you were looking for a battery for your hearing aid."

Now she was angry. *Impossible! Had she actually missed that most crucial fact in the entire case because of her hearing? It couldn't be!* "Rafael, you never told me that. If you had told me that you had complained to the auditor, we'd have told Gilmore! But we didn't because you never told me!" She was beside herself. "Why didn't you tell him?"

Rafael didn't understand why she was so upset. He looked bewildered and scared. "I only answered his questions. That's all I was supposed to do. You never told me to tell him, and he never asked who else I told, so I never said anything."

Alexa threw the forks on the counter and slammed the cabinet door shut. Lupe came running into the kitchen. "Is everything all right?"

Alexa only looked at her and nodded. To Rafael, she said, "My God, Rafael! You actually complained to the auditor?"

"Yes! I was really concerned."

In her frustration, she couldn't help repeating herself. "Why didn't you tell Gilmore when he asked why you didn't talk to the lawyers? And why the hell didn't we put it in the proffer? Or add it as a question on the polygraph?"

He shrugged. "I told you, and you didn't say anything, so I figured it wasn't important. I don't know." Then, "Is it important?"

She sat at the breakfast table. "Come here." Rafael followed her. "Sit down and tell me exactly what you said."

"I showed him the security agreement and the funding agreement TriWorld had with Bank of Taiwan and told him I was concerned about them. I had just realized that we were probably matching funds."

Alexa went to the kitchen cabinet, opened a drawer, and brought out a spiral pad and a pen. She sat back down at the table. "Who was the auditor? What was his name?"

Rafael rubbed the back of his neck. "I'm not sure. I'd never seen him before. He had a Russian-sounding name that started with a 'D', something like Dombrowski, Dobinski, Dembinski...," he shook his head in frustration. "It had a 'ski' at the end. But I showed him the parts I had highlighted in yellow."

Alexa was scratching the names down on the little pad. "When was this? What was the date?" She waited, anticipating his answer, ready to note it. When he didn't answer right away, she looked up at him. Rafael sat with his legs stretched straight out, his arms folded. His lips were pushed out as he tried to recall. He looked down, then his head swung up to the ceiling. "I don't know," he finally said, shaking his head. "Whenever the regular audit took place. It was some time in the fall... or winter. The last audit before I was fired."

"When? What year?"

"Before this whole thing started. Let's see, I was fired in February of 2025, so it was during the last audit of 2024."

"Okay. It was the last time the bank was audited before you were fired." He nodded. "And who was there when you told him?"

Rafael answered, shrugging as if the answer was all too obvious. "No one, just him and me. I wanted to talk to him alone, away from Steman and Jason."

Alexa ripped the piece of paper off the pad and sat looking at Rafael. Unable to decipher the look on her face, he asked, "What is it? Something good?"

Alexa smiled. "Sounds like whistleblowing to me," she said.

42

They went back to Alexa's office with two cups of coffee and apple pie on a tray. Alexa was too excited to eat. They were now in a way different ballpark. This could be a very substantial case, an international bank with untold assets scapegoating a whistleblower.

The first order of business was to make certain that Rafael understood he needed to retain the right lawyer to litigate the case. When he begged her to represent him, she told him the reasons for her decision.

"But, Alexa, you know all the facts!" Rafael argued.

"I'll turn everything over. They'll have the whole file, and you can fill in the gaps," she said.

"But you've lived it. You brought me this far. You can't walk away."

"Watch me."

Rafael eyed her then. "That's it, isn't it? It's because of what happened on Friday. Because you let your guard down and slept with me. I lived on it the entire weekend. It was food for a starving man. And now, you're punishing me like this. You want distance."

Alexa allowed her frustration to show. "No, Rafael. Everything is not about that. If you trust me so much, then trust that I should not be the attorney who takes this to trial."

"Like you shouldn't have been the attorney that represented me with the Federal Reserve?"

"This is different!"

"How?"

"I told you. This is a huge case, and as tough as the Federal Reserve was, it was *just* the Federal Reserve."

"And the Justice Department," Rafael broke in.

"Yes. But Justice would only have moved on you if they'd found you at fault; you didn't have to contend with them at the same time."

He was stubborn. "There was everyone at TriWorld and their attorneys."

Alexa rolled her eyes in frustration. Rafael moved his head slightly, and she took that as a sign of at least momentary acquiescence and continued. "When you go to trial, you'll have the Bank's attorneys opposing you; you'll have the judge whom you'll have to persuade to grant your umpteenth motions on legal grounds with the Bank's attorney arguing against you – and by the way, I come up way short on knowledge of civil procedure – and you'll have to persuade the jury. I might be able to persuade a jury. But to get to them, you have to jump over a million hoops, and I can't." Alexa had the feeling Rafael had actually been listening to her. She stopped to let that all sink in.

"And besides, I stopped doing court work because of my hearing loss. Remember that? I can't hear well. I friggin' didn't hear you when you told me you had spoken with the auditor! Even with these new aids, which seem to be really good, I wouldn't take the chance that I might not hear what the judge says, or what opposing counsel says, or that I'd have to keep asking witnesses to repeat themselves.

"And by the way, it's going to be extremely costly to try this case, and I can't carry that cost. You won't have to pay them an hourly fee or a retainer. But there will be costs for things like depositions, and you'll need to take lots of them. You need a firm that can invest that kind of money – thousands of dollars in your case – because they believe in it and they have the money."

"I absolutely insist you stay on the case," Rafael said. "We can look for another attorney to work with you. But I only trust you, Alexa. You have to stay a part of this. You need to stay on the case. You need to make sure they're getting it right. You can't just leave me in the latch."

Alexa threw her hands up. "Lurch," she said impatiently. He looked baffled. "Leave you in the lurch, not latch. Damn it, Rafael! When will this end? I don't want to do this!"

And then she sat down at her computer and drew up a new retainer agreement for wrongful termination against public policy for whistleblowing against TriWorld Bank.

She wondered if Rafael would ever cease being part of her life.

43

Rafael waited patiently while Alexa went through the entire new retainer agreement with him, explaining all the provisions before allowing him to sign it. Then she made a list of LA attorneys who had won wrongful termination cases involving whistleblowing. Together, they went to visit several of them.

Happily, Roger Prince, the third attorney they met with and the one both she and Rafael liked the most, had been Alexa's classmate in law school. From time to time, they'd gone to study at the UCLA library together. She didn't tell Rafael that Roger had had a crush on her. In any event, she'd heard he'd married. The photo on his office desk showed an attractive woman holding an infant. Another photo on the wall showed a sandy-haired and freckled boy, a beaming toddler.

Roger's most recent win had been the case of a whistle-blower-bookkeeper he'd represented who was awarded over two million dollars in an action against her employer, a clothing manufacturer who had fired the plaintiff for squealing on him to the IRS, having informed the agency that he was making regular payments to family members, as well as his mistress; all that had been fraudulently written off.

Alexa was glad to see that Roger was still brimming with that surplus of energy she recalled he'd had in his younger days. His large firm, his string of wins in wrongful termination cases, along with his ready smile and warm personality, made him the perfect choice.

Roger Prince worked with the firm of Randall and Stoll in Sherman Oaks. It was the firm's policy to attach all lawyers to a partner. Prince was attached to Boyd Carter, a senior partner, whom Alexa guessed to be in his 60s. As Alexa and Rafael were to learn, Boyd liked to spend a good part of his day walking around the office, greeting everyone, and stopping to chat.

The firm of Randall and Stoll was excited to take on Rafael's case. The way they saw it, the lawsuit had all the trappings of a big win. The defendant had very deep pockets, which translated into a lot of money, and the Federal Reserve's investigation proved that Rafael had been scapegoated. It was an archetypal case of the little guy being screwed by the really big bully.

The day Rafael decided to retain Prince, a relieved Alexa was in no rush to head back over Mulholland to her office. She deposited her attaché into the trunk of her car parked on the street and suggested that she and Rafael take a walk in the park across from Prince's office building and share their perceptions of Roger before parting ways.

"What do you think?" Rafael asked.

"I think that's the right firm, and I think he's the right attorney. They have the manpower to deal with the slew of paperwork we'll be getting from the bank in discovery, and they've got a good record of success. Roger seems to grasp the case, and he's optimistic enough to invest in the case, though it will be pricey. And there was no problem associating in with me."

Rafael nodded. "He likes you."

"I like him, too. He was one of the few guys in law school

that I'd even talk to." Rafael put his hands in his pockets, put his head down, and kept walking.

The complaint filed against TriWorld alleged wrongful termination in violation of fundamental public policy, conspiracy to wrongfully terminate in violation of fundamental public policy, breach of implied contract, breach of implied covenant of good faith and fair dealing, and failure to pay wages.

It asked for punitive as well as compensatory damages.

44

As the discovery process began, Alexa was heartbroken to witness her mother's condition deteriorating. Over the weekend, Giselle and Madlynn had spent an evening at Alexa's house, and Giselle had tried covering up her inability to remember the names of both Lupe and Reggie, though she had no trouble recalling her daughter's name or Savannah's. Alexa spoke briefly with Madlynn in the kitchen and learned that Dr. Mindox had recently added a mood elevator to her mother's memory enhancer, as Giselle had been showing signs of depression, as well as outbursts of anger and continued paranoia.

Alexa wished her brother were in town. Not only because Mike would be somewhat knowledgeable about Giselle's condition and able to spend time with her. Also, because she felt the need to commiserate with her older sibling. As it was, all she could do was update him via email, and after Giselle's last visit, she sent him another email and asked when he intended to return to Los Angeles.

Rafael's trial was to take place in Santa Monica. Alexa was pleased because she loathed going to court in downtown Los

Angeles. The freeway traffic was always miserable. The downtown maze of one-way streets frustrated her. Parking was a nightmare. The area depressed her. The government buildings seemed to be surrounded by derelicts, and some had fallen into the sort of poor maintenance and ill repair one would expect to see in third-world countries, badly in need of paint. Some offices had boxes and boxes of files stacked and overflowing into hallways. Vending machines that were out of order were never repaired, and entire buildings had no cafeterias, no food, and no drink, not even functional water fountains.

In contrast, the two-story Superior Court located at 1725 Main Street in Santa Monica, known for many celebrity cases including the civil cases against O.J. Simpson, Lindsay Lohan, and Michael Jackson, was easy to get to and had convenient parking. Unlike the LA Superior Courthouse in downtown Los Angeles, the Santa Monica Courthouse sat on a pretty street, a wide greenbelt only a few short blocks from the beach and within walking distance to a slew of shopping choices. Smaller, it had a more informal feel. The individual courtrooms were far less imposing than those downtown. This was the venue where Rafael's fate against TriWorld would be decided.

On the day pretrial motions began, Alexa had her first view of TriWorld Bank's lead attorney. Ann Lacey was an attractive blonde in her late 30s or early 40s, a Southern belle with a tantalizing figure and a peaches-and-cream complexion who spoke in a warm voice with the mildest of Southern accents. She was joined by co-counsel, Nathan Baxter, a man somewhere in his 50s, balding, with a permanent expression of apology. Alexa wondered if Baxter was the engine that drove the pretty girl, then reprimanded herself for what she realized was a chauvinistic thought. Attorney Lacey was undoubtedly an excellent lawyer.

Alexa noted how Lacey's eyes had lingered on Rafael seconds longer than needed the first time they met, then found herself looking for a wedding ring on Lacey's hand; there was none. She told herself that many married female attorneys didn't wear wedding bands to court in order to make themselves more attractive to male jurors. Or was it the other way around? Didn't unmarried attorneys wear wedding bands in order to ward off unwanted advances from leering judges and opposing counsel? Roger interrupted her attempt to unravel her momentary confusion.

"Remember, Alexa, I'm counting on you. I need you to let me know if I forget something."

"Definitely," she said. She looked at Rafael. He was looking at Lacey, but his expression told her nothing.

The pretrial judge, Richard Ha, was a middle-aged Asian man who looked to Alexa like he'd just sucked on a very sour lemon. His eyes seem to drift to the bank's lady lawyer more often than needed. The white sheath she'd worn that day was most flattering.

Alexa had explained to Rafael that Ha would not be their trial judge. He would only rule on pretrial motions. Among those motions, TriWorld had requested a Summary Judgment based on their contention that Rafael's pleading had failed to allege the makings of a case. If Judge Ha had granted that motion, Rafael's case would have been blown right out of the water, and there would have been no trial. Their request was – as expected – denied.

The discovery phase and pre-trial motions dragged on. The Bank flat-out denied producing almost everything requested by Prince during this discovery phase, including routine documents such as Rafael's employment files, his annual reviews, and the Bank's Code of Conduct. They forced Prince to file Motions to Produce for everything requested. Lacey, in turn, filed motions requesting the court to limit what her client had to produce. It was mandatory for Prince to file a motion in response to every motion Lacey filed and to file a response to every one of the bank's motions to limit discovery. Not all documents were of equal importance. They included things like the application for employment Rafael had submitted to TriWorld almost ten years ago. Others were out of Rafael's reach due to various privileges, yet Prince fought for the right to review them anyway. It seemed to Alexa that these pretrial battles were more a show of power and endurance between the two sides, and she was glad to see that their side was faring well.

Then they suffered their first blow. It came from an unlikely place and hit them hard. TriWorld subpoenaed the proffer Rafael had delivered to the Federal Reserve, and Prince, inexperienced with communication to the Reserve, handed it over. That was a mistake. When Prince then subpoenaed the documents TriWorld Bank employees had submitted to the Federal Reserve, Lacey refused to turn them over. Prince filed a Motion to Compel in an attempt to force production, and Lacey filed an objection on the grounds that they were privileged as governmental documents and that only the Federal Reserve could agree to waive that privilege. The court agreed and denied Prince's Motion to Produce. Prince and Alexa were aghast. Alexa felt humiliated by their ignorance and could only imagine the look on Lacey and Baxter's faces when they'd received Rafael's proffer, a document to which they had no legal right and that clearly outlined Rafael's position on the subjects it addressed. Prince offered the court the equitable argument that what was fair for one side was fair for the other, but the court remained unpersuaded.

They had fallen into a trap with their eyes wide open. Prince then contacted Attorney Gilmore at the Federal Reserve, requesting that the government waive its privilege and allow them to examine those documents.

His request was met with interest. "So, Mr. Lamon is suing?" was Gilmore's tongue-in-cheek response. In the end, their request was denied.

"The Federal Reserve does not involve itself with lawsuits," was how Gilmore put it.

Prince was apologetic; Alexa was extremely upset. They had walked right into a trap set by their ignorance. It had been a big mistake, and they couldn't afford to make mistakes. They would have to be a hell of a lot more careful from here on out. They couldn't allow the other side to benefit again from their lack of knowledge. Rafael didn't truly understand this game of privilege, but he felt like he'd been kicked in the stomach. Meanwhile, what was done was done, and there was nothing to do but go on.

Then Lacey had the gall to serve a subpoena on the Law Office of Alexa Starr for production of "any and all documents passed to the Federal Reserve on behalf of Rafael V. Lamon." She actually wanted more! That would have pointed to the polygraph exam Rafael had taken and its results. Of course, Alexa objected to their production based on the same privilege that Lacey had invoked; she had learned that one. The question of whether Prince would introduce them into evidence was still open.

Once both sides had received all the documents they were going to get, depositions were scheduled. Both sides wanted information from potential witnesses who might be called to testify at trial.

Though historically, depositions were memorialized by a court reporter taking down every word spoken at a deposition, then typed up for the attorney to read and use, some attorneys preferred to video the deponent. What was said by someone during their deposition could be used at trial if needed, perhaps to refresh a witness's recollection, or to impeach or discredit their testimony at trial if that testimony varied from what had been said during their deposition. After all, depositions are given under oath. They're expensive and videotaping only adds to the cost, but potentially high-value cases are thought to justify the expense, and so both sides videotaped all the depositions.

When the date was set for Rafael to be deposed by Lacey and Baxter, Alexa explained to Rafael that it would be the first opportunity the opposing side would have to see and gauge how he would be viewed when he testifies at trial.

By viewing the tape later, they can study how he will appear to a jury, study his manner, and his affability. Does he appear honest? Likeable? Defensive? These things would be considered and added to the mix if and when a possibility of settlement before trial arose. Not that anyone expected TriWorld to settle, and Rafael felt no inclination to settle at this point. He had been hurt. His ego, his dignity, his reputation, his family name, his finances, and his financial security had all been damaged. He wanted to expose what TriWorld had done to him, how low these people had stooped to scapegoat an innocent man. Both Alexa and Prince were present at Rafael's deposition. It took two full days and spilled into the morning of a third.

Understandably, a huge amount of time was spent grilling him about his conversation with the auditor. Lacey asked all sorts of questions, from the auditor's name, his physical description, the date, time of day, and exact location where they'd spoken, and – more germane to the lawsuit – why Rafael had not mentioned anything about an auditor to the Federal Reserve in his proffer as the bank's attorneys had hat proffer. Rafael answered the question honestly in the same way he had answered Alexa when she'd asked the same question: No one had asked. He had told his attorney.

During a deposition, questions that could be properly objected to if asked at trial can be properly asked and answered so long as they are not privileged and "appear reasonably calculated to lead to the discovery of admissible evidence." Rafael had weathered the stress well and had answered all the questions honestly and openly, except on the few occasions when counsel directed him not to answer due to privilege. He seemed relaxed and confident. When it was over, Rafael was exhausted and feeling insecure despite his attorneys' reassurances that they were pleased with his bearing during the ordeal.

When Alexa and Roger deposed the array of bank employees, one of the goals was to obtain the exact name of the auditor whom Rafael had complained to, so they could subpoena him. His name was probably Dublowski. But try as they might, neither they nor their personal investigators could locate him.

Finally, with any possibility of settlement out of the question, the date was set for trial.

45

Alexa and Rafael were having lunch after another marathon meeting at Prince's office. Prince wasn't able to join them. They were seated at a Chinese restaurant Prince had suggested, both with a healthy appetite. Their faces were in the menus.

"Alexa, I'm paying for lunch," Rafael said looking over his menu at her.

"By all means," Alexa said. "I'm just about tapped out from feeding you. No longer part of my job." Having made her selection, she put down her menu. "By the way how is your job?"

"Oh, didn't I tell you?" Rafael said. Having made his selection, he also put down the menu. "I'm not working any more. I quit."

"No, you didn't tell me. When?"

"When the depositions started. I quit. The lawsuit is my job now." And then he smiled and his eyes lit up. "Besides, I detested that job and hated going there five nights a week." He poked his chin out at Alexa. "You need shoes? They were having a three-for-two sale when I left."

Alexa chuckled. "No, thanks. But I'm sure the women will miss you."

Rafael gave her a sleepy-eyed look across the table. "Feet are not my favorite part of a woman." The waiter came by and took their order.

"By the way, Rafael, have you told the entire banking world that I was responsible for winning your case?"

"Me? No. Why?"

"I've gotten three calls from bankers wanting me to represent them in various matters."

"Really? The Federal Reserve?"

"No, other things." She looked across the table at him somewhat suspiciously. "I don't know how the word got around, but it did."

"So now my Alexa is a banking lawyer."

"No, your Alexa is not a banking lawyer. Never was. And I couldn't take the cases if I wanted to. I'm too busy with yours."

"How are things with your mother?" Rafael asked, changing the subject.

Alexa put down the chopsticks she'd been playing with. "Not good. She seems to be getting worse every day. She constantly repeats herself, and when she meets someone, she doesn't remember whether she knows them. She bluffs a lot. She's smart. She'll ask questions that sound innocuous, but she's trying to figure out who they are. It's sad because she can't. And she keeps repeating the questions."

Rafael reached across the table and took her hand. "I'm sorry, Alexa. I lost my mother when I was in my twenties, and I still miss her. A mother is – well, you're a mother, and you love your own mother; you know what I'm trying to say. I'm just really sorry. I hate to see you go through this."

Alexa nodded. "Thank you." A tear started to trickle down her cheek. Rafael's hand moved to her face, wiping away the tear. His genuine care and sympathy had touched her deeply and brought out her sadness.

"How are the twins?" He asked, hoping to change her mood.

"Oh," she said, forcing a smile. "They're fine." She was ready for a change of mood as well. "You know, I used to think that all that talk about girls being so different from boys was silly talk. I thought it was all about how they were raised." She laughed as if at her own ignorance. "Wow! Was I wrong! I have a boy and a girl, and from their earliest days, they were completely different."

Rafael was hanging on her every word. The chicken in lettuce arrived. They both wrapped some ground chicken in a lettuce leaf, drizzled sauce over it, and took a big bite. "This is delicious," he said. He swallowed, then took another bite. "I only have a daughter, so explain."

"Reggie was a macho man from day one. His first word was 'ball.' He studied every kind of dinosaur there is and learned every truck on the road, and even some he had never seen before he was three. He loves all the superheroes and plays with cars and trucks. Savannah was born a ballerina. She's all pink and bubblegum, cotton candy and ice cream. Give her a coloring book, paints, and dolls, and she's happy. She sings and dances all day. And she loves makeup." Alexa stopped to take another huge bite of the appetizer.

"I see what you mean," Rafael laughed.

Alexa joined in his laughter with her mouth full, waving her hand for him to wait until she swallowed to hear more. When she could talk again, she pointed to the remains of the chicken in lettuce on her plate. "This is really good! So, last night at the dinner table, Reggie burped really loudly. I looked at him and said, 'Reggie! Say, excuse me!'" He looked back at me like I was stupid and very calmly said, "Mommy, it's okay, men buwp." The two continued laughing.

Their entrees came then, and they both dug in. Rafael had

ordered a beef and vegetable dish, and Alexa was truly enjoying her shrimp in black bean sauce when Rafael spoke between mouthfuls. "Alexa, I want to marry you."

Alexa gasped, choked, and started coughing. Rafael quickly came to her and began tapping her back. She put both her arms up as she had learned to do, then took a sip of water. Eventually, she was all right. At least, she was no longer choking. But she wasn't sure she was truly all right. Had she heard correctly? "What did you say?"

"I want to marry you. Will you marry me?"

Alexa shook her head as if to shake herself awake. "Excuse me, but aren't you already married?"

"I don't mean now," he said. He went back to sit across the table and motioned to her plate. "Eat." Alexa watched him take a forkful of beef to his mouth. She looked at him in disbelief. How could he expect her to eat after he's just told her that he wants to marry her? She couldn't touch another bite. He had sounded calm, but he talked crazy. She waited.

"I can't leave Viviana now. Sofia is just married. And we don't have money. But when I win this lawsuit – if I do, I'll have money. Then I can. I want to, and I will."

He put his fork down and went on speaking as though he was sharing his plans to take his car in for servicing that afternoon. He saw Alexa look at him as if he were insane. "Alexa, don't look at me like that. You know I love you. You've made the worst time of my life the best time of my life just because I've been around you like this." Alexa was starting to feel nauseous. He went on. "You know what my relationship with Viviana is like. She's a nice person and a good mother. But I have nothing in common with her; I never did. I'll give her the house and enough money to make sure she's okay." He put his fork down and took her hand. "Please, say you'll marry me."

So, this is what their relationship had led to; she was a home wrecker. Alexa wanted to get up and run. Rafael actually expected her to cause Viviana heartbreak and Sofia sadness. These things passed through her mind, as did the fact that his proposal was conditioned on winning his lawsuit. And he was still, again, her client.

True, she had not slept with him during the time she had represented him before the Federal Reserve, nor had she slept with him since he'd signed her retainer that named her his legal representative in the lawsuit against TriWorld Bank. But that was almost a technicality. In that short interim, that celebratory Friday afternoon, she had revisited a little piece of heaven, and damn it, this was the result! She desired him, yes – but did she love him? Lately, it seemed that question kept popping up like the Cheshire cat. Now, it loomed before her. He was waiting for her to say something.

"Rafael, I don't know what to say."

"Say, yes."

"You have a way of making me say yes to whatever you want. But this time it's not just about you and me," she said.

"Alexa, if you're thinking about Viviana, don't worry. She won't even miss me."

Alexa flinched at that. The Viviana she knew was a woman who cared very much about Rafael. But Rafael knew her far better than Alexa did. Was he uncaring, or was he right? Was he being selfish and kidding himself? "How can you say that? She's been your wife for what? Over 20 years!"

"Actually, 23 years. And it boils down to this: she just wants a paycheck. She never talks to me. She goes to lunch with friends, comes home and watches the Spanish soaps on television, talks to Sofia, to her sister, and friends on the phone, maybe plays cards at one of their houses, makes dinner, then watches television again, and comes to bed after I'm asleep."

Alexa said nothing. That did sound like a rather sorry way to live. She had no idea what to say. She couldn't begin to think clearly.

Then she ventured to speak. "Rafael. If you want to leave your wife, leave her. Don't leave her because of me. When I left Ben, it wasn't to run to someone else. I wasn't happy, so I left. If you're not happy, leave. Then we'll see how it goes. Maybe we'll date. If that goes well, maybe we'll live together for a while and see if we're compatible out of bed for a sustained period. Or maybe with enough time living together, we'll just get one another out of our system."

Rafael looked angry. "Living together is out of the question. I want you forever. I'll never get you out of my system. Alexa, marry me. We've made love only twice, I know, but I miss it. When you're there, and I'm part of you, I don't know or care what time or place it is, who I am, or what anything is. And I won't leave Viviana unless you say yes. I'm a man who needs to have a woman in my bed."

That stung Alexa. But how could she be hurt when he'd just told her he loved her and always would? When he just told her that he wanted to leave his wife and marry her? She was incredibly confused. "Since the trial hasn't even begun yet, we have some time to think about this," she said.

He pressed her hand in his, and she wondered how she went about without his hand on hers. "Okay, we have a date. The day that the case is over — no, there'll be too much going on that day. The day after the case is over, we have a date. You'll let me know then. Okay?"

Before she could answer, the waiter came by to check on them. Alexa asked to pack her barely touched lunch to go. The bill was presented along with two fortune cookies. Rafael took the bill and read his fortune. It read, "Start today to reach for the stars." He smiled. When he showed it to Alexa, he said, "It should say, reach for the Starr." Alexa was almost afraid to read hers. It read, "The dragon smiles."

"Oh, that's Lacey," Rafael said. "The day after the trial. Okay?" She nodded.

46

Alexa was looking forward to the trial, even though thinking about it made her extremely anxious. Her blood would feel heavy, and she could actually feel her heart tremble. It was exciting to finally have David confront Goliath in court.

It was an important civil trial because Rafael was seeking justice. Hopefully, justice would prevail, and he would win, perhaps even be awarded a significant amount of money. She certainly hoped so. Not only for Rafael. By now, she had a significant lien on this case, and if he won, she could get paid for all that time spent with the Federal Reserve. She'd also receive a modest portion of the attorney fees that would go to Prince's firm. Maybe she could put some money away. She'd had to turn cases away to concentrate on Rafael's case. Just that morning, she'd refused to represent a client in a substantial upcoming arbitration hearing because of the upcoming trial.

She wished she weren't so nervous. She was insecure about being in a courtroom again after so long. She would be sitting at the plaintiff's table. Prince would handle all the legal pleadings, but he insisted that she take a very active role in the trial, addressing the judge, jury, and witnesses. He liked pitting a woman against a woman and had a very high regard for Alexa's courtroom abilities.

But she couldn't count on hearing important words spoken by key players. Alexa wasn't shy about the fact that she wore hearing aids. When a battery died, she had no problem removing the aid from her ear to change the battery and replace it wherever she was. She couldn't see a difference between needing aids to help boost hearing and needing glasses to boost vision.

Still, she would die of embarrassment if she misheard or failed to hear something the judge said or in the witnesses' testimony. She actually had not heard Rafael tell her that he'd spoken with the auditor! What if she failed to hear or misheard something else of importance? Of course, when she hadn't heard what Rafael had said, she had one of her aides out, and they were the old ones. Her new hearing aids were far superior; she hardly ever had to ask anyone to repeat anything. Besides, Prince would be there, and he knew she had a hearing deficit. But how would he know when she missed something?

In addition, there were key differences between civil and criminal trials, and Alexa lacked the knowledge a civil litigator like Prince had. He had all the tools of civil litigation down. For example, the Fifth Amendment protection against self-incrimination afforded a witness in a criminal trial doesn't apply in a civil proceeding. In fact, if a witness in a civil trial refuses to answer a question invoking that protection, the judge instructs the jury that they may well infer the witness's response would have been adverse to him or her. Likewise, the right to a speedy trial and the right to have an attorney appointed do not apply in civil trials. *What other differences did she not recall?*

Alexa was used to being on top of her game, and she was feeling, once again, as she had when she agreed to represent

Rafael before the Federal Reserve, insecure. To a great extent, all trials were similar. You represented your client and communicated his or her story to the judge or jury as clearly and as persuasively as possible. Alexa had won many criminal trials in her career. But she'd never litigated a civil trial. It was the differences – subtle and not so subtle – between civil and criminal procedure that made her nervous. Truth and justice aside, she would have to hope and pray that with substantial leaning on Prince, they would win against the mammoth corporation that was TriWorld. No wonder she was anxious. How could she not be?

On top of all that, Rafael had told her that if he won this case, he expected her to marry him! He was planning to give Viviana a portion of the money he would be awarded and leave her. Thinking about that, Alexa's heart began to pound. He would be her second husband and her children's stepfather, their new daddy. Her heart rate accelerated, and her breath caught at the thought. Her face suddenly felt hot.

How could she allow him to leave his wife for her? How could he do such a thing?

Would he? She shook her head. Maybe it would be better for everyone if he lost the trial. Ideally, he would win the wrongful termination case and be awarded compensatory damages, but not punitive damages. That would mean the jury would find he was wrongfully terminated, but not because of whistleblowing. If that happened, Rafael would not be entitled to the really big money. Maybe that would keep him at home. Alexa didn't want to be a home breaker.

Damn it, if Rafael wanted to leave his wife, why couldn't he just leave her? After that, they could date, get together, and go from there. How could she know if she wanted to marry the man? She'd only slept with him two times and represented him in two cases. They'd never dated. She hadn't really thought of him as a potential husband. She'd already made a mistake once and paid for it with a divorce that left two children with parents who lived apart. She wouldn't jump into another marriage without being sure. Ben had been unfaithful. Rafael was being unfaithful.

But this was Rafael…

47

With the pretrial motions over, the case moved to Judge Marlene Darnell's courtroom in Department J, on the second floor of a newer annex outside the main courthouse. Entering the courtroom, Alexa was hit with the sight of maple everywhere. An intimate circle was formed with the jury box, the witness stand, the court reporter and the plaintiff's table where Alexa, Prince and Rafael were to sit. The attorneys for the defense, Lacey and Baxter, sat at the table to the judge's left.

Judge Darnell took her seat, the Great Seal of California behind her. She was a grey-haired Black female who apparently did not share the view that a woman should always smile.

It had yet to be seen if Lacey would be the lead attorney at trial. Alexa guessed that Ann Lacey's good looks would not make points with this this judge and wondered if the obvious fact that she was from the South might work against her, if only subliminally.

Judge Darnell welcomed the attorneys as they introduced

themselves. The first order of business was to select the jury that would decide whether Rafael had proven he'd been wrongfully terminated by a 'preponderance of the evidence.' This was different from the 'beyond a reasonable doubt' required in criminal cases.

If they managed to convince the jury that TriWorld had not, in fact, proven Rafael guilty of the illegal activity by the preponderance of the evidence introduced, the bank would be liable for compensatory damages. The jury would then be asked if they believed that the wrongful termination was in violation of public policy – in other words, if it was in retaliation for whistleblowing. If so, the Bank would be liable for punitive damages as well. Finally, evidence would be introduced to help the jury determine the amount of punitive damages to award. That's where the vast amounts available in TriWorld assets would be put into evidence, leading – hopefully – to a large award.

And so, it began. The clerk called the jury pool into the courtroom from the third floor. As the members of the pool filed into the courtroom, many seemed self-conscious, as if aware they were on display, being judged by the attorneys like farm animals at a county fair. They looked like a hodge-podge of extras from some casting agency. A surfer with his cap on backward and a backpack came in behind an elderly man in a lightweight suit and spectacles. He was followed by a young Asian woman, Alexa thought she'd seen at her manicurist's, and behind her was a middle-aged black man wearing some kind of khaki-colored uniform that had his name – Vernon – stitched in red across his shirt pocket. Rafael would have been amused by the cross-section of people, had his life not been in their hands.

From the initial general questions and expressions of hardship, almost half of the pool was excused, leaving thirty-five people.

Once these thirty-five were seated, Judge Darnell greeted them. She explained that 12 jurors and alternates were needed.

Though two alternates could be deemed sufficient, this was not a case she would want to declare a mistrial in. "Last thing I want to happen is to be in the midst of this trial and find out that a third juror has to be absent." To avoid that, she would set three alternatives.

The potential jurors stated their information as required. The judge gave a very brief outline of the case in a sentence and introduced the four attorneys, asking them to stand and face the potential jurors. "Do any of you know any of these attorneys?" she asked. Heads went from Lacey to Baxter to Alexa to Prince. As the judge called out their names, heads were shaking, and there were murmurs of "no." She next asked if anyone had business with the law firms the attorneys belonged to. No one responded. Then a juror, an older man in dark pants and a golf shirt, raised his hand. "I had a legal case and don't recall what firm the attorneys were from. I can go home and look it up."

"No," Darnell said. "That won't be necessary. My concern is that your knowledge of the firm might sway your decision in this case. If you can't recall as you sit here, then it's not a problem."

She asked if anyone knew her. Apparently, no one did. Next, she asked if anyone had an account at TriWorld. It would have been surprising if anyone did, as these people were all supposed to be U.S. citizens. Again, there was no response from anyone. She asked if anyone held a power of attorney on an account at TriWorld, and again, no one did. Next, she asked, "Has anyone here ever sued a bank?" Two people raised their hands. After confirming that it had actually been the case, the judge dismissed the two individuals without further conversation.

The attorneys took over then. Each side used the peremptory challenges allowed to them, as well as challenges for cause, excluding jurors one side or the other believed to be unable to decide the case in their favor. Relevant questions were asked to assess potential bias in either direction.

Alexa noticed the woman sitting by Lacey, busily making notes on a page she held lengthwise, scribbling anew as each potential juror was questioned. The woman was a jury consultant hired by TriWorld to gain an additional edge. Her specialty was human behavior. Jury consultants are supposedly adept at reading people by their dress, body language, mannerisms, general behavior, and objective facts, and believe they can predict how a particular juror will vote given the facts of a case. This woman looked to Alexa to be in her fifties. She wondered how much TriWorld had spent to engage her services.

To Alexa's surprise, Lacey questioned a few potential jurors about the television shows they watched. It seemed that with the slew of shows modeled around the courtroom and the law, it was fair game to question a potential juror's feelings about Judge Judy, Law and Order, The Good Wife, Orange is the New Black, and even Breaking Bad. Apparently, Lacey's thinking – or the jury consultant's thinking – was that people who didn't watch Breaking Bad or Orange is the New Black and perhaps didn't even watch cable TV would prove to be more conservative and friendlier to pillars of the establishment such as TriWorld, whereas a juror who watched those shows would be sympathetic to the underdog as often the underdog was championed in the shows. There were also questions about the source of news that a potential juror most often relied on. Throughout the voir dire, the jury consultant sat scribbling up a storm, obviously supplying Lacey with questions to ask and coaching her on which jurors to accept and which to nix. The defense attorneys were busily taking notes and passing whispered comments back and forth.

For his part, Prince wasn't surprised to see the jury consultant. "Apparently, the Bank sees the case as worthy of all these expenses," he said. But Alexa didn't think having an expert on the other side was such good news. Once the jurors were impaneled, the consultant might conduct intensive research on each one, looking into anything and everything they could discover about them to give Lacey ideas on how to pitch them based on what they uncovered. She had probably also coached the Bank's witnesses on how to sit and gesture while testifying to maximize their credibility and likability to the jurors. Alexa tried to rein in her anxiety.

Alexa and Prince based their decision to keep or challenge potential jurors on their general appearance, their age, their job, and their race, as well as their answers to questions posed – in short, on stereotypes and gut instinct. The trick was to take their answers regarding their life experience and translate them to determine if they had a predilection to believe that Rafael had been the target of wrongful and malicious termination. Would they believe that an entity as powerful and as prominent as TriWorld Bank would do such a thing?

The juror profile they did not want on the panel was a white, male executive who would relate to the corporate world of TriWorld. They wanted young people, blacks, laborers, immigrants – anyone who could relate to being treated unfairly and wanted the chance to kick back vicariously through Rafael. These people would have reason to empathize with the little guy who had been stomped on by the Big Bad Bank, and they could believe Rafael had been treated unfairly. Alexa believed that women would be more compassionate.

"Historically, women are tougher when it comes to awarding damages," Prince said. "They're generally more conservative with money. But I think they would relate to a husband who's lost a job unfairly."

As Alexa spoke to the potential jurors, she used this first interchange as an opportunity for the jurors to begin to know and like her. She spoke clearly and tried to seem relaxed. Her tone was friendly, and she could see the jurors begin to relax with her. To Rafael, the two sides were playing legal Ping-Pong.

The woman was thirty-three. Questioning revealed she was

married with no children. She slouched, spoke softly, and, in fact, seemed hesitant to speak. Her husband had his own business. He was a computer repairman who made house calls and did some programming on the side. She held a part-time job as a receptionist in a neighborhood auto repair shop. Rafael guessed she would be an ideal juror. Then Lacey asked, "Mrs. Gallan, do you like your bank?"

The woman smiled, and color came to her cheeks. "Oh, yes! We'd be lost without their help. They gave us the loan that started my husband in his business. We were really in a bad way – financially, I mean – that is, we had to pay for his parents and my parents – well, my mother – they hadn't been doing well... and the man at the bank was wonderful." Her voice had risen, and she was speaking faster now. "He gave us the loan without any problem. We were so surprised, and we were so grateful."

Lacey smiled, accepting her, and then cast Alexa a sideways look, expecting that she would use a challenge to exclude Mrs. Gallan as a juror based on her response that evidenced such a fondness for her bank. Without looking at Prince, Alexa smiled at Mrs. Gallan without hesitation and said, "I'm so happy for you, Mrs. Gallan, and your husband." She had no intention of excluding her. Rafael was as surprised as Lacey was.

Christopher Johnson was a sixty-one-year-old black doctor. Though belonging to an ethnic minority, the fact that he had his own private practice made him immune to the danger of being terminated, wrongfully or otherwise. He was well dressed and looked to be a man of means, which one would assume would align him with a pillar of the establishment.

"And do you believe that people will lie to extract money from defendants?" Lacey asked.

Dr. Johnson frowned and pursed his lips as if in thought. "Well," he mused, "I do. In fact, I recently had a dream about that very thing."

"Really," Lacey sounded bemused.

"Yes," Dr. Johnson said in his deep voice. "Happened with my wife. Her niece denied taking the money, but after that dream, I pulled the truth out of her." He folded his hands in front of him. "I put a lot of stock in my dreams. They don't lie. I guarantee you, if I dream about this case, I'll know the truth, and it won't matter what anyone says."

Lacey excluded him before Alexa had the chance to.

Finally, they had their twelve-person jury and three alternates. The clerk swore the jurors in, and they swore they would listen to the evidence, render an honest decision, and reach a verdict based only on that evidence.

There were seven women and five men. There were two Asians, three African Americans, three Latinos, a Middle Easterner, a European Jewish woman, a male with what Alexa thought was a French accent, and two Caucasian native Californians. The youngest juror was an Asian male, twenty-one, and in college, studying to be an electrical engineer. The oldest was the sixty-six-year-old housewife, probably Jewish.

Judge Darnell congratulated the men and women who would be her jury and thanked them for the service they were about to perform. "I expect the trial you are about to be part of to proceed with professionalism and expeditiously," she said. "My role is to determine questions of law if there are objections and to instruct you. But you will decide questions of fact. You are the judges of the facts. The attorneys may poll you after the verdict is reached, asking how you came to your decision; however, for the length of the trial, they may not interact with you in any way outside this courtroom.

"Realize that you must decide this case on the basis of credibility. Not just what a witness says, you must believe that they are telling the truth; that they saw and heard things correctly, and that they are speaking the truth. The court reporter's notes prevail over any notes you may take. You must be able to hear and see everything, so if you cannot, speak up, change your seat, stand up, do what you must. If you have questions for a witness, write them down with your name or seat number and give them to the clerk. The attorneys will see them and, if they have no valid objection, will ask the question. Perhaps not exactly as you write them, but they may be asked." Alexa noted that the jurors were totally attentive.

The judge continued, "Once you leave this courtroom, you are to put this case out of your mind completely. You are not to speak about it to anyone at all until it is over. You are not to talk about it amongst yourselves until you deliberate. You are not to do any research, refer to any reference materials, or contact any experts. Nothing outside this courtroom can influence your decision in this case. At the end of the case, I will instruct you. You will follow my instructions when you deliberate, even if you do not agree with those instructions." She then warned them not to speak with any of the attorneys or parties in the case. "If you are approached by any of the attorneys, witnesses, or anyone connected with the case in any way, you are to immediately notify me. Is that understood?" She passed a look at each individual juror as they nodded.

"Okay, ladies and gentlemen. You may go upstairs and have your parking validated, then leave. Please return to the jury clerk on Monday morning. We will start this trial at nine o'clock sharp."

Rafael, all wound up from anxious expectation, invited his two attorneys for a drink after court. They were all tired, but the thought of sitting down with a cold drink was too tempting to pass up. Besides, it was four thirty on a Friday, and the freeways would be more miserable than usual in all directions for the next few hours. They decided on the restaurant bar a block away from the courthouse and hadn't been seated a minute before a waiter approached to ask what they'd like.

"Roger, you like champagne?" Rafael asked Prince.

"Why don't we wait until there's something to celebrate?" Alexa suggested.

"Actually, I'd rather have a vodka on ice," Prince said.

"And I'd like some tequila," Alexa said. "A margarita, blended."

"Well, since champagne is not meant to be drunk alone," Rafael said, "I'll have a martini." The waiter took their orders, nodded, and left. Rafael looked at his two attorneys. "Tell me. What do you think of the jury?"

Alexa waited to hear what Prince would say. She knew what Rafael was thinking. As calm as he appeared, he knew that today the group of men and women had been chosen who would decide his case against TriWorld, his future fate, and possibly hers as well.

"I'm happy," Prince said, nodding slowly. "It looks like a hell of a good jury to me."

Rafael smiled broadly. He looked at Alexa. "You hear that? Do you agree?"

She knew it was a good jury. It was better than what she could have expected. Though she knew there were problems with several of the jurors, she had no doubt that Roger knew that too. "Roger knows more about this than I do," she said.

Rafael turned back to Prince, a bit more relaxed, or rather, relieved. "Why do you think it's such a good jury?"

Alexa saw Prince hesitate for the slightest second. Then he said, "They're pretty much what we wanted. Most of them are the oppressed: blacks, immigrants... housewives whose husbands are employed or they're employed in nine-to-five jobs themselves." He looked around the room then and nodded. "The fear of termination is something these jurors relate to. We're in good shape." He looked at Alexa then, and they passed a knowing smile.

"Alexa, why didn't you excuse the woman who loved her banker?" Rafael asked. He turned to Prince. "Do we want her?"

"I think so." Prince said, nodding again. "She's emotional and seems to be a follower."

"And I think she knows what it's like to get screwed," Alexa added.

Rafael sighed. "I have to believe you guys know what you're doing," he said.

48

The twins were with Ben that weekend and Lupe was spending the weekend at her daughter's house. Alexa took her power walk on Saturday morning and met Sheyanne for an early lunch at an outside table at Il Pastaio on Canon Drive. Sheyanne looked radiant as only a woman wearing the engagement ring she had so longed for can look. They kissed, hugged, and ordered lunch. Alexa opted for pasta. Sheyanne ordered a salad with dressing on the side. "I'm trying on wedding dresses," she said, rolling her eyes. "My selection of dresses is small because it's such short notice, so I have to lose weight."

The wedding date was set for late July, two months away, in Malibu. Joshua's sister, also a friend of Sheyanne and the original link between bride and groom, would be the maid of honor. Alexa was to be one of two bridesmaids. The other was a longtime friend of Sheyanne's from college.

Through most of their lunch, the two spoke about wedding plans but as the meal wound down, Sheyanne was anxious to hear about Alexa's life now that the biggest time-consuming part of it, Rafael's matter before the Federal Reserve, had ended. Alexa told her about the wrongful termination case filed against TriWorld and the potential to be awarded punitive damages because Rafael was a whistleblower.

"That's fantastic!" Sheyanne said. "I mean, if you still need to be his lawyer, at least you'll get paid if he does." Alexa nodded. "Well, it's not like you don't deserve it," Sheyanne said.

"I know," Alexa said.

"Why do you say it like that?"

Their waiter was at their table asking if there was anything else he could get them. He gave them their check. Both women reached for their credit cards. They looked at one another and silently decided to forgo arguing about who would pay for lunch. Two credit cards fell on the bill. The waiter bowed slightly, took the bill and two cards, and walked away.

Sheyanne eyed her knowingly. "So, girlfriend," she said cautiously, "why am I getting the feeling you're being weird?" Alexa shook her head as though trying to shake off her anxieties. "Come on, Lexie, tell Mama all about it. What's up?"

Alexa looked at her best friend sitting across the table from her and realized she wanted desperately to tell her of her confusion about Rafael, tell her of his insane proposal, and how she couldn't make heads or tails of it. "Rafael asked me to marry him." She watched Sheyanne closely for her reaction.

Sheyanne appeared stunned. She was silent for a moment, then said, "You mean, he wants to leave his wife?" Alexa nodded as she raised her glass of bubbly water and took a sip. "Whew! Alexa! What did you say?"

Alexa put her glass down and shook her head. "I don't know what to do," she said. "I know Viviana. I like her. She's nice to me, and I think she's a good person. I don't want to do that to her. When I think that she doesn't know that I've slept with her husband, I want to cringe." Tears welled up in her eyes.

Sheyanne passed her a fresh napkin and waited as Alexa

dabbed the tears from her eyes. "Look, Lexie, I'm Jewish. We're all martyrs. But you know I'm not really religious." Alexa's tears gave way to a tiny smile, and she chuckled and nodded. "Anyway, I know this. According to Jewish law, you haven't committed a sin," she said, making air quotes around 'sin.' "You're not married, so you haven't committed adultery; he has."

"I still feel terrible," Alexa said. "How could he do that? I mean, it's one thing to have an affair, a two-night stand, a fling or whatever, and that's terrible – I divorced Ben because of that – but to leave his wife who loves him after so many years as soon as he comes into money?"

Sheyanne sat back in her chair. "So, you don't respect him."

Alexa hadn't thought of it that way. "I guess I don't. I really feel bad for her."

Sheyanne leaned forward again and spoke forcefully. "Look, Lexie. If you don't respect him or love him, that's one thing. But if your only problem is Viviana, forget it. It's typically you. You're everybody's lawyer. You feel you need to rescue everyone who's getting a raw deal." She had Alexa's attention. "You are not Viviana's lawyer! For once in your life, advocate for yourself! You haven't said anything about how you feel about Rafael. Do you love him?"

Tears began to well up in Alexa's eyes. That was the very question Alexa dreaded, the question she had been asking herself, the question without an answer. She hadn't wanted to believe she felt anything more than a huge attraction for Rafael. But the attraction hadn't ebbed; instead, it had grown.

Why?

She tried to be honest with herself, but she was at a loss. Had emotions formed because of his situation, deep emotions that had enhanced their physical relationship? Was it because she feared intimacy after having been burned by Ben, and viewed Rafael as a married, unattainable man, and that made him safe?

Rafael had been honest and vocal about his feelings for her. Why hadn't she done the same? Maybe she wasn't even being honest with herself. She was too afraid. She answered tentatively. "I think so."

"Then, goddamn it, girl, go for it. You're entitled to have a loving relationship. Let Viviana fend for herself. If she wants him, she'll fight for him. Don't fight her fight for her. Fight your fight."

Alexa felt a fog lift from her brain. Sheyanne made sense. Having found her friend's advice to be clear-headed and rational, she hurried to tell Sheyanne all of it, eager to get her view. "He's leaving Viviana to marry me – if he wins this case," she said.

"And?" Sheyanne looked at her, waiting for more.

"I feel pressured. I've made one mistake already. It wouldn't be fair for the kids or me if I made another. I mean, okay, there are no guarantees, but I'd want some time with him after he's away from her." She couldn't bring herself to say 'divorced.' "We've never dated. Our dates have been in my office talking to the Federal Reserve, and now, in court."

"And in bed," Sheyanne added.

Alexa nodded. "Yes, but those aren't dates. We haven't really done anything else together. You only met him one time, and that was for a minute when you happened to knock on my door. He doesn't know my friends or my mother, and I don't know anything about his friends… You know, things people know about one another. I'd like to live together for a while."

"Okay, I get it. You want to pull a Joshua." Sheyanne said. "What's the problem?"

"That's the problem," Alexa said. "He says he won't leave his wife unless it's to marry me, not date me or live with me. Marry me."

"Hmm." Sheyanne looked around at the other al fresco diners and took a sip of her iced tea. "That is a problem."

"Yeah."

"Well, okay. But promise me you won't *not* marry him because you'll play advocate for Viviana. You're over that, right?" Their waiter returned, and both women signed on their charge cards, adding a generous tip. "Alexa? Look at me. Are you done playing her attorney?" Sheyanne asked when the waiter left.

"I think so," Alexa said. "You make sense." She nodded and smiled to signal her appreciation of her friend's advice.

Sheyanne looked at her watch. "Okay, I've got to go. This is my day off, and I'm meeting my mom. We have to get to at least four or five bridal shops this afternoon. I have to find a dress. I'd love you to come with me."

"I'd really love to see you in wedding dresses and give you my two cents, but I need to see my mother and talk with Madlynn about some things."

"Okay. I'd love to come see Giselle for a minute, but I'm really late. Give her my love."

Alexa nodded. Her heart ached. She would not relay Sheyanne's message of love to her mother.

Giselle would have no idea who in the world her daughter's old friend was.

49

When Alexa parked in front of Giselle's house, her mother was outside taking a daily walk with Madlynn at her side. Alexa sat in her car watching the two women as they made their way down the sidewalk. Her mother had aged a great deal in the short time since her diagnosis. The woman who had always looked younger than her years, vibrant and filled with energy, was now walking slowly and holding on to Madlynn's arm. Alexa bounced out of her car and greeted them cheerfully. "Hi, Mom! Hi, Madlynn."

Madlynn responded immediately, twisting in Alexa's direction and returning her smile. Giselle did not react at all. She continued to look at the ground ahead of her. Alexa went to stand by her mother. She gently tapped her shoulder. "Hi, Mom," she repeated. She hugged her.

Giselle reacted to the touch, looked up, and saw Alexa. Alexa could see there was no hint of recognition in her mother's eyes. Her heart missed a beat. She kissed Giselle on the cheek. "It's me, Mom. It's Alexa."

Alexa was amazed to see her mother turn to Madlynn as

though for an explanation. Madlynn smiled and held Giselle's hand. "It's Alexa, your daughter. Say hello."

Giselle turned back to Alexa and smiled a little smile. "Hello," she said, with a sudden smile, faking enthusiasm.

"We were just taking one of our walks," Madlynn said.

"Can I walk with you?" Alexa asked.

"Sure. Come on my side, though, so we don't confuse your mother."

This was not what Alexa had expected, and she didn't really understand, but she trusted Madlynn, so she moved away from her mother to walk alongside her caregiver. As it turned out, this position made it easier for Alexa to ask the caregiver her questions.

"How is she doing?" she asked.

Madlynn's expression didn't change. "As you see," she said.

"She didn't recognize me."

"No, I don't think she did." Madlynn stroked Alexa's back with her free hand. "But she probably will in a few minutes or an hour or tomorrow," she said. "Her memory comes and goes."

Alexa nodded. She had witnessed as much. She swallowed and asked about her mother's physical health. Giselle had been to her internist the day before.

"She's okay," Madlynn said. "She's healthy."

"And she's taking her meds?"

Madlynn informed her that her mother no longer clung to her handbag, but she was still prone to displaying seemingly unprovoked bursts of anger and temper.

"Yes, she is, and they're helping a lot. She's okay. Believe it or not, this morning we were singing together.

"And she's eating well? Sleeping well?"

"She's eating a lot." Madlynn chuckled. "She's gained weight. Yesterday, the doctor said I should be careful so that she doesn't gain more. She forgets when she's eaten." Madlynn seemed uncomfortable then. "She sleeps well, but the last few nights I've been sleeping with her."

"Why?" Alexa asked, almost afraid of the answer. It couldn't be good.

"She has accidents, and it wakes her up, and then I need to change the sheets. Now I put something down like what they do in hospitals, then remove it in the morning. But I'm going to go to the drugstore today and buy some Depends."

Alexa shut her eyes. This was all too much for her to digest. The woman who wouldn't be seen unless she was immaculately groomed would be wearing diapers. Alexa had researched Alzheimer's from the day Dr. Minton first gave her the news. She'd learned it was generally accepted that Alzheimer's, the most common form of dementia, had seven stages, and with this latest news from Madlynn, she realized her mother had passed to the fifth.

Alexa thought her reading and the research she'd done on the internet had prepared her to witness her mother regress socially as well as physiologically as the disease progressed, but it didn't lessen her shock or her pain.

She'd read that in the population of people who were, like Giselle, over the age of sixty-five, one in ten had the illness. Four million Americans suffered from Alzheimer's or "ALZ," and almost forty million Americans knew someone diagnosed with ALZ. Those statistics were expected to increase at an alarming rate as baby boomers continued to age. As her mother's illness advanced, her loss of memory reached further into her past, leaving her with no memory of the events she'd seen, the things she'd experienced, and the people she knew. Alexa was glad that her father wasn't there to witness this. *How long before her mother would not have been able to recognize the love of her life?*

The three women continued walking around the block, then returned to Giselle's house. Alexa wanted to stay, to sit and have a cup of tea with her mother, embrace her, or just hold her hand.

As Alexa prepared tea for the three of them in the kitchen, she noticed that Madlynn was helping her mother to her bedroom. Alexa put the kettle on to boil and brought out three cups before Madlynn came into the kitchen.

"Where's Mom?" Alexa asked.

"She's napping," Madlynn answered. "The walks tire her out." Alexa put the cups back into the cupboard and turned off the stove.

"Okay, I guess I'll be going then," she said. She gave Madlynn a hug. "Please call me. Let me know how she's doing. Let me know if she asks for me. I'll be here in minutes. I'm in trial now, but I'm home this weekend."

She left her mother's house depressed. There were errands she had to do; she wouldn't have time to get them done during the week. There was dry cleaning to pick up, a few things she needed from the beauty supply, and milk for the children. She made only one quick stop for milk and told herself that the rest would have to wait. She drove home in a funk. Alone until Monday, she spent all day Sunday doing as little as possible. She stayed in bed late and didn't take a power walk. She hardly ate, and when she did, she finished off the pint of ice cream in the freezer and topped that off with chocolate chip cookies. She called Sheyanne and left a message, wondering if she'd found a dress and telling her what a great time she'd had at their lunch.

The most ambitious thing she did was to take a shower and wash her hair. She needed this day of rest, a throwaway day. If she couldn't take a vacation, she owed it to herself to give in to her depression and let herself wallow in her funk when the twins weren't around.

Tomorrow would be another day and the start of trial.

50

Monday morning, as Vivian set about getting ready for court, she again wondered what to wear. It was the first day of the trial and the jury's first look at Rafael's wife, the plaintiff's spouse, the woman whose husband had been so wronged by the defendants.

She had first thought to wear a black suit with a white blouse and short black heels. She would look conservative and demure, the way she used to look. Before. But she longed to wear one of her new dresses. On hearing the news that the Beverly Hills branch of TriWorld had been shut down and that it had been decided Rafael would sue the bank for wrongful termination, Viviana had gone shopping with a credit card for the first time in a very long time – other than for her daughter's wedding reception when she'd bought the dress her husband hadn't noticed at that catastrophic party.

She bought herself several dresses in her now-smaller size to complement her new, lighter hair color. She'd also bought herself the most expensive handbag she'd purchased since coming to America, along with two pairs of the newest in high heels from Nordstrom's, where Rafael used to work. She longed to introduce the new Viviana to Rafael, and what better time than on the first day of the trial, she hoped, would change both their lives?

She wanted to see the look of surprise on his face. She also wanted to see the look on Alexa's face when she saw the new Viviana.

Viviana liked Alexa. She'd liked her from the day they'd met. She knew Alexa was a dedicated mother and a good lawyer. But if Alexa thought Viviana was stupid, she was wrong. Viviana was well aware that Rafael's relationship with his lawyer was more than strictly professional. Alexa was a beautiful woman. And she was smart. Viviana was smart too. She knew her husband well and knew he was smitten with his attorney. She'd guessed they'd had an affair.

But did he love Alexa?

Viviana was far more certain than she would have liked that he did love her.

Would he leave her for Alexa?

Winning this case would bring in money, and Sophia was now married and safe from the dangerous stigma of being the child of divorced parents. But Alexa had two young children. *Would Rafael want to step into a household with two young children? Would he be able to live with a strong, independent American woman?* And the children's father would always be in the picture. *Would Rafael want to deal with another man in the background?*

Alexa was not the first woman Rafael had bedded outside their marriage. Viviana had seen how women threw themselves at him. He was charismatic. In his efforts to get customers for the bank, he was always meeting rich, spoiled women who were used to getting whatever and whomever they wanted. Viviana had accepted that because she loved him and knew she had no choice in the matter. Her husband was highly sexual, whereas she was sure that her own sexual appetite was less than average.

The affairs had been short, and he'd always been discreet. But Rafael was very emotional, and here was this lovely, caring, smart, and pretty young woman who had shared deep emotions with him throughout his greatest trauma. She knew her husband well enough to know that he had invested deep emotions in Alexa, and she had a strong sense that their relationship had developed into something more. Then she had seen them together at the party, and her worst suspicions only solidified. It was as though the two were on a date, and she had been no more than a bystander.

Viviana not only loved her husband; she needed him. Without him, she was lost. She was not the kind of woman who could survive on her own. She was raised to marry, have a home, and take care of her children and husband; her husband would take care of her. There was no way she could let Rafael leave her. She had witnessed Sarita, the Argentinian she'd known, go through a divorce, then move to a small apartment, enter a spiral of depression, and vanish.

Their party for Sofia had been a very rude wakeup call. The realization that it was time to act had hit Viviana hard. The very next day, she started a diet and scheduled daily training sessions at the gym. She'd restyled and lightened her hair and spent an afternoon with Sofia at Sephora learning how to do her makeup. She learned that the colors of a spring garden suited her best. And she clandestinely read every article she could find in certain magazines on different ways to please a man.

She ultimately decided to wear the orchid-colored dress with a lightweight lavender jacket and the new pair of neutral high heels. Rafael was almost ready to leave for court, and she didn't want him to have to wait for her. She hurriedly applied a touch of makeup as she'd been taught, brushed her hair into a simple, elegant roll, and met Rafael at their bedroom door.

When Rafael saw her, he whistled loudly. "Pareces sensacional!"

"Gracias, senor," Viviana replied with a smile and a warmed heart. And then in English, she added, "I hear a whistleblower." They laughed as they made their way down the hallway. Rafael was feeling good after their lovemaking last night. Seeing her, he confirmed he hadn't been dreaming. Viviana had definitely proved surprising. It was as if she had become another woman in bed, not the modest and demure wife of twenty-three years. He was baffled, but content.

Vivian had served him tea after dinner, and, as they sat together on the couch, she began asking him questions about the day in court instead of turning on the television. As he spoke, she began rubbing his feet! Rafael was surprised and appreciative; he loved having his feet rubbed. To his surprise, when he rose to go to bed, rather than staying in the living room to watch television, Viviana joined him. He lay turned away from her between the sheets. Soon, she lay down as well and began to massage his neck. Rafael started to relax. After a few minutes, she began to caress his nape. Then she nibbled at his ear ever so gently and set soft kisses on his cheek. Rafael turned his face around, and she kissed him on the lips. When he put his arm around her and drew her close, he discovered she was naked. Rafael was stunned. This was the first time he could remember in all their married life that Viviana had come to bed unclothed. He wanted to say something about it, but there were other priorities at the moment.

Now, walking down the hall toward their front door with her, Rafael was still in shock. And look at her now! She was beautiful. When they got to the front door, Rafael opened it and followed his wife out of the house and to the car.

When was the last time he saw her from this rear view? She certainly looked good, slimmer than she'd been and rather shapely in the clothing she wore. And he didn't recall seeing this purple dress either. His eyes traveled down to her shapely legs and then to the heels. He shook his head.

When had this transformation taken place? Where had he been?

At the car, he fumbled then found his keys and unlocked the doors. He opened Viviana's door and watched as she got in, her legs moving gracefully, swiveling inside. Walking to his side of the car, he raised his head to the sky. It was a good day.

On the way to court, Viviana asked what Rafael expected to happen that day. Viviana noted his relaxed attitude. "How does Alexa feel about it?" she asked. She watched his face as he answered.

"She thinks it will go well," he said. Neither his voice nor his face showed any emotion.

Viviana pushed. "She's quite remarkable."

Rafael looked over his left shoulder and changed lanes as he said, "Yes, she is."

"She's so... dynamic. I don't know how she manages the law and raising children. She has two children, I think."

"Yes," her husband answered. "They're twins. A boy and a girl."

Viviana knew that from conversations with Alexa. "You've met them?"

Rafael answered casually. "Yes. Her office is at her house now."

"Oh," Viviana said easily.

Noting that the jurors smiled at Alexa, it had been decided that she would be the one to question the witness with Prince backing her up and taking notes, so on the opening day of the trial, her anxiety level was understandably high, even before she glanced over at the defense table and saw a total of five – yes, count them! – five attorneys. Three other attorneys, all middle-aged males, had joined Lacey and Baxter at their table. The cadre of attorneys was intimidating.

"Five?" she said to Roger.

He seemed unfazed. "Our reputations have obviously preceded us."

Alexa looked back at them and frowned. The defense table was crowded, and attaches were everywhere, files already covering the table, legal pads out, pens ready. Lacey and Baxter would have been enough of a challenge.

Noting Alexa's continuing discomfort, Prince chuckled. He covered his mouth and said to her, "Big mistake. It only adds to the image of a bullying Goliath. The jury will wonder why they need so many lawyers."

Alexa looked at him and deadpanned. "Because they want to win."

Prince shook his head. "Don't you see? They're only making us look even more like the underdog, and the jury will sympathize."

"Well, I hope you're right," Alexa said.

"I am. You think anyone on that jury could afford to pay five attorneys?"

As the jurors entered and made their way down the aisle to take their seats, they eyed the defense table with curiosity, noting three new lawyers.

Then Rafael entered, Viviana at his side. Viviana watched as Alexa automatically smiled at Rafael as though she had not recognized Viviana. Then her eyes widened in recognition. "Viviana! Good to see you," she said.

"Hello, Alexa," Viviana said.

The two exchanged brief kisses on both cheeks, and Viviana put her hand out to Prince. "Hello, I'm Mrs. Lamon." Roger Prince introduced himself, and Viviana was aware of Alexa exhaling, her face going slack as she gazed at her, then at Rafael, who was smiling. Viviana gave her husband a peck on his cheek before taking a seat in the first row of the spectator section.

She studied the members of the jury. These twelve people seemed so ordinary.

How could they understand what TriWorld had done to her husband, to her, to his reputation, and to their standing in their community? Would they be simpatico? She knew they had to be U.S. citizens to serve on the jury, but she strained in vain to find one who might have had a South American heritage.

Seeing Viviana, Alexa's anxiety vanished and was replaced with total shock. The woman looked stunning. Why, she barely looked like the same woman Alexa had last seen just months ago at her gathering. She'd changed her hair color and her hairstyle, and she was dressed in a gorgeous outfit, something Alexa would never have expected to see her in.

It was like one of those total makeovers Alexa had seen on television. The woman had gone from a plain-looking, understated, middle-aged wife to a fashionable and extremely attractive woman. She must have lost fifteen pounds! Alexa was aware of Rafael's attention to his wife and the new look in his eyes when he gazed at her. Alexa recognized that glimmer. She knew it well.

Alexa had been prepared to harden her feelings toward Viviana after her conversation with Sheyanne. After all, Sheyanne was right: Viviana could fend for herself. Now, seeing this version of the wronged woman made Alexa feel as if *she* was the one who had been somehow betrayed. *What the hell?*

Rafael was looking over at the defense table. "My God," he whispered to Alexa. "Five attorneys?"

51

The bailiff instructed everyone to rise. Judge Darnell entered the courtroom and took the bench. "Lamon v TriWorld Bank," she announced. "Are the attorneys present and ready to begin?" It was time for Alexa to turn all her attention to the trial.

The seven attorneys made their presence known. Immediately before the trial, both sides had submitted a brief to the judge outlining their arguments and a list of the witnesses they would call as well as the documents and exhibits they would introduce as evidence in support of their position.

"All right then, let's begin with opening statements." Her Honor turned to face the jurors. She explained that the opening statements they were about to hear from both sides were simply what the two parties, the plaintiff and defendant, hoped to prove. There would be no testimony contained in them, and the statements made were not necessarily factual.

It had initially been decided that Prince would make the opening statement. But due to Rafael's urging, arguing that the jurors would pay more attention to a woman, and with Alexa's okay, that plan changed. Alexa now rose from her seat at the plaintiff's table.

"Good morning, Your Honor," she began. The judge nodded her head in Alexa's direction. Alexa turned to face the jury. "Good morning ladies and gentlemen and welcome. Thank you for being here and participating in the outcome of this case. My client appreciates your efforts." She paused before continuing. "This is a civil case of wrongful termination. The plaintiff in this case is Rafael Lamon. He is represented in this matter by both Mr. Prince and me, Alexa Starr, so you'll be seeing and hearing from both of us.

"The case you're about to hear is about a man who was wrongfully and maliciously fired. We will show you through the evidence and the testimony of witnesses that Rafael Lamon worked at TriWorld Bank for almost eight years. During that time, he was a model employee. He consistently received glowing performance reports and raises.

"At some point, he was shown paperwork by his superiors that he believed was in violation of common sense and most probably against banking laws. He questioned his immediate superior and the bank's general manager about them. Both assured him there was no problem. Still not comfortable, he brought it to the attention of the auditor visiting the Bank to perform a regularly scheduled audit.

"The auditor communicated the information he received from my client to the Federal Reserve. As a consequence, the Federal Reserve began an investigation into activities at TriWorld Bank. In an effort to head off the investigation, TriWorld, which had engaged in illegal activities, not only abruptly terminated Rafael without any explanation, but further scapegoated him, telling the Federal Reserve that it was Rafael Lamon who was their man.

"By firing Rafael Lamon, they hoped the Federal Reserve would believe he had been the guilty one, end the investigation, and their problems would be over. After all, they had found the criminal and terminated him. On a Monday morning, when Rafael showed up to work, he was terminated – without cause, without warning, without any explanation – and escorted off the property by a security guard, humiliated, and forbidden to return to the Bank. TriWorld misrepresented to the Federal Reserve that Rafael Lamon was the culprit and that he alone had been guilty of the wrongdoing.

"Thus, Rafael's termination with the explanation that he was, quote, involved in illegal activity, thrust Rafael Lamon into the hands of the Federal Reserve and the Justice Department to suffer undeserved punishment for a year and a half. He suffered undue financial stress and emotional distress, a damaged reputation... great loss in every aspect of his life.

"In fact, Rafael was never involved in the slightest in any illegal activity whatsoever. By definition of his job, he was a relationship officer, charged with acquiring new clients for the bank. He had absolutely no power to fund or to have any part in funding. He was completely innocent.

"Nonetheless, Rafael Lamon suddenly found himself without a job, and with limited funds. He also found himself the main object of interest to the Federal Reserve and the Justice Department, and faced civil penalties of over one million dollars and a possible jail sentence for a crime he did not commit and had no part in. In fact, as I stated, he was the one who had initially informed the Federal Reserve of the illegal activity through his discussion with an auditor who had visited the bank.

"Rafael could not find another job as no one would hire him. He had to seek professional help for his mental and emotional state. His marriage was stressed. Eventually, he found a job as a part-time shoe salesman in a department store – and he was happy to take it.

"After depleting his funds, sacrificing his health, stressing his marriage and suffering unwarranted damage to his reputation, the truth became obvious to the Federal Reserve. But it was a long road. It took a good year and a half to vindicate himself of guilt as everyone from TriWorld conspired to point their finger at him. Today, we hope to secure restitution for Rafael Lamon for what he was deliberately subjected to. More than that, we hope to punish TriWorld for the intentional and malicious act of terminating Rafael Lamon and scapegoating him simply because he acted as any good citizen would when he blew the whistle to the auditor, showing him signs of the illegal activity conducted at the bank. When he did that, he became a whistleblower, and to terminate an employee because of whistleblowing is against public policy and deemed to be worthy of significant punishment." She walked even closer to the jury box.

"Now, you will hear language about basis points, matching funds and other banking terms. Please, don't be confused. They will be explained so that you understand them all. Ladies and gentlemen do not lose sight of the fact that this is, in reality, a simple case. It is a case of David and Goliath. It is a case of a giant believing it can unfairly and unjustly squash the small man. We hope that you will agree that this time, it didn't work." She paused. "Thank you for your time."

Alexa could have paraded all her exhibits to the jury then as well, projected them onto the screen, and discussed the importance of each, but both she and Prince had decided it would be best to introduce them via the witnesses, explaining their significance and putting each into context. Besides, she didn't want to go on and on. It was better to be brief, be bright, and be gone, so she headed back to the table.

It had been years since she had spoken in open court and she'd just done so without any notes. She had spoken the knowledge she had lived for almost two years. She thought she'd said everything she'd meant to. Because she had been doing the talking and hadn't had to worry about not being able to hear anyone, her anxiety level had been down and her confidence level, up. When she was done, she felt exhilarated.

Prince moved in his seat as though making space for her to sit down and whispered, "Good job." Rafael, on her other side, didn't have to say anything; his shining eyes said it all. She realized she was excited. She had enjoyed herself.

"Ms. Lacey, please proceed with defendant's opening statement," Judge Darnell said.

Ann Lacey stood. She was holding a legal pad. "Yes, Your Honor." Alexa couldn't help noticing again how attractive Lacey was. The soft light-blue designer dress, edged with turquoise piping, looked well on her. Her blonde hair was down, falling in big, loose curls just past her shoulders. As she walked, her gray high heels clicked on the wooden floor with every step. Alexa had to hand it to her. Those heels were higher than any she would dare wear to court. She wondered how the women on the jury would perceive her. She thought she could guess how the men did. Lacey certainly had the jury's attention.

She stopped at the lectern only to deposit her legal pad there. "Ladies and gentlemen, I represent TriWorld Bank." Lacey extended her arm out to the defense table. "Co-counsels, Mr. Baxter, Mr. Blank, Mr. Sheffield and Mr. Alvarez you see seated at the defense table will be assisting me throughout this trial." Alexa realized the truth of what Prince had said. The presence of so many attorneys made her seem somewhat incompetent, as if she needed the assistance of four males to do her job.

She began to walk alongside the jury box. "Now, we all heard everything that Mr. Lamon's attorney said to you in her opening statement. And it sounded good." She was nodding her head. "The story of David and Goliath. The poor little man squashed under the foot of the big bad giant." She turned and looked at the plaintiff's table. "It makes you feel sorry for poor Mr. Lamon." She turned back around and continued her walk up the jury box. "I understand. So wronged. A heart-wrenching tale."

She suddenly turned on her heel. "But a fairy tale." She paused. "Like Alice in Wonderland and the Three Little Pigs. A fairy tale." She took a few steps back down the jury box. Alexa noticed that all the jurors had their eyes locked on her. "We will show that Rafael Lamon is not as innocent as counsel would have you believe. We will show that the Federal Reserve has in fact, not found Rafael Lamon innocent. We will show that Rafael Lamon was, in fact, guilty of participating – if not orchestrating – illegal loans in violation of banking laws."

Lacey walked back to the lectern and retrieved her legal pad. She glanced at it, and Alexa knew she was scanning it for points she needed to address. After a few seconds, she put it down and continued speaking as she returned to the jurors. "Rafael Lamon's attorney has told you that he was wrongfully and maliciously terminated. We will show that he was terminated for engaging in illegal activity. That is not wrongful termination and certainly not malicious.

"Beyond that, Rafael Lamon is alleging that he was terminated in violation of public policy because he was a whistleblower. We will show that he was not, in fact, a whistleblower. That is a figment of the same imagination that created the entire fairy tale.

"TriWorld has not harmed Rafael Lamon. This lawsuit is a simple case. That's true. It's a case of a man and his attorney – pardon me, his attorneys – trying to milk a bank for money that is undeserved and which will not be awarded. Thank you." With that, she sat down.

The trial was about to get popping.

52

Since this was Rafael's party, he was first to present his case against TriWorld.

The first witness Alexa called to the stand was the security guard, Ed Monroe. As the witness was sworn in, and Alexa made her way to him, she felt the eyes of the five defense attorneys on her. She greeted the security guard and asked about his place of employment. Monroe answered, "TriWorld, Encino." Alexa asked where he had been previously employed, and Monroe answered, "The Beverly Hills branch of TriWorld."

Alexa established that Ed Monroe had been the security guard on duty the day Rafael was fired. Yes, he knew Rafael Lamon and was stationed at the door when he had entered the Bank on the morning he was fired. Ed didn't recall the exact time but guessed it was nine a.m. as Mr. Lamon was consistently punctual. His demeanor seemed normal when he arrived. No, he did not seem stressed.

Monroe testified that the next time he saw Mr. Lamon was less than half an hour after he'd arrived, when he was told to go into his office by the bank manager, Mr. Stamen, and escort him to his car. Mr. Stamen had called Ed into his office five minutes earlier and told him to wait in the hallway until he called him into Mr. Lamon's office. He was to take Mr. Lamon's keys and walk him to his car. He guessed that Mr. Lamon was being terminated. Stamen didn't tell him why. Ed had always liked Mr. Lamon. He'd always greeted Ed and was always smiling.

"Mr. Monroe, when you went into Mr. Lamon's office, what did you see?"

"Well," Monroe leaned forward a little as if sharing something confidential. "Mr. Stamen and Mr. Alandro were leaving Mr. Lamon's office, and Mr. Lamon was sitting at his desk."

"And how did he look to you?"

Monroe scratched his cheek. "He looked kind of stunned, you know? He was shaking so bad, I had to take the key off his keychain for him. I guess he wasn't expecting it."

"Objection!" Lacey was on her feet. "Speculative."

"Sustained. The jury will ignore the witness's last comment," the judge said.

"Did he say anything?"

Monroe thought. "Not that I can remember. I told him he had to take whatever he wanted with him because he wouldn't be allowed back on the premises. He didn't take much. I think he was in shock." Lacey made no objection this time.

"And what did you do?"

Monroe shrugged. "Nothing. I did what I was told to do. I took his key, got a box for him to put his stuff in, and then walked him downstairs to his car."

"And have you seen or heard from Mr. Lamon since that day?"

"No, not till today, seeing him here in court." He gestured to Rafael sitting at the plaintiff's table.

"Were any other employees at that branch fired that day or soon afterward that date?"

"No ma'am, not to my awareness."

Alexa waited a beat. She wanted the jury to process what he'd testified to so far. "Mr. Monroe, you are no longer working at the Beverly Hills branch?"

"Yeah, that's correct."

"Why is that?"

"It was closed down."

"Mr. Monroe, do you know why it was closed down?"

He shrugged. "Only that the Feds closed it down. They pretty much stormed the place and shut it down, told everyone to leave and go home."

Alexa was surprised that Lacey didn't object.

"Are you aware of the reason it was shut down?"

"Only what I read in the papers."

"Was Mr. Lamon working there at the time it was shut down?"

"Oh, no. He'd been fired long before that."

"Thank you for coming here today, Mr. Monroe. That's all the questions I have for you."

The judge asked Lacey if she wanted to cross-examine Monroe.

She declined. Despite Lacey's objection, their first witness had helped establish that Rafael's termination had been a complete surprise. He'd also testified that the branch had been "shut down" by the Federal Reserve when it "stormed" the premises. The jury also heard him testify that only Rafael had been fired and that the branch had been ordered closed long after he had left it.

The next witness called was Michael Bowen, Head of Human Resources at TriWorld's California office. It was Bowen who had communicated with the Employment Development Department, telling them that Rafael had been fired for funding illegal loans. Bowen was probably quite experienced and may have been meticulous with his paperwork, but he was nothing much to look at, stocky in an ill-fitting suit and a clipped bowtie, his sparse wheat-colored hair combed over his almost hairless head, and perspiring before he even got to the stand.

In speaking with the security guard, Alexa had referred to her client as "Rafael Lamon" or "Mr. Lamon." But from here on, and beginning with Bowen, Alexa tried to remember to refer to her client as "Rafael" as she had in her opening remarks. She wanted the jury to think of him as one of them, because he was.

After the oath was taken and the preliminaries were over, Alexa dove in, stating Bowen's name and position at TriWorld. It was established that he was the person at TriWorld who regularly communicated with the EDD, informing them whether a terminated employee was eligible for benefits. He did so in Rafael's case.

Prince projected the document received from EDD, marked as 'Exhibit A', onto the screen so that it was easily visible to the jurors, and Alexa asked Bowen to identify the handwriting. Bowen took his glasses out of his suit pocket, put them on, and confirmed it was his. The foundation was laid as he confirmed that he had sent this to the EDD, as was his obligation whenever an employee stopped working at the bank, to determine their eligibility for unemployment benefits. Then she directed him to read aloud the handwritten sentence in the upper left corner.

He adjusted his glasses and read, "Employee was terminated for illegal conduct. He funded illegal loans."

"Do you recall making that statement to a representative of the Employment Development Department?"

"I probably did."

"What was your understanding of why Rafael was fired?"

"I was told he was involved in illegal activity."

"What sort of illegal activity?"

"Well, what it says there," Bowen pointed at the screen.

"You mean, you were told he was funding illegal loans?"

"That's correct. That he was involved in that."

"Mr. Bowen, when you say, 'involved' in that, are you implying that there were others involved as well?"

"I don't know. Or, well, I didn't know at the time."

"Was anyone else fired along with Rafael?"

"You mean at the same time?"

"Yes, in that same time period. Were you in communication with the EDD about anyone else at TriWorld who had been terminated along with Rafael for "being involved in illegal activity" or "for funding illegal loans?"

"Not that I can recall right now."

Alexa asked if Bowen had discussed the reason for Rafael's termination with anyone before he communicated anything to the EDD. Bowen shot a glance at Lacey, then said he had received his instructions from Attorney Redwood, TriWorld's legal counsel. She then asked Bowen if TriWorld had a Code of Conduct that was distributed to employees, setting out what was expected of them.

Bowen nodded confidently. "Yes."

"And as Head of Human Resources for the California office of TriWorld, were you familiar with the contents?"

Bowen smiled. "Yes, of course. Thoroughly. I was asked for my comments. I thought it was extremely well put together."

"And did all TriWorld employees have the Code?"

He smiled again, more broadly this time. "Absolutely. Every single employee is given one at the time they are hired." Then, as an afterthought, he added, "And they are instructed to read it and become familiar with it."

"Thank you. And according to that Code of Conduct, what is the protocol to be followed when an employee's conduct falls short of what was expected of him or her?"

"Well, they would first get a verbal warning from their superior or the branch manager. The second time, they'd get a written warning, like a memorandum. If they persisted, they'd get something in their file."

"And what would it mean to them to have something in their file?"

"Well, it could mean a lot. When it was time for performance reviews, it wouldn't look good."

"And how often were performance reviews conducted?"

"Once a year."

"In your capacity as Head of Human Resources, you were familiar with the files of employees at TriWorld?"

"Well, yes, of course."

"Were you aware of any written notes of that type in Rafael's file?"

Bowen squirmed slightly. "I can't say." He blinked several times. "It's been a few years since I've seen that file."

"Of course. But to the best of your recollection?"

Lacey shot up. "Objection, your Honor. The question has been asked and answered." Judge Darnell sustained the objection.

At that point, Alexa went to the table and returned to face Bowen with a file in her hands. "This file is marked as 'Exhibit B.' Mr. Bowen, do you recognize this file?"

He took it, looked at it, opened it, and scanned the pages. "Please look through the file and see if there are communiqués of any kind – notes, memos – that served as a warning to Rafael or that stated anything negative about him. Take your time. Go through it carefully."

After a full minute, he closed the file. He shook his head. "No, I saw nothing."

"And please look through the file again and tell us how long Mr. Lamon was employed at TriWorld."

Bowen reopened the file and answered within seconds. "He was employed at TriWorld for eight years or so."

"And in all that time, previous to the instructions you were given by Mr. Han to relay to the EDD that Rafael was involved in funding illegal loans, had you ever heard or had reason to believe that he was anything short of a model employee?"

Bowen's eyes drifted, and he frowned as he thought back. Then he answered, "No."

"Thank you, Mr. Bowen." Then, to the judge, Alexa said, "I have no more questions for this witness, Your Honor."

Rafael could have kissed Alexa right there in the courtroom. She had again shown her smarts when she realized the importance of having him go to the EDD in person to file for unemployment.

Judge Darnell said, "Very well. Ms. Lacey, do you wish to cross-examine this witness?"

There was a moment of discussion at the defense table, and then Ann Lacey smiled. "I do, Your Honor." She approached Bowen and said, "Good morning, Mr. Bowen. I just have one or two questions for you. As you described the protocol that was followed when an employee was engaged in conduct in violation of TriWorld's Code of Conduct, you stated that the employee first received a verbal warning. Is that correct?"

Bowen nodded. "Yes, that's right."

"And in the time that Mr. Lamon was employed at TriWorld, did he receive a verbal warning in regard to conduct that was in such violation?"

Bowen shrugged. "I have no idea."

"So, you don't know. Is that right?"

"Yes."

"And is it conceivable that a written document in an employee file could be lost?" Lacey asked.

Bowen shrugged. "Unlikely, but conceivable, I suppose."

"I see. So, it is possible that Rafael Lamon received verbal and written warnings regarding conduct he was engaged in at TriWorld that was in violation of the bank's code of conduct, although there was no write-up in his file, or no write-up in his file that you presently remember as you sit here. Is that correct?"

"Yes. That's correct."

"Thank you, Mr. Bowen." Lacey smiled at the man. Now, assume that the conduct in question is flagrantly illegal. Do you mean to tell us that when such flagrant illegal action is uncovered, the employee first receives a verbal warning and then a written memorandum?"

Bowen's face flushed. He stammered. "I – I guess not. I'm not sure. I guess not."

"I see. Let me ask you this, Mr. Bowen. As Head of Human Resources, would you normally, in the course of your work, have any reason to know of illegal funding of loans occurring at the bank? Let me be clearer. Does your department have any knowledge of funding, whether legal or illegal, that went on at the Beverly Hills branch of TriWorld?"

"Oh, no. We have nothing to do with that part of the bank's operations."

"Thank you. That's all for this witness, Your Honor."

Alexa and Prince agreed there was no reason to ask the witness any further questions, and the judge dismissed him.

Alexa found herself in a sea of emotions. As she'd expected, all her nervousness had disappeared as soon as she was on her feet and talking. Nonetheless, today was the first time she'd ever examined witnesses in a civil case, and the first time she was in open court in years. She was unsure of how well she'd made the necessary points, and she wanted feedback on how she'd come across to the jurors; they'd have to like her and stay with her if they were to win. Prince reassured her that she'd done very well on both counts. Rafael looked very pleased as well.

She thanked God that her new hearing aids worked so well, the batteries hadn't died, and she'd heard everything. But she couldn't even think of resting easy yet. This was only the beginning of what she knew would be an uphill battle. TriWorld was not about to roll over and die.

Judge Darnell called a recess. As the jurors filed out, the

elderly female juror stumbled as she came to the bar's swinging gate and gasped, "Oh!"

Instinctively, Prince shot up and put one hand on the juror's back and held her arm with the other until she found her balance. She whispered, "Thank you." The juror behind her, an Asian woman, smiled broadly at him. Prince smiled back. Alexa realized that little episode was the sort of gold star scored that neither evidence nor money could buy.

And then Viviana was at Rafael's side. "Do you have time to get some fresh air?" she asked her husband.

Rafael turned to Alexa and Prince. Prince answered. "Sure, take your husband outside for a few minutes. It will do him good. Just don't forget to bring him back." Alexa forced a smile and looked down at her papers on the table.

For the next few minutes, Alexa and Prince reviewed questions for their next witnesses, and Alexa changed batteries – just to be sure they wouldn't die soon.

53

When the court resumed, Alexa called Favio Melo of Bank of Taiwan to the stand. Melo was a young, good-looking man who could hardly be mistaken for anything other than Italian from his swarthy complexion to his confident step as he walked to the witness stand wearing a slim, Italian-cut suit. Rafael was surprised to see how young he was. His voice on the phone had not betrayed his youth. He took the oath, then sat and crossed his legs, putting his ankle atop his thigh. He folded his hands and was ready to answer Alexa's questions in accented English.

Alexa needed Melo to explain to the jury that whereas TriWorld could not make loans to U.S. citizens, Bank of Taiwan, a domestic bank, could and did. And that TriWorld made loans to banks, including his bank. He testified that TriWorld sent Bank of Taiwan customers, and when they did, Melo dealt with those customers.

"Mr. Melo, why did TriWorld refer customers to your bank?" Alexa asked.

He nodded. "They couldn't offer them loans."

"Why not?"

He shrugged. "They were U.S. citizens. So, they sent them to us."

"I see," said Alexa as if she hadn't known that long before Melo had just told her. "Now my understanding is that these people who were referred to your bank held a power of attorney on accounts at TriWorld."

"Yeah."

"And they were able to borrow from Bank of Taiwan against those accounts. Is that right?"

"I guess so. I mean, TriWorld pledged the money in the account to us."

"What do you mean when you say TriWorld 'pledged' the money to your bank?"

Melo shifted in his seat. "See, they send us a U.S. citizen who has power of attorney on one of their accounts. Say, for instance, you have the power of attorney on an account at TriWorld with three million dollars in it."

"Yes?"

"Okay, you come to us and borrow, perhaps, a million dollars. See? TriWorld pledges one million dollars to us to cover your loan if you don't pay."

"So, your bank, Bank of Taiwan, takes no risk. And was that legal?"

Melo waved his arms, and a killer smile broke out on his face. "Hey, I dunno know! I just do what I'm told."

The smile was not lost on Alexa. She set her gaze on the jury. "Mr. Melo, when these customers were referred to your branch, how did you know they came from TriWorld in the first place?"

Melo pressed his lips together and shrugged again, as his brows went up. "They tell us. And then the forms come."

"The forms? Could you explain? What forms?"

Melo cocked his head. "Two forms. One pledged the money that was in the TriWorld account to us in the amount of the loan we gave to them, like I said, so we'd be okay. Whatever happened, we would be paid." Alexa nodded as if to say, I see. "The other was a document that said they would fund our bank."

Alexa asked, "What exactly do you mean when you say, 'okay, whatever happened?'"

Melo smiled again, the same dazzling smile. He uncrossed his legs, sat up straighter, and looked over at Judge Darnell. "Ah, I'm sorry. I forget the legal word." He looked back at Alexa. "If, you know, if something were to go wrong, we wouldn't lose the money."

"I see," said Alexa. "Does that mean that if your borrower didn't pay – defaulted – on the loan – that TriWorld would reimburse your bank?"

Melo nodded. "Yes. It was like that."

"So," Alexa said, "in effect, you were lending your customers TriWorld's money."

"Yes."

"Is that legal?"

"Objection! This witness has no –"

"I withdraw the question, Your Honor."

"Mr. Melo, I have two exhibits I'd like you to take a look at and tell us if these are the documents you just described. Let's take them one at a time. Your Honor, I'd like to present 'Exhibits C and D'." The judge nodded. In turn, Alexa nodded to Prince, and he projected Exhibit C onto the screen.

Melo nodded. He snapped his fingers. "Yes, I couldn't think of that word. It's a security agreement. It says, "Security Agreement" at the top."

"And is that the same document that was given to Bank of Taiwan for each loan made to these customers with a power of attorney on a TriWorld account?"

"Yes. For sure"

"Thank you. Let the record show that the witness identified

Exhibit C as the Security Agreement." The screen was taken up with another document. "Your Honor, this is marked as 'Exhibit D.'" She turned to Prince. "Okay, Mr. Melo, please look at this."

Again, the witness responded without being asked. "Ah, yes. This is the one that funds Bank of Taiwan," Melo said.

"So, is this document the Funding Agreement?"

"Yes."

"Thank you. Let the record show that the witness identified Exhibit D as the Funding Agreement."

Alexa knew that on cross-examination, Lacey would dwell on the fact that Rafael was Melo's contact, so she wanted to be the one to establish that. "Mr. Melo, do you know Rafael Lamon?"

Melo craned his neck, looking behind Prince to see Rafael seated at the table with Prince. "I see him today for the first time. But we have spoken on the phone."

"And have you called him or has he called you?"

"He would call me."

"What was the purpose of his calls?"

"He called to ask me what the interest rate was that we were charging on our loans to customers."

"And did you tell him?"

Melo shrugged. "Of course, why not?"

"Yes. And do you know why he wanted to know that?"

"No, it's not my business. I was told to tell him, so I did."

Alexa walked away from the witness box and looked at Prince, who shook his head so slightly that only Alexa understood. She turned to the judge. "That's all the questions I have for this witness, Your Honor."

"Ms. Lacey? Will you be cross-examining this witness?" The judge asked.

"Yes." As Lacey walked toward the witness, Melo watched her with obvious appreciation. He straightened his tie and pulled at his shirt cuffs. A smile played on his face as he looked at her, and his eyes danced.

Lacey was all business. "Good morning, Mr. Melo."

"Good morning." He spoke low and liltingly as though inviting her into his den.

"Now, you told us that you spoke with Mr. Lamon on the phone."

"Yes, I did." He ran his finger across his lower lip.

"Did you speak with anyone else from TriWorld?"

Melo's eyes were pinned to Lacey's chest. "No."

"How many times did you speak with Mr. Lamon?"

Melo was still staring at her chest. He took a breath. "Five, maybe six."

"In what length of time?"

"Melo's eyes hadn't moved from her chest. "What? Oh." His shoulders bounced. "A year or two."

Lacey had become aware of what Melo was staring at. She made an about-face while asking, "And in all that time you spoke only to Rafael Lamon about the customers your two banks had in common?"

Seeing her from behind, Melo sighed deeply and loudly, then exhaled audibly. He didn't answer. He sat staring, apparently lost in his dreams of love. Lacey turned around and saw his expression.

Her face reddened. "Mr. Melo!"

"Yes?" He didn't want to upset this beautiful woman.

"I asked you a question."

He adjusted himself in his chair and sat up straighter. "I'm sorry. Could you repeat, please?"

Alexa glanced at the defense table. The male attorneys were shifting in their seats, and she wondered if they were reacting to Lacey's momentary loss of control or to the witness's gall.

Judge Darnell spoke to the witness. "Please try to pay more attention to the questions asked."

Melo looked up at the judge peevishly. "I'm sorry."

Lacey swallowed her impatience. "You said you spoke to Mr. Lamon three or four times a year. In all that time, you spoke to no one else at TriWorld about the customers your two banks had in common?"

"No. Yes. I mean, yes, that is correct. I spoke only to him."

"No more questions," she said before abruptly walking away and taking her seat.

Rafael was smiling. He had enjoyed that interplay between the healthy young man and his attractive interrogator. Alexa had no redirect. The witness was excused, and the judge called a recess for lunch.

As the courtroom emptied, Alexa saw Viviana and realized she would most likely be present for the duration of the trial. Alexa watched as she smiled at Rafael, and Rafael answered with a hesitant smile, aware that Alexa was watching. It was obvious the woman was fighting to keep Rafael. Alexa decided she no longer owed Viviana anything. She wondered if Viviana knew that Rafael wanted to leave her. *Had they talked about it?*

Did Viviana know Alexa had slept with him?

Well, Alexa's own husband had been unfaithful, and she had divorced him. If, after all this time, Viviana didn't know that she and Rafael had more than a professional relationship, she damn well ought to. If she did know and had chosen to fight for him rather than divorce him – which seemed to be the case – she had apparently chosen to live with it.

It was agreed that Rafael and Viviana would lunch together while Alexa and Prince would grab a bite at the café in the nearby hotel and discuss their afternoon witnesses. Alone together for the first time without Rafael, they both felt awkward for the first few minutes as they adjusted to their client's absence. Then, it was as if the space he had emptied made it possible for them to become more intimate, and their conversation couldn't help but take a personal turn.

"So, you've been keeping busy," Roger said as they walked to their destination.

"You haven't done badly," Alexa remarked.

Prince nodded. "Law's been good to me."

"And you married and have a son."

A shadow passed Prince's face. "Yes, he's five – well, almost six."

"That's great. I have a five-year-old son and a five-year-old daughter."

"Twins," he noted.

Alexa nodded. "I divorced three years ago."

Roger nodded in understanding. "It's tough to raise children alone."

"Yes," Alexa said. "Are you divorced, too?" she asked.

"No." He shook his head. After a few seconds, he said, "My wife died." The statement stung Alexa. Surely, she must have been too young to have died.

"I'm so sorry!" She took a breath. They were almost at the hotel entrance. "Was she ill?"

He nodded. "She had uterine cancer. She was diagnosed while she was pregnant and opted to postpone treatment until after delivery. By then…" he looked at Alexa. "… it was too late."

"I'm so sorry," Alexa said again. She couldn't think of what else to say.

"Oh, don't feel bad. It was really sad, but time heals. It's been almost six years. Lily will always be in my heart, but I've tried to move on."

As they ate, they discussed what lay ahead.

"Roger, I really think you should be the one to question Alandro and Stamen," Alexa said.

"Why not you?" he asked

"They're both key witnesses. I don't want to screw up with them."

"Alexa, I've been watching the jury. They like you. They follow you. It's like they get you." It warmed Alexa's heart to hear that. Then he went on to say, "And you won't screw up. You're doing a great job. You're a natural, a born litigator." Alexa stared at him. "What is it? You're hearing everything, aren't you?" Prince asked.

Alexa nodded. "Yeah. I mean, I'm pretty sure I am. I think these new aids are good."

"Alexa, you can do this," Prince assured her. "And I'll be right there. If you need to have me take over, say the word."

They had sandwiches and discussed the points to be covered with Alandro and Stamen. Walking back to court, they reviewed what they wanted the two witnesses to testify to on direct examination.

As they entered the courthouse, Roger said, "I enjoyed our talk. Let's spend some time alone like that again. It was nice."

54

Alexa reentered the courtroom with her adrenalin pumping. Alandro would be a key witness along with Stamen and Han, the President of TriWorld, and she wanted to perform well. She felt that mixture of excitement and fear that actors call stage fright. A lot was riding on her ability to remember her goal with Alandro and deliver her lines effectively. Court resumed.

"Your Honor, I'd like to call Jason Alandro to the stand."

Alandro took the oath, took a good look at Rafael and sat in the hot seat. He had his arms and legs crossed. Surely, Alexa thought, the attorneys had coached him not to sit like that. Why, the jury consultant would surely have been adamant that all their witnesses sit with both their feet firmly on the ground and their arms open, the sign of an open and honest person. Alandro, all crossed up, looked guarded and defensive.

It was quickly established Alandro had been the Executive Director in charge of new accounts at the Beverly Hills branch of TriWorld.

"You were Rafael's immediate superior, were you not?" Alexa asked.

Lacey was on her feet. "Objection. Leading question." Leading questions seem as though they're meant to put words in a witness's mouth and are generally not permissible in the direct examination of a witness but are acceptable when examining a hostile witness.

Alexa was surprised that Lacey would object to such a harmless question concerning something so unimportant. She must have known the judge would overrule her. She was obviously being difficult. Alexa stood her ground. "Your Honor," she said, "I would like permission to treat this witness as a hostile witness, in which case leading questions are permissible."

"Your Honor," Lacey said, "this is Ms. Starr's witness. How can she say he is hostile?"

"Counsel is correct. I did call Mr. Alandro as my witness. However, we understand that he has been aligned with the defendant's position from the start of the investigation. On that basis, I would like to treat him as a hostile witness."

"Objection overruled. You may continue, Ms. Starr." It was a small victory, but Alexa savored it, nonetheless.

Rafael focused his full attention on Alandro. He was one of the people whose testimony Rafael was most interested in. What would his immediate supervisor say?

Alandro answered that, as Executive Director of New Accounts, he had been Rafael's immediate superior throughout the seven-plus years Rafael had been at TriWorld, while Rafael was the Director of the South American accounts. No, he had not hired Rafael. He had heard of Rafael before Rafael began working at TriWorld.

"We had been looking for someone to head up our South American accounts, and Carlos Aman at United had mentioned Rafael had a following in that community as well as banking experience."

"So, TriWorld approached Rafael?" Alexa asked.

Alandro nodded. "Yes, I believe that was the case."

Lacey pounced. "Hearsay." Apparently, this was information Alandro had heard from someone else.

"Sustained. The jury shall disregard the witness's comment about TriWorld approaching Mr. Lamon."

Alexa could have worked her way around the objection by reframing the question, but she let it slide. Meanwhile, the jurors had heard it. She continued. "As Rafael's superior, was it your job to oversee his performance?"

Alandro visibly wiggled in his seat. "Yes. To the extent that I was aware of his conduct."

"And were you responsible for issuing performance reviews on a regular basis?"

Alandro answered cautiously. "That's right."

"And did you issue them?"

"Yes."

"How often?"

"Once a year."

"What was the purpose of these reviews?"

"After completing my appraisal, I would meet with the employees to discuss their strengths and their weaknesses, what they needed to work on, and we'd set goals for the coming period."

"And would you say that you were objective in completing these reviews?"

"I did my best," Alandro answered, gathering his dignity.

"And, I would imagine you were honest?"

"Yes." Alandro drew the word out as he began to guess what was coming.

"Were these reviews also used to determine if an employee such as Rafael would be getting a raise in salary in the next period?"

"Yes. If there was a raise, it would be annual."

"Okay. Thank you." Alandro nodded and actually smiled. Alexa walked over to her table and waited until Prince had projected Rafael's most recent performance review onto the screen.

"I would like to present the following in evidence as 'Exhibit E.' Mr. Alandro, I ask that you look at this document marked as Exhibit E." she said. "Would you please identify it?" Prince had it on the projector.

"Yes. It's a performance review that I issued for Mr. Lamon."

"You recognize the handwriting as yours?"

"Yes."

"And what is the date on that?" "December of 2015."

"That was the last performance report you completed for Rafael; the final one before he was fired."

"Yes. He was fired in early February of 2025."

And you've said it is your custom to answer these performance reviews honestly and to the best of your ability?"

"Yes."

She pointed at the screen with her laser. "Now at the top of the page, you see a line with 10 demarcations and a box at each. There's a check placed here, in the box at the number nine. Did you place that check?"

"Yes. Yes, I did."

"And what is the significance of that check in that box?"

"I suppose I felt at that time that Rafael – Mr. Lamon – was performing at that level."

Alexa faced the jury box and spoke loudly and clearly. "And what grade did you gave him on his job performance?"

"Nine."

"Nine. That's a nine out of 10?" Alandro looked down.

"Yes."

"I'm sorry, Mr. Alandro. Would you please speak up so the jury can hear you?" Rafael smiled.

"I said, yes!" He boomed.

"You gave him a nine out 10 for his job performance. Thank you. Now, beneath that you're asked to write what you base your assessment on. Is that correct?"

Alandro answered, "Yes."

Alexa said, "Please read what you wrote there."

Alandro grunted. He read, "Mr. Lamon has an excellent record –"

Alexa interrupted him. "Excuse me. Your Honor, please ask the witness to speak up so the jury can hear him." Judge Darnell did so.

Alandro sighed, took a deep breath and began again, obviously feeling put out, speaking louder. "Mr. Lamon has an excellent record bringing in new business to the bank. He has outstanding rapport with his clients, understands their needs and stays in communication with them. I recommend him for future managerial promotion."

"Thank you. And finally, you'll see there is a sentence below that. It reads 'Goals'." She pointed to the area with her laser pointer. "Could you please read what you wrote here?"

"Let's see," Alandro mumbled. Then he read aloud. "Rafael needs to be more aggressive in selling additional bank products to his existing clients."

Alexa smiled. "So, at his last performance review the only weakness you found, as Rafael's superior, was that he was not aggressive enough in selling more bank products – like credit cards – to the clients he brought into the bank. All told, you graded him a nine. Is that correct?"

"Yes. As I just read for you."

"Mr. Alandro, did you show this performance review to anyone?" In the silence that followed, Alexa added, "Did you discuss Rafael's excellent performance review with Bob Stamen, the General Manager?"

"Yes. I was required to do that in terms of possible future bonuses and other considerations."

"What would those other considerations be?"

"Well, you know." He waved an arm dismissively. "Talking about his weaknesses and his strengths." He shrugged. "We went through that that with all the directors."

"And at that time, did you or Mr. Stamen bring up the possibility that Rafael was making illegal loans?"

Alandro looked surprised. "Why, no."

"Mr. Alandro, did you have reason to suspect that Rafael Lamon was making illegal loans?"

The witness was in catch-22. If he said yes, then as Rafael's supervisor, he would have had to do something about it. "No," Alandro said, sounding insulted.

"Was making loans part of Rafael's job description?"

"It wasn't supposed to be," he answered.

"He was strictly a relationship officer, was he not?"

"Yes."

"And could you tell us the function of a relationship officer? What his duties were in general terms."

"He's supposed to build relationships for the bank," Alandro said. "Go out and get us business."

"Is that all?" Alexa prodded.

"Yes. That's all he was supposed to do," Alandro said. "And sell the bank's products."

"Again, the date of this last review is December of 2025. Rafael was fired in early February of 2026. That was about two months later. In that two months did you come to believe that Rafael funded illegal loans?"

"I was told that he did."

"By whom?"

Alandro looked at the defense table but got no help there. He squirmed a little then said, "From management."

"Would that be Mr. Stamen, the branch general manager?"

Alandro nodded. "Him, and then others."

Alexa needed to educate the jury. "Other than what you were

told by others, did you yourself have any independent knowledge that Rafael was involved in any illegal activity?"

Rafael took a deep breath. "No," Alandro admitted.

"Are you still presently working at the Beverly Hills branch of TriWorld?"

"No, I am not."

"Why is that?" Alexa asked.

The answer was immediate. "The branch is closed."

"When was it closed?"

"I believe it was this past May."

"And do you know why it was closed?" "Yes."

"Would you please tell us –"?

Baxter shot to his feet. "Your Honor, I object! Irrelevant."

Alexa shot a look at Prince who gave her a subtle nod. She spoke calmly. "Your Honor, it is most relevant."

Baxter moved away from the defense table. "Your Honor, may we approach the bench?"

Judge Darnell spoke to the courtroom. "There will be a short recess."

She turned to Alandro. "You are not excused; you'll be returning to the stand after the recess. Please wait closeby in the hallway and do not speak to anyone." She struck her gavel and the courtroom emptied of everyone but the attorneys.

Alexa and Prince were not surprised at the defense efforts to keep the information as to why the Beverly Hills branch had been closed away from the jury. But they were curious to see how Baxter would argue irrelevance. It seemed he was fighting a lost cause. Prince and Baxter joined Alexa and Lacey at the judge's bench as did the other three attorneys for the defense.

Judge Darnell looked at Baxter. "It's a little crowded here. You have a problem with Ms. Starr's question?"

"Yes, Your Honor. This trial is about Rafael Lamon. He is alleging that he was wrongfully terminated due to whistleblowing. If the witness answers that the Beverly Hills branch was closed because the Federal Reserve Bank found that it was guilty of carrying on illegal practices even with the plaintiff terminated, the meaning to be inferred is that he was not guilty of funding illegal loans. That is a big jump and prejudicial to the defense."

The judge looked at Prince. "Counsel?"

"Your Honor, I find the defendant's argument defective in several ways," Prince said. "First, the inference he stated is, in fact, exactly what we believe to be the correct inference. This case is about having singled out my client and scapegoating him for the acts of others. The jury can infer any number of things from all the evidence they see. If Your Honor wishes to guide them in that area your instructions can do that. That aside, Mr. Baxter is not objecting to the question itself but to a line of questioning that I have not yet embarked on, though I may well. But this is about my client's life, reputation, and dignity, and I think the jury should have as much information as possible."

It was quiet as Judge Darnell mulled over the issue. She clasped her hands and Alexa noted her dark red nail polish was chipped. Her hands separated and she directed herself to Baxter. "As this case alleges a malicious act on the part of the defendant which may be against public policy, I tend to agree that the jurors should have all the information legally and reasonably available to them to make their decision. If they believed that life went on as usual at the branch and that it was closed because a decision made internally by TriWorld, or perhaps because of Mr. Lamon's alleged illegal acts that would also be prejudicial. However, that would work against Mr. Lamon, would it not?"

It was Lacey who responded. "But your Honor, what this witness knows to be the reason the branch closed is hearsay."

Alexa spoke. "Your Honor, if I'm not mistaken, defense counsel did not object on the basis of hearsay."

Judge Darnell nodded. "That's true. It may be hearsay. We'll see. Meanwhile, you are correct. That's not the objection defense raised. I'm going to overrule the objection."

With that, she instructed the bailiff to bring in the jurors and to return Alandro to the witness stand. Alexa noticed Baxter smiling broadly to the jurors as he and Lacey returned to their seats at the defense table. The judge went back on the record and reminded Alandro he was still under oath. Then she overruled Baxter's objection.

Alexa repeated her question. "Mr. Alandro, do you know why the Beverly Hills branch of TriWorld was closed?"

"Yes."

"Would you please tell us how you know?"

"I saw the notice the Bank received from the Federal Reserve Board."

"You read the notice yourself?"

"Yes. I did." That killed any hearsay objection.

"And when and where were you at the time?"

"I was at the Beverly Hills office. It was the last day we were open. Bob Stamen had been fired so I was taking care of things and I received the notice."

You said Mr. Stamen was fired."

"Yes. That's right."

Alexa nodded. "Go on, please."

Alandro shrugged. "Federal agents came in and shut us down."

"Okay. Thank you. Now let's jump to February of 2026. Were you present the day Rafael was terminated?"

"Yes. Stamen wanted me there with him when he fired Rafael."

"Can you tell us what happened?"

Alandro shrugged again. "What do you mean? He fired him."

"I'm sorry, I wasn't clear. I'd like you to tell us where and how Rafael was fired. Was he called into Stamen's office?"

Alandro wiped his lips. "No. We went into his office."

"Do you recall what time of day it was?"

Alandro tilted his head. "Morning. Early."

"And did Stamen tell him why he was fired?" Alandro shook his head.

"No."

"He gave no reason?"

"No."

"Did Rafael ask why he was being fired?" Alandro shrugged lazily.

"I don't recall."

Rafael smirked, thinking Alandro was a spineless weasel, afraid even now. Even when it's all over and the man has no reason to be beholden to Stamen, he's dodging the truth. He had seen how shocked Rafael had been to hear he'd been fired.

Alexa didn't like that answer either. "Please try to remember. The Bank's General Manager walked into Rafael's office with you and fired him. Did Rafael appear to be surprised?"

"Oh, yes. He was surprised all right. I'd say he was shocked." Rafael exhaled. There was hope.

"And can you now recall Rafael asking why he was being fired?"

Alandro winced. "Yes. Yes, I do. He did."

"And do you recall Mr. Stamen's answer?"

Alandro's hand went to his chin, his lips slanted and he nodded, recalling. "Bob said he'd find out later."

"And he was escorted off the property?"

"That's right."

"When?"

"Immediately."

"Without notice?"

"Yes. As far as I know, he had no notice. That's why he was so surprised." Alandro said.

"As far as you know, was it the practice at the branch to

escort people who were terminated off the property immediately and without knowledge of why they were being terminated?"

"No, but this was a special case." Rafael, who had his head down at the moment in relief of Alandro's honesty, herked his head up in attention.

"Special in what way?"

"Well," Alandro said casually, as if what he was about to say was general knowledge. "Bob wanted to get ready for his meeting with the Federal Reserve that morning."

Rafael blinked, his jaw falling open. Alexa's body tensed suddenly as if in shock. Gilmore had never mentioned any meeting at TriWorld that morning. This was new and vital information. It was Important with a capital 'I' and she had to follow up with more questions. She restrained herself from looking over at Prince with a telling look, certain he had heard Alandro and had registered that bit of news. No doubt, Rafael had as well.

"And how soon after Rafael was escorted off the property did the meeting with the Federal Reserve take place?"

"Oh, very soon. Within the hour, maybe the half hour."

This was a gift of pure gold and she could have kissed Jason Alandro right then and there. *What better reason to fire Rafael when and how Stamen had?* He wanted Rafael gone before the Feds came in! She took a breath.

"Mr. Alandro, during the almost eight years that Rafael worked under you at TriWorld, did you have reason to meet him outside of the office?"

"Yes."

"And based on your interactions did you form an opinion about his honesty?"

"I liked Rafael. I always liked him. This was as shocking to me as it was to him."

"Before that day you just described that he was fired, did

you have knowledge of any illegal funding or any illegal acts that Mr. Lamon was engaged in?"

"No."

"Sir, it is my understanding that Rafael Lamon was the TriWorld's go-between for Bank of Taiwan. Is that correct?"

"Yes."

"And was that your decision? Did you delegate that job to him?"

"No."

"Do you know who did?"

"Yes. That was Bob Stamen."

"The general manager of the branch?"

"That's right."

"You sound so sure. How do you know that?"

"Bob and I discussed it."

"And do you know what he was supposed to do in contacting Bank of Taiwan?"

Alandro nodded. "He was supposed to find out the rates that Bank of Taiwan was charging on loans."

"Did Mr. Stamen tell you that as well?"

"Yes"

"And did he share with you the reason he wanted Rafael to find out that information?"

"Yes." Alandro moved in his chair as if to get more comfortable before continuing. "You see, TriWorld loans money to Bank of Taiwan and many other banks on the global level. Bob said he wanted to know how much interest Taiwan was charging on their loans so TriWorld would be able to charge them a few basis below that."

"I'm sorry, but I imagine few of us if any know what a basis point is. Could you tell us what that is?"

"A basis point is a tenth of a point. One-tenth of a percent."

"I see. So, the idea was that TriWorld would find out what rate Bank of Taiwan charged their borrowers so TriWorld could charge them a few basis points below that on the money they loaned Bank of Taiwan so that both could make a profit?"

"That's right."

Alexa nodded to Prince and he placed another document, previously marked as Plaintiff's 'Exhibit C' onto the screen. "Please look at this document, entitled 'Security Agreement,'" Alexa said. "Have you seen this before?" Alandro nodded. "Please answer with a yes or no."

"Yes."

"Can you tell us what it is?"

"It's the Security Agreement. TriWold secured the loans Bank of Taiwan made to those with power of attorney on our accounts with the monies in those accounts in case of nonpayment."

"Did you compose it?"

"No, I did not. Absolutely not. It was handed to me by Bob Stamen."

"Was it your understanding that Rafael Lamon composed the security agreement?"

"No, Bob told me that it had been drawn up –" Lacey was on her feet.

"Objection. Hearsay."

"Your Honor," Alexa said. "It's important to know this witness's state of mind, what he believed to be true about this document. It bears on my client's case."

Lacey said, "Your Honor, so long as the witness stated it was not his belief that Mr. Lamon prepared the document, who he believed composed it seems irrelevant."

Alexa persisted. "Your Honor, we would like to show that our client's understanding was most reasonable and in fact, was not different from that of this witness."

"I'll overrule the objection," the judge said. "Please answer the question."

"He told me it had been drawn up by the lawyers for the bank."

"Bob Stamen told you the Security Agreement had been drawn up by TriWorld attorneys. Is that correct?"

"Yes. That's what I said."

"And did you show this agreement to Rafael?"

"Yes. Bob told me to. It was his job to get it to TriWorld for each of its borrowers who held a power of attorney on our accounts."

"Rafael Lamon was handed the Security Agreement and instructed to use it?"

Alandro nodded. "Yes."

"And was he to sign it as well?" Alandro nodded again.

Alexa said, "Please note the witness answered Yes." Then she directed herself back to the witness. "To the best of your knowledge, did Rafael ever object to this document?"

"Yes. He complained to Bob and me. But Bob told us that the lawyers had written it and that we had been given the 'go ahead.'" Hearing this, Rafael was absolutely delighted. He was being vindicated.

"Mr. Alandro, was Rafael a relationship officer or a financial officer?"

"I told you, he was a relationship officer."

"And did relationship officers have the ability to move money at TriWorld, to accept requests for loans or lend money to other banks?"

"No."

"If he wanted to, could he have?"

Alandro smirked. "I don't know."

"Doesn't an institution as important as TriWorld have safeguards in effect that would render that impossible?"

Alandro shrugged and said, "You would think so."

Alexa paused. She simply stood still for several seconds, wanting this information to sink into the juror's minds. Then she changed subjects, veering back to something the witness had said earlier.

"Mr. Alandro, when did you first meet with agents of the Federal Reserve?"

Alandro's eyes moved up and to the right, trying to pull the answer from his memory.

"Objection! Irrelevant." Lacey was on her feet once more.

"Your Honor, I assure you, this information is *not* irrelevant. Any communication that the witness has had with the Federal Reserve prior to or close to the time of my client's termination is relevant as it may have had a bearing on his termination."

"Objection overruled."

"I don't recall exact the date."

"Let me ask you this. Was it before or after Rafael was terminated?

Alandro answered easily, tossing out the answer with a shrug. "It was the day he left. Right afterwards. He walked out and they came in."

Alexa turned her back to the jurors, shot a glance at Prince, took a breath, then turned back to the men and women of the jury. "Mr. Alandro. I'd like the jury to be clear on this point. The very morning that Rafael Lamon was terminated, without warning and without being given a reason for his termination, and escorted off the premises with a security guard apparently to ensure his departure, agents of the Federal Reserve met with you and Bob Stamen, the General Manager of the branch at TriWorld. Is that your testimony?"

"That's right."

"Was this a scheduled appointment? Was their visit expected?"

"Yes. Yes, of course." He sounded impatient.

"And my understanding is that only you and Bob Stamen met with them?"

"That's right."

"Bob Stamen, the general manager of the branch and you. And where did you meet?"

"In the conference room."

Lacey again objected on the ground of irrelevance but Judge Darnell overruled that objection when Alexa contended it was relevant to explore how the Federal Reserve came to focus attention on Rafael.

"Can you tell us what was discussed?"

"Sure. The irregularities found at the branch. Violations."

"And how did that meeting conclude?"

"Well, Bob told them that he'd fired Rafael. He said Rafael had been the problem and he'd been terminated."

"And how did the agents of the Federal Reserve react to that information?"

"They wanted to speak to Rafael. But Bob told them he wasn't there. We gave them his contact information."

"Then it was Bob Stamen at that meeting who brought Rafael Lamon to the attention of the agents of the Federal Reserve?"

"Yes."

"Thank you." Alexa turned to the judge. "I have no further questions for this witness."

Alexa was absolutely thrilled. Her examination of Alandro had uncovered extremely valuable information that, incredibly, had not come out during his deposition. She now knew that TriWorld was expecting to meet with the Federal Reserve the same morning that Rafael was fired. Alandro had also testified that the Federal Reserve had no prior independent reason to believe that Rafael had been involved in illegal activity. It was Bob Stamen who had put them on his tail. If she'd had this information in her talks with the Feds, she could probably have short-circuited the entire harrowing experience. As for Rafael, things were beginning to fall into place in his mind as well.

Lacey had no desire to cross-examine Alandro but reserved the right to call him back. Alexa then asked Judge Darnell for a brief recess. She would have liked to just sit for a few minutes and process what Alandro had testified to and talk to Prince about it. She'd have asked him to take over the next witness. The judge refused the request. "We have time for one more witness this afternoon, counselor. Let's not take up the time with a recess."

Alexa looked at Prince and then at Rafael. Both were beaming.

55

His attitude hadn't worked for him, so he had obviously resolved to mellow it down. As Stamen's large frame ambled into the witness box, Alexa looked at the defense table and happened to catch the eye of one of the three male attorneys who joined Lacey and Baxter for the trial. She didn't know him by name but though his look was piercing, she realized she was no longer intimidated by the men at the table. She was totally focused on her job and had forgotten all about them.

The one thing that was a puzzle was why Stamen would put together the illegal scheme. *Why would he go out on a limb to allow TriWorld to in ensure loans to the US citizens who held Powers of Attorney on their accounts? What did he have to gain?*

Stamen opened the button of his suit jacket, sat down, and crossed his legs, cowboy-style. He had his hands on his lap, chin forward, and lips tightly pursed, all signs of a witness loath to cooperate, a witness who was not anxious to provide spontaneous testimony. After establishing that, yes, Stamen had been the general manager of TriWorld's Beverly Hills branch since the bank first opened, and yes, he had terminated Rafael Lamon in early February 2024, Alexa asked why he'd done so. Stamen answered that he'd had reason to believe that Rafael had been involved in illegal funding.

"Were you aware that TriWorld was involved in illegal funding in violation of federal laws and matching funds in violation of federal banking law?" Stamen looked past Alexa at Lacey. His gaze lingered. "Mr. Stamen?" Alexa said.

"Look," Stamen said. "I don't want to get into the legalities of all that."

Alexa looked up at Judge Darnell. "Your Honor, would you kindly ask the witness to answer?"

Judge Darnell complied. "Answer the question."

Stamen turned to the judge. "Your Honor, do I have to? I mean," Stamen's large frame wriggled in his seat. He bit his lower lip. "It's a delicate question."

"Sir, I'm ordering you to answer. If you don't, I will both direct the jury to infer the least favorable answer, and I will also charge you with contempt." Stamen wriggled some more and seemed to be deciding on what to do. "Mr. Stamen?"

"It was brought to my attention."

"Mr. Stamen, when did you first meet with the Federal Reserve on this matter?"

"I first spoke with them on a conference call with the bank president, Mr. Han. That may have been in February."

"Of what year?"

"2024."

"And when did you first meet with them in person?"

Stamen began wriggling again. He apparently hadn't realized that Alandro had just testified to the meeting with the Federal Reserve the same morning Rafael had been fired. "Um, let me see," he said, with his hand poised at his mouth. "I can't recall."

"Are you sure?" Alexa asked, sounding as harmless as she could.

Stamen's hand came away from his mouth. He uncrossed his legs and shook his head. "Sorry. I don't recall."

Rafael swallowed a chuckle. Alexa took a step forward. "What if I were to tell you that you met with the Federal Reserve on the very day in February of 2025 that you fired Rafael Lamon, and within minutes of the time Rafael was escorted off the premises. Would that refresh your recollection?"

Stamen turned red. "Maybe," he said.

"Maybe?" Alexa said. "Are you still unsure?"

"I said, I don't recall."

Alexa heard a male voice grunt, and then Ann Lacey's voice was heard. "Your Honor, I strongly object. Ms. Starr is harassing the witness. He's already said he doesn't recall."

Judge Darnell looked at Alexa, awaiting a response. When she said nothing, the judge pushed. "Counsel?"

Alexa answered, so disgusted with Stamen she wanted to scream at him. "Your Honor," she said, turning away from Stamen and trying hard to keep her expression impassive, "the witness is hostile, and I believe he is being intentionally evasive."

Lacey had more to say. "Your Honor, I further object as to the time of the meeting, as it has already been put into evidence."

"Your Honor, rather than dispute the fact, I'll abandon this line of questioning," Alexa said.

"Very well, but I'm going to overrule the objection," the judge said.

"Mr. Stamen, do you recall the content of that first meeting held at the Beverly Hills branch office with the Federal Reserve agents?"

"What do you mean?"

"Do you recall why the Federal Reserve wanted to meet with you?"

"Yes."

"Can you tell us what that reason was?"

"They were concerned about possible violations of banking regulations."

"And did you know they were coming to the branch that morning at a scheduled time?"

Stamen nodded, apparently comfortable with this line of questioning, and seemingly unaware of the danger. "I was expecting them at some point."

Alexa knew she was walking on a vein of pure gold. "And were you able to tell them that you had taken care of the problem by firing Rafael Lamon?"

A rustle was heard at the defense table. Stamen looked offended. In fact, he looked insulted. "Yes. Yes. I did. And I believed I had."

Alexa couldn't believe the man's gall. "Are you presently working at TriWorld?"

"No."

"Can you tell us why?"

"I'd rather not."

"Isn't it true that you were fired?"

"I-"

"Isn't it true that you were fired as a result of the findings of the Federal Reserve in this exact matter that we are speaking of, and that you scapegoated Rafael Lamon, hoping to make him pay for violations he did not commit?"

Lacey shot up.

Alexa beat her to it. "I withdraw the question, Your Honor." She paused a moment for the heat to dissipate, then continued, "Mr. Stamen, Mr. Alandro testified that he conducted regular performance reviews, and he confirmed the last performance review he conducted for Rafael Lamon. Were you aware of the results of that review?"

"I don't remember."

"I'm not asking if you recall the specifics of that review but rather if you recall Mr. Alandro sharing the results of that review with you."

"No. Not that I recall."

"Well, let me ask you this. Was it customary at your branch at TriWorld for Executive Directors like Mr. Alandro to conduct performance reviews of the directors under them?"

"Yes."

"And did TriWorld's corporate protocol require those Executive Directors like Mr. Alandro to share the results of their reviews with you as the branch General Manager?"

"I guess so."

"You guess so? You're not certain?"

"Yes."

"Yes, what?"

Stamen bristled. "Yes, they shared the results."

"Then wouldn't it be safe to assume that Mr. Alandro shared the results of his performance review of Rafael Lamon with you?"

Stamen made a flickering motion with his hand as if removing lint from his trousers and shrugged. "Yeah, I guess."

"And are you aware, as you sit here today, that Mr. Alandro's most recent review gave Rafael Lamon a 9 out of 10 in overall performance of his duties?"

Stamen simply looked at Alexa with dead eyes, showing as little interest as if Alexa had just scratched her arm. "So?" he asked.

"You have told us that several times that you suspected Rafael Lamon was involved in illegal funding and illegally pairing funds. Why is that, sir?" Alexa asked.

Stamen folded his arms and answered. "Because he was the person in touch with Bank of Taiwan."

"And who delegated that job to him?"

"I did." No one could see Stamen's right foot begin to shake except for Alexa and the judge. The judge winced and looked away. It annoyed her, and she would have liked to ask him to stop.

Alexa looked at the jury and back at Stamen. "You believed that the man you delegated the job of dealing with Bank of Taiwan was guilty of illegal activity because he was the person dealing with Bank of Taiwan?"

It didn't take much to realize Stamen was being mocked. He tried to defend his position. The smile was gone. "Well, I didn't expect him to do anything illegal. I just wanted him to ask what the interest rate was that Taiwan was charging on loans."

"Why would that be important?"

"So that we could set our interest rates a few basis points below whatever they were charging on their loans. But then, hell, I don't know what happened."

The judge spoke. "Mr. Stamen, please watch your language in my courtroom."

"Sorry, Judge," Stamen said. He ran his fingers down his tie, and it flopped in place over his shirt. Then his hand went to his brow, and he rubbed.

"One last question for you, Mr. Stamen. What bank are you presently employed at?"

Alexa was taking a chance, pretty sure that the Feds had banned Stamen from the banking world. "I'm not working right now," he said.

"Why is that?"

"I thought I'd take some time off," Stamen shrugged.

"Time off?" Alexa asked. "Isn't it true that the Federal Reserve has enjoined you from seeking employment at a bank?" Stamen was silent. "Mr. Stamen?"

"The defense objects to counsel's badgering of the witness," Lacey said.

"Objection overruled. Answer the question, Mr. Stamen."

"I refuse to answer."

"On what grounds?" It was the judge asking, saving Alexa the bother.

"I don't want to answer. I take the Fifth."

Judge Darnell didn't want to hear that. "Well, sir, in that case, I will instruct the jury to assume the more damaging answer to that question."

Stamen twisted around to face Judge Darnell. "You can't do that. It's my right." Then, amazingly, he addressed the defense table. "She can't do that! Object!"

Judge Darnell struck her gavel down hard. "Sir, control yourself. This is a civil case, not a criminal case, and I can and will do exactly that."

Stamen looked from the judge to Alexa, glaring at her with unmasked dislike. Then he looked up at the ceiling, sighed, and said, "Yes. It's true."

"Thank you. As a result of their eighteen-month-long investigation, the Federal Reserve has forbidden you to work at a bank." She paused, then asked, "Are you aware that they have not taken any such measure against Rafael Lamon? In fact, they have imposed no penalty on him at all. Nothing."

"Well," Stamen said, leaning forward slightly. His next words were very clear. "Good for Rafael," he said. Rafael was gloating. All he could think as his insides were bursting was that this was the man who had single-handedly caused him all that misery. *Damn you, Stamen!*

Alexa took a chance then. "Mr. Stamen, did you hold a power of attorney on any of the accounts at TriWorld?"

Stamen glared at her. Alexa felt a jolt of electricity shoot down her spine. She had hit gold. Again. "That's irrelevant," he said.

Judge Darnell smirked. "Mr. Stamen. Let's leave it to the attorneys – I count five of them for the defense – to object. Meanwhile, you just answer counsel's questions."

Stamen's pleading eyes moved to the defense table. No one

objected. "Mr. Stamen?" Alexa said, her heart beating fast. "Would you like me to repeat the question?"

His eyes eventually found their way back to Alexa. They were filled with disgust. "No, I heard you."

"Well then, please answer."

"Yes, little lady. I did."

Rafael instinctively slapped his thigh. *The bastard!*

Alexa could hardly contain herself. "And did you have loans out at Bank of Taiwan?"

Stamen chortled. "What do you think, little lady?"

"Your Honor, would you kindly direct the witness to answer?"

"Mr. Stamen!" The judge was losing her patience. "You will answer the questions put to you!"

"Yes." He was sarcastic now. "I had loans out at Bank of Taiwan." Then, as if surrendering, he became smug. "I had a few loans."

Alexa walked over to the table and touched a legal pad covered with random notes before returning to the witness. She was hoping he would believe that she knew the answer to the next question. "And could you tell us the total amount of loans you had?"

"Five and a half mil."

"Five and a half million dollars?"

"Yeah."

Now, Alexa was curious. "And please give us the name that was on the TriWorld account?"

"What do you mean?"

"Well, Mr. Stamen. I understand you are a U.S. citizen, and TriWorld only held accounts for non-U.S. citizens. Isn't that correct?"

"Yes."

"So, my question is, who held the account? Who was the non-U.S. citizen?"

"My wife and her father."

Paydirt!

"You mean you held power of attorney on more than one account at TriWorld and took more than one loan out at Bank of Taiwan?"

Alexa was certain Stamen would have killed her if he could. "Yeah."

"So, your wife and your father-in-law had accounts at TriWorld. You held the power of attorney on both those accounts. You then borrowed money from Bank of Taiwan and used the money in their accounts to secure the loans and indemnified your possible default with that money. Is that correct?"

Alexa saw Lacey put her hand over her forehead as though to hide, as she scribbled on the notepad in front of her. "Thank you." She turned to Judge Darnell. "Your Honor, I have no further questions of this witness."

"Ms. Lacey, any cross-examination of this witness will have to wait until tomorrow."

The judge excused the jury, slammed down the gavel and court ended for the day.

56

Rafael had sat throughout the trial, legs crossed, hand folded on his lap, listening to the testimony of the various witnesses. He sat taking it all in, and with each witness his disgust at what had been done to him grew and with it, his confidence. Let the jury see how blameless he was.

He'd heard much of the witnesses' testimony from prior depositions. But the gems in the testimony of Alandro and Stamen were new revelations and they were gems, pure, precious and astounding.

He was disgusted by Alandro's flippant willingness to concede to Stamen at every turn. He realized that Jason's acquiescence was probably in large part the reason the man had risen in the branch, working right under Stamen. He was simply the general manager's "Yes man."

And Bob Stamen. The Culprit. That was more than obvious. The man was bad. He was a criminal. And he had tried to hide behind him, Rafael, an innocent man.

Rafael had taken his job to heart and had persistently done the best he could for the bank, bringing in wealthy clients and continuing to hold their hand, cajoling them when they needed extra attention, all to ensure that they were happy with TriWorld.

How dare Stamen blame Rafael for his own wrong acts and throw him to the dogs? He had scapegoated Rafael! That was the word Alexa had used. *Scapegoated.*

And Alexa. What a marvel she was. Rafael could see that the jurors liked her. In fact, they seemed to be captivated by her. Prince was obviously aware of the great job she was doing. And she said she couldn't represent him well in a courtroom. *Hah!* The woman was a smart tiger. Or was it tigress? Whichever. There was no end to her ability.

When court adjourned for the day, and his attorneys were loading up their attache cases, Rafael burst out indignantly. "My God, Alexa! Those bastards *knew* the Federal Reserve was coming in."

Alexa nodded. "Right! And Stamen sent them straight to you! Can you believe that? Now we know why Bloom told you the Feds had said that the bank gave you to them in a gift box."

Rafael shook his head. "Unbelievable. He's really bad," he said.

Viviana was at her husband's side. She hugged his arm and stroked his shoulder. "It's over now, *querido.*" She turned to Alexa with a warm smile. "You are doing a very good job, Alexa."

Viviana's compliment chafed. Alexa directed herself to Rafael. "We'll get them," she said. "Rest up. See you tomorrow." She managed a smile as the Lemons said goodbye and took their leave of the courtroom.

"Have time for a bite?" Prince asked her.

The two of them went to Josepi's. Over pizza, salad, and red wine, they discussed the afternoon's events. Alexa had examined five witnesses that day. She was rightfully exhausted.

But she was too excited o realize it.

57

The following morning, Lacey declined cross-examination of Stamen. But, as with the other witnesses, she reserved the right to call him to the stand. Alexa couldn't really blame Lacey. The defense had no doubt decided that the less time Stamen was before the jury, the better.

Alexa longed to put Gilmore from the Federal Reserve on the stand and question him before the jurors. Certainly, his testimony alone would suffice to show the extent of TriWorld's baseless and malicious defaming and scapegoating of Rafael. Of course, that was impossible, so she continued on that day, questioning Jim Redwood next, the attorney for TriWorld, who had conducted the in-house investigation pursuant to the alert from the Federal Reserve of its pending investigation.

When questioned about the two documents already marked as exhibits, the Pledge Agreement and the Security Agreement, Redwood testified that neither document had been composed by TriWorld's legal department. No, neither he nor anyone in legal had been consulted about them or even known of their existence prior to the Federal Reserve's investigation. Yes, he was absolutely certain of that.

"Mr. Redwood, let's focus on the Security Agreement. Is that an agreement that you would have composed if asked to by, say, a branch manager?"

"Absolutely not."

"And why is that?"

Redwood let out his breath. "It's illegal. Not to mention bad business. It's preposterous. It purports to hold money in our account as security for a loan by another bank – in this case, Bank of Taiwan. The money in our account does not belong to the power of attorney, and there is no consent form showing the owner of that account agrees to use their money to secure another person's loan."

"I see. And what about the Indemnity Agreement?"

He shook his head. "Absolutely not. Completely illegal. It holds the Bank of Taiwan harmless from any and all losses it might incur in the normal course of business by making loans to its customers who happen to hold a power of attorney on one of our accounts. It comes down to us giving them the money to loan to their borrowers." He looked at Alexa in bafflement and put his hands up, shrugging. "Why would TriWorld do that?"

"So, do you have any idea why Mr. Alandro and others believed that Mr. Stamen, the General Manager of TriWorld's Beverly Hills branch, had received those two documents from TriWorld's legal department?"

"I do not," Redwood said with finality. "He certainly did not get them from us."

"Michael Bowen, Head of Human Resources in the California office of TriWorld, communicated to the Employment Development Department that Rafael had been fired for funding illegal loans. Did he get that information from you?"

"I initially was told by Mr. Han that it had been discovered that Mr. Lamon had been involved in the illegal activity. At some very early date, I may have transferred that information to Mr. Bowen when he asked what he should say to the EDD."

Alexa was not surprised that Lacey didn't object to any of that testimony on grounds of hearsay.

"In other words, you based your statement that Rafael Lamon was funding these loans and that he had composed the security agreement and the indemnity agreement on Mr. Han's statement to you? Is that accurate?"

"Yes. That's correct."

"And Mr. Han is the President of TriWorld?"

"That's correct."

"Would you say that was unfortunate?"

"Ye-

"Objection!" Lacey bolted from her seat.

Before she could state grounds, Alexa withdrew the question.

"Thank you, sir. I have no further questions for this witness."

Once again, Lacey declined the opportunity to cross-examine the witness, reserving the right to call him back.

The bailiff went to fetch Lee Han, the President of TriWorld, who, like the other witnesses, had been absent from the courtroom throughout the previous testimony.

Curious eyes turned to him as he entered the courtroom. He was as short as a comma, no taller than five feet if that. Like a comma, he was important enough to give pause. He wore glasses with a dark blue tint, so his eyes were unseen. His black suit was obviously custom-cut to suit his slim frame. Every hair of his thick, straight, raven-black mane was precisely cut and placed. His navy-blue tie lay proudly atop his starched white shirt. He passed through the bar and crossed Alexa to take the witness stand, and she noted his shoes, the black leather that looked soft enough to have come from a calf born that day. She remembered that Rafael had said Han was an extreme germophobe and realized how much of a strain this court appearance must be for him. As he took the oath, Alexa noted his cufflinks, a gold T and W artfully tied together. He sat with his feet flat on the floor and his hands on his thighs.

Judge Darnell addressed him. "Are those glasses necessary?"

Han looked at her and answered in clipped speech. "They are prescription lenses."

The judge's lips twitched. "Very well," she said.

To Rafael, the man was a cartoon character.

Alexa went through all the information she had already gathered from the other witnesses. She took Han through a chronological review of events at TriWorld from the first contact with the Federal Reserve about improprieties at the Bank to the closing of the Beverly Hills branch. There was really nothing new to be added to the evidence from Han's testimony. It was more a matter of tying up all the players, having the jury take a look and listen to each as they told the same tale, which she hoped was now sounding pathetically biased and malicious. It only served to ingrain it in their minds.

She went through Han's meeting with Redwood, during which he told the attorney that Rafael was the culprit. "I'd had multiple discussions with Robert Stamen, the branch manager, on the subject of the illegal loans. He convinced me that Rafael Lamon was the guilty party, the rotten apple. I am still not sure he was not involved."

Again, Alexa was unsurprised when Lacey didn't object to this testimony as hearsay, though it obviously was; but it was admissible as it was being presented to justify Han's state of mind when Rafael was fired rather than for the truth of the statement. "Mr. Han, I understand the General Manager of your Beverly Hills branch was fired and barred from working in the banking arena. Is that correct?"

"Yes."

"And the branch was shut down by the Federal Reserve?" Han nodded. "Does your nod signify a Yes?"

"Yes."

"Did TriWorld receive any admonishments from the Federal Reserve?"

"Yes."

Alexa thought for a moment. As much as she would have liked to show Han that she could pounce on that statement, continue with this line of questioning, and point out that Rafael remained unscathed from the investigation, she decided to hold off until she had Rafael on the stand.

"If you believed that Rafael was involved in illegal funding, why wasn't he told the reason he was fired the day he was terminated?"

Han shrugged. "I can't answer that. I didn't know he wasn't told."

"Are you telling us that it was Bob Stamen's own decision not to disclose to Rafael the reason for his termination?"

"It seems that way."

"Were you aware that agents of the Federal Reserve would be at the branch that morning?"

"Yes."

"And you were aware that Mr. Stamen planned to terminate Rafael Lamon that morning?"

"Yes."

"Thank you. That's all the questions I have." '

Rafael wanted to stand up and applaud.

True to her now standard m.o., Lacey reserved her right to call Han back to the stand at a later time. As he walked back up the aisle and out of the courtroom, Rafael chuckled at the thought that the germaphobe was on his way to shower and change clothes

"Your Honor, the plaintiff calls Larry Bloom."

Alexa and Prince had thought long and hard about when to call the attorney to the stand. There was merit to calling him at the very beginning of their case as well as immediately before or after either Stamen or Han. They'd finally decided to wait until the jury had heard from all the bank employees, then hear what Bloom had to say.

Alexa quickly laid the foundation for his testimony, establishing that, as an attorney specializing in banking, he had initially been retained by Rafael to represent him before the Federal Reserve and that he had made the first telephone call to the agency on Rafael's behalf.

"And do you recall whom you spoke with at the Federal Reserve?"

"Yes, it was Attorney Gilmore. I believe there was also someone from the Justice Department on the phone with us, but I don't have a name."

"And what did they tell you?"

"They told me that TriWorld had given them – and I quote – Rafael Lamon in a gift box tied with a bow."

"Objection. That is both hearsay and privileged."

"And both objections are overruled," said the judge. "Continue, counsel."

"Thank you, Your Honor. And what did you take that to mean?"

Bloom grunted. "That they had pretty much screwed Lamon. They had fingered him, blamed him for the illegal activity going on."

"Thank you, Mr. Bloom. That's all."

Lacey said the defense wanted to cross-examine Bloom. There was a flurry of papers as the five defense attorneys passed notes and whispered among themselves. Then Lacey rose and faced Bloom.

"Why did your representation end?" she asked.

Bloom smirked. "Mr. Lamon decided he no longer wanted me to represent him."

"Could it be because after hearing the facts and speaking

with the Federal Reserve you did not believe that he was innocent?"

Alexa was about to object to the question when Bloom quickly answered, "No! I most emphatically object to that implication. I never believed that he was guilty. He seemed to me to be a fine man, honest and completely innocent, and I had no reason to believe otherwise. I believe it was a financial decision. His assets were limited."

"Well, of course, Mr. Bloom, I respect your professional ethics in trying to shield a past client but –"

"Your Honor, I object! Counsel is badgering the witness. The question has been answered."

Judge Darnell interrupted Alexa. "Objection sustained."

"Yes, Your Honor," Lacey said. She looked at the four co-counsels sitting at her table. They were no help. She had nowhere to go.

"No more questions," she said and sat back down.

58

Having laid out for the jury what the defendants had done to her client, Alexa now turned their attention to the resulting damage. She first called on the psychologist Rafael had been seeing.

Leave it to Rafael to find an attractive psychologist. That was Alexa's first thought when she saw Angela Romero, the young, petite Argentine with strawberry blonde hair and green eyes.

She wore a dark green suit with a cream-colored silk blouse. Her bearing was professional, and she spoke clearly but with an accent, which Alexa found charming. After reciting her rather impressive qualifications as a psychologist, citing her studies both in Argentina and the United States, she went on to say that Rafael had come to her due to emotional problems he was suffering as a result of his termination from TriWorld. Her testimony was protected by the psychotherapist-client relationship, but Rafael had waived that privilege, allowing her to speak freely about him.

"You see," she explained, "unfortunately, in the Argentine

culture, a man is nothing if he is not a breadwinner." She tilted her head and smiled a bittersweet smile.

She continued. "A man is defined by the work he does. Rafael – Mr. Lamon – had been respected for his work as a Director at TriWorld, his television show, and his lectures. When he was fired, he was disgraced, humiliated.

It is a macho culture, and in such a culture, a man's ego will be devastated; Rafael's was. He couldn't cope. He felt not only betrayed by those he had worked with for all those years, he felt victimized by the world. For well over one year, he'd wake up every morning and go to bed every night wondering if he would ever be free of the stigma that had wrongfully befallen him; if he would be jailed and owe massive amounts of money to the government.

He may as well have been branded a criminal.

He was shunned by his friends, by his peers... by the community at large. And all of this was during his daughter's engagement. He had no money and had to borrow from family. He couldn't afford to pay for her wedding. He couldn't afford to pay his bills. He had spent all his money on legal fees. And at the time his daughter is marrying, well, that's a time when a man's reputation is most vulnerable."

"And what about his own marriage? Did that suffer?"

"Yes. Of course. How could it not? Such a thing affects a man in every way. He no longer felt like a man. He was totally broke. He lost his appetite. He lost weight. He couldn't sleep. He was anxious and nervous all the time. He was afraid he might not be believed; that he would be arrested and go to jail. Under such stressful conditions, he lost the ability to function in many ways and to perform the functions of a husband.

"Did he take medication?"

"He didn't want to. He fought it. But he was so terribly depressed that he decided to try an antidepressant. I prescribed one for him."

"And did that help?"

The psychologist smiled wistfully. "Well, it helped, but not as much as one would hope. The problems he faced didn't go away with a pill. They were very real. And very frightening."

Alexa could see that the jurors liked Angela. More importantly, they seemed to trust her, caught up in her depiction of a man in emotional pain.

"Did Rafael confess his guilt to you during those meetings?"

The psychologist shook her head. "He professed through it all that he was completely innocent and had been victimized. And because there were so many powerful fingers pointed at him, he felt powerless."

The next witness was an economist who testified as a financial expert regarding Rafael's loss of income resulting from his termination.

This testimony, along with the psychologist's, would go to Rafael's compensatory damages, an amount meant to make Rafael monetarily whole for the injury suffered at the hands of the defendant's conduct. In contrast, most emotional pain and suffering were deemed general damages, as there could be no clear dollar amount assigned to them, whereas loss of earnings was listed as special damages, as it was presumably quantifiable.

The economist testified to Rafael's lost earnings and the present value of future lost earnings, accounting for future inflation, then reducing the income by the probable taxes that would be paid on the income.

It wasn't sexy testimony; it was boring, all about numbers, but it was important. After all, the case was about money.

Norman James had an easy way about him. He looked comfortable on the stand and spoke fast with the confidence of an expert. Alexa had expected him to speak to the jury, but he directed himself instead to the court reporter, aware that she would be taking down his every word. Yet the jurors seemed attentive to what he had to say.

Alexa took that as a sign they were considering awarding Rafael a sum of money.

If the jury found that Rafael had been wrongfully terminated, he would be awarded an amount based on compensatory damages. Regardless of what that figure might be, whether low or high, Rafael, Alexa, and Prince hoped that justice would be served; that the bank would be held liable for punitive damages as well as compensatory damages, punishing TriWorld for its conduct as a deterrent to similar future acts.

But to get punitive damages, the jury would first have to find that Rafael was wrongfully terminated and award compensatory damages. Only then could they proceed to determine that the wrongful termination had been malicious, intentional, and against public policy, warranting punitive damages as well.

The economist stated that using the formula he described, the amount of compensatory damages due Rafael would be approximately two and a half million dollars.

James was the one witness that Attorney Baxter cross-examined, and Alexa quickly noted that his goal was to poke holes wherever he could in James' testimony by splitting hairs.

As an example, when James said that Rafael's background and experience rendered him overqualified for many jobs, Baxter retorted, "But it's possible he could get something, right?"

59

The final witness Alexa called was Rafael. For three days, the jury had seen him sit in the courtroom, and they watched for his reaction as he listened to the various witnesses. They had seen his wife come in with him and stay for the duration. They were understandably curious about him, and now they were about to hear him speak and listen to him tell his story.

The courtroom was silent as he took the witness stand. The first words he spoke were the affirmation of the oath, and then his name and Alexa knew from those words and his body language that he was ready, calm, feeling secure, yet not overly confident.

He sat with his feet on the floor, his hands relaxed all short and direct. He was the Rafael she knew and the jurors would be his.

She took him through the preliminaries, asking his age, educational background, degrees and such, mentioning his daughter's recent marriage, his early working experience, his time in the media both in Argentina and in Los Angeles, his years with other banks, and then the sign-on bonus he was given to start with TriWorld. He spoke of his regular raises and excellent job reviews and arrived at the day he was terminated after having worked at TriWorld two months shy of eight years.

Rafael described the scene in his office when Stamen entered, with Alandro tagging behind him, and summarily fired him without warning or explanation despite Rafael's questions, ordering him to leave the premises immediately and not return.

He spoke of the utter confusion and panic he felt upon leaving TriWorld, escorted by the security guard, suddenly without a job and without a reason.

He spoke of his position as a Director and his job description as a relationship officer. No, he had nothing to do with loans; that was a separate department he knew nothing about.

Alexa projected the two infamous documents on the screen. He described his problems with the Indemnity Agreement and the Security Agreement and how he had complained about each when he was first presented with them, believing them to be illegal.

He explained that he was given the documents because Stamen had instructed him to sign them on behalf of TriWorld, along with someone from Bank of Taiwan for each of the loans made to Americans given powers of attorney.

Rafael described his discussion with the auditor to whom he also complained about the documents, how he had shown him the phrases, which the jurors could see were highlighted in yellow, and why he'd had problems with them both. He described the meeting in Stamen's office where the general manager instructed him to contact Favio Melo at the Bank of Taiwan and interrogate him about the interest rates his bank was charging its borrowers.

The jurors' attention was riveted on Rafael, and even the sound of the courtroom door opening and closing, which normally diverted their attention, did nothing to shake their interest or break their gaze from him.

"Rafael, did you do anything illegal at TriWorld?"

"No."

"Were you involved in any illegal funding of loans?"

"No. Never."

"Did you hold a power of attorney on any account at TriWorld?"

"No."

"Did you take out any loans from Bank of Taiwan?"

"No, I did not."

And later, "What happened when you showed the auditor the two documents and told him your problems with them?"

"He thanked me and made copies of both."

And still later, "Did you know why you were terminated on that day well over a year ago?"

"No."

"You truly had no idea?"

"That's right."

"What did you do when you were fired?"

"I didn't know what to do. I called you."

"Did you look for another job?"

Yes, he had applied to banks, but he was turned down everywhere. He was reduced to applying for jobs that required none of his experience and finally felt lucky to have gotten a job as a shoe salesman since he needed the money, especially after paying for his daughter's wedding.

He confirmed everything that the psychologist had said, sounding matter-of-fact rather than self-pitying, and ended by saying that he was pleased he had been vindicated and was now able to finally have his day in court.

"Thank you, Rafael. Your Honor, I have no more questions for this witness. The plaintiff rests."

"Very well," Judge Darnell said. "Ms. Lacey?"

Lacey arose. "I have some questions for Mr. Lamon, Your Honor."

60

The jurors shuffled in their seats, readying for the face of the lion, the predator on the tail of its prey.

Alexa went to her table, feeling as confident as she could that Rafael would take care of himself. But she couldn't kid herself. Lacey didn't get to be TriWorld's litigator for nothing.

As she had approached her seat, she'd locked eyes with Viviana, and they held for a meaningful second. They both knew that the next minutes could decide the fate of the case.

"Mr. Lamon, good morning." Her smile was unmistakably ingratiating.

"Good morning." Rafael still looked and sounded fine.

"Sounds like you've been through a lot," she said.

"Yes."

"Tell me, has the Federal Reserve sent you or your attorney a letter telling you that you have been vindicated? I believe that was the word you used."

"No."

"Who is representing you before the Federal Reserve?"

"No one any longer. Larry Bloom represented me at first.

Then Alexa Starr did. But again, no one is representing me any longer."

"Why is that?"

"Because they're finished with me."

"How do you know? Did they tell you that?"

Rafael smiled. Alexa was surprised at how well he was doing. Despite all that was riding on his testimony, he seemed composed. Though there was little doubt that he was nervous, he looked calm.

"Ms. Lacey, you know if the Federal Reserve is not finished with you." There were smiles and stifled chuckling from the jury box.

"Would it surprise you then if you were to discover that the Federal Reserve believes you were involved in illegal funding?"

"It would more than surprise me," Rafael said. "I wouldn't believe it."

"And yet you have not received notification from them of any kind that they believe you to be innocent."

"The Federal Reserve is under no duty to tell you that they believe you to be innocent. But after examining me for about 18 months, they would certainly let me know if they believed I was guilty. If not them, then I would have heard from the Justice Department."

"But it is possible that the Federal Reserve still believes you were involved in illegal funding."

Rafael shook his head, smiling. "No, Ms. Lacey. When the Federal Reserve thinks you're involved in something, they let you know for as long as they think it's a possibility."

There was silence. Rafael filled it. "I believe they've come to the results of their investigation. The Beverly Hills branch of TriWorld has been closed. Bob Stamen has been fired, as we've heard, and the branch has received a cease and desist notice."

Alexa gave Rafael the win.

Lacey, who had been standing at Rafael's left, facing the jury box, made no response as if what Rafael had just said had no real import. She turned on her heel and took a few steps, then turned back around. "Mr. Lamon, you have testified that you complained about the Security Agreement and the Indemnity Agreement to the auditor who came to TriWorld."

"That's right."

"When was that?"

"During the branch's last audit when I was still there. That would have been the last part of 2024."

"And who was this auditor that you spoke with?"

"Phil Dublowski."

"Are you sure of that name, Mr. Lamon?"

"I believe that was the name. I couldn't recall his exact name. I recall it began with a Dub-something. My attorneys told me we were given the name Dublowski by the defense."

"And what exactly did you say to Mr. Dublowski? I know you told us that you spoke with him, but I'd like you to be as specific as possible at this time." Lacey's tone was unmistakably sarcastic.

"I told him that I had been told that the attorneys for the bank had drawn up the two documents, and I pointed out the parts in each document. I had highlighted them, and I told him I had problems with them and asked if he agreed."

"And what did he say?"

"He said he would look into it. As I said, he made copies of them."

"And did he get back to you?"

"No." There was a pause, and then Rafael went on. "But it's likely that the audit led to the investigation by the Federal Reserve." He paused again before adding, "which led to my termination."

"Did you contact TriWorld's legal department to ask about the legality of the documents?"

"No. I should have, but at the time, I didn't believe that I had access to them. Besides, Bob – Mr. Stamen – told me that they had been drawn up by our legal department."

Alexa wanted to get up and start dancing in the courtroom. Rafael had caught Lacey in a net of truth. But Lacey wasn't ready to go down.

"Mr. Lamon, you and Ms. Starr, your attorney, composed a 28-page proffer at the request of the Federal Reserve in which you purportedly explained why you were innocent of any wrongdoing. Is that correct?"

Alexa wanted to kick herself. Lacey was referring to the document, which by all rights she should never have received from them. It was a privileged document, and only the Federal Reserve could have waived that privilege. Now they were being paid back for their mistake.

"Yes, that's right."

"So, could you tell us why there is no mention at all in those 28 pages of your meeting with an auditor? Isn't that meeting a fabrication that you and Ms. Starr have cooked up in an attempt to get punitive damages?"

Rafael remained cool as an ocean breeze.

"Ms. Starr is hard of hearing. She wears hearing aids in both ears. Unfortunately, when I told her that I'd told the auditor, her hearing aid was out. She was changing the battery, and so she didn't hear me. She didn't know until I happened to mention it again after the Federal Reserve matter had ended."

Lacey tried to do the best with what she had been given. She laughed. "Mr. Lamon, you must be joking! You don't really want us to believe that."

"It's the truth."

Lacey sneered and turned on her heel ever so slowly. "It must have been difficult for you to work with an attorney who couldn't hear you."

"Alexa– Ms. Starr– doesn't hear well, but she's an excellent lawyer."

"I'm sure she is. But if she couldn't hear you say something as crucial as the fact that you told the auditor about your misgivings, don't you wonder what else she didn't hear?"

"No, I don't."

"Mr. Lamon, are we to understand that you were questioned by agents of the Federal Reserve for a year and a half?"

"That's right, more or less."

"And why is it that in all that time you never mentioned your conversations with the auditor?"

Rafael shrugged. "I never told the Federal Reserve because they never asked. It just never came up. They questioned me about the illegal activity at the bank; they never asked about the auditor. It's possible that they had that information from their files and never told me."

"No further questions," Lacey said. Alexa noticed that Baxter's head was down.

"Ms. Starr?" Judge Darnell said.

Alexa was done. Rafael didn't need resuscitation. "Your Honor, the Plaintiff rests its case."

61

It was time for the defense to knock down the plaintiff's case with their own witnesses – except that all their witnesses had already been called by the plaintiff's lawyer, and the defense apparently had no other witnesses.

Lacey, Baxter, Blank, Sheffield and Alvarez put their heads together. When they came apart, Lacey announced, "Your Honor, the defense calls Alexa Starr to the stand."

At the plaintiff's table, Alexa gasped and looked at Prince. If they wanted her on the stand, it could only be to erode Rafael's credibility on the issue of his encounter with the auditor. Lacey wanted the jury to hear why there had been no mention of Rafael's meeting with an auditor in the proffer.

Prince rose. "Your Honor, we object. Ms. Starr does not appear on the list of witnesses. Furthermore, the defense is not permitted to call the plaintiff's attorney to the stand."

"Your Honor, in the pursuit of truth, there is no bar to examining plaintiff's attorney," Lacey said. "Attorney Starr was not placed on the list of witnesses because we did not think it would be necessary to call her. Also, in the event that it would be necessary, we thought it best not to alert her, again, in the interests of furthering justice."

Alexa sat silently, allowing Prince to manage this surprise maneuver. "If it please the Court," he said, "we would ask for a continuance to allow submission of a brief on the matter."

Judge Darnell sighed. She was loath to stretch the trial out any longer, yet she had no alternative. There was no way around it. Never before had this issue arisen in a case before her. She dismissed court, telling the attorneys she expected their briefs the following morning at nine a.m. The jurors would reconvene directly following her ruling on the matter.

Prince and Alexa returned to Prince's office and worked on the brief. They discovered that the law that ruled attorneys as witnesses was rooted as much in legal ethics as in evidentiary law.

The next morning, Prince recited Model Rule 3.7(a) to the court.

A lawyer can act as a witness at a trial where the lawyer's testimony relates either to an issue not challenged or to the nature and value of the legal services rendered in the case or where failure to testify would work a substantial hardship on the client.

None of these are present here, Your Honor. Attorney Starr is barred from testifying."

"Ms. Lacey?" The judge asked, turning to defense counsel.

"It is interesting that learned counsel alludes to Rule 3.7(a), Your Honor. Allow me to continue to quote from that rule:

A lawyer shall not act as advocate at a trial in which the lawyer is likely to be a necessary witness. Where the lawyer representing the client was the client's former attorney – as Ms. Starr was in this case – the client's former attorney may likely be a necessary witness at trial. Unless the attorney testifies, the opponent is provided with no basis to object.'

"So, actually, Your Honor, contra what Mr. Prince has said, Rule 3.7(a) operates to disqualify past attorneys in a future representational capacity; it does not bar their testimony as witnesses. If anything, it bars Ms. Starr from having represented Mr. Lamon in this case since, as his former attorney, she would most likely be called on as a witness as was Attorney Bloom."

Prince answered. "Ms. Starr represented the plaintiff in another matter. And there was no reason to think she would be a necessary witness in this trial. But, if, as you say, she is a necessary witness, why wasn't she on the list of witnesses?" Prince countered.

Lacey, apparently certain of the strength of her last argument, didn't answer. Judge Darnell frowned. She sighed. She was not happy. Not happy at all.

She grunted, then said. "This is a messy situation. Ms. Lacey, if you had a problem with Ms. Starr's representation of Mr. Lamon, why didn't you bring it up? Even now, I want the record to be clear that you are not objecting on the grounds that she ought not have represented plaintiff, so you can forget a mistrial on that basis. You are simply arguing that you should have the right to call her as a witness. And, at this time, although I strongly rebuke you for not putting her on your list of witnesses, in the interest of justice, I shall grant you the opportunity to examine her on the stand. I find for the defense." Baxter and his cohorts smiled.

With that, the jury was called back in, and court reconvened. Lacey continued from where she'd left off. "The defense calls Alexa Starr to the stand."

Alexa rose from her table and took the oath before sitting. She had never testified at a trial before. She sat, waiting, remembering everything she'd told others to do on the stand. Things looked very different from this perspective.

"Good morning, Ms. Starr."

"Good morning, Ms. Lacey."

"You represented Mr. Lamon in the matter with the Federal Reserve?"

"Yes, that's correct."

"And are you still representing him?"

"As Rafael told you, he's no longer involved with the Federal Reserve. It's a closed matter."

"Oh, you mean he's been vindicated."

"Correct."

"Have you received a letter to that effect? I know your client has not."

Alexa smiled. "No."

"Then is it not possible that the Federal Reserve still believes your client, Rafael Lamon, was involved in the illegal activity at TriWorld?"

"Absolutely not."

"You seem so sure."

"I am sure. The Federal Reserve is not shy, Ms. Lacey, as I'm sure you know. If they want you, if they want to continue talking to you, they do. Furthermore, they're aware of this proceeding, and if they believed Rafael was involved they would have acted to prevent it when we filed– if they believed he was involved and this case was frivolously filed– they would have somehow let us know; I assure you."

"Ms. Starr, how long have you known Mr. Lamon?"

"Let's see. About three years."

"And Mrs. Lamon?"

"The same." Alexa felt her stomach tumble but remained outwardly calm.

"I see. Now, this idea that your client met with the auditor," Lacey said, rolling her eyes, "it's something you and your client cooked up, isn't it?"

"Absolutely not," she said calmly.

"Well, I can't understand why you failed to mention it in your 28-page proffer to the Federal Reserve. Why is that?"

She remained serene. "Because I wasn't aware that Rafael had spoken with the auditor until the Federal Reserve matter was over. As he testified, he had told me early on; but, unfortunately, I hadn't heard him."

"Yes," Lacey said. Her tone became biting. "He mentioned that you don't hear well."

"I wear aids in both ears, and I hear quite badly without both of them in. When Rafael told me that he'd spoken with the auditor, one of my batteries had died so I couldn't hear him. And he wasn't facing me."

Lacey folded her arms, looked up, and made a tight smile. It was obvious she thought this was pure gibberish. "Ms. Starr, please forgive me. I don't mean to question your statement, but would you mind if I were to ask that you show the jury that you are, in fact, wearing hearing aids?"

"Certainly." Alexa noted that the jury was most attentive. She took out one hearing aid and held it up for Lacey, the jury, and the judge to see, then took out the other and did the same. The high-pitched sound of feedback could be heard momentarily. "That sound is feedback," she said.

Lacey, probably embarrassed, had turned her back to the witness as she asked, "How long have you worn hearing aids?" she asked. Everyone in the courtroom heard the question except Alexa. She didn't hear her and simply waited. Lacey turned back to face her.

"Ms. Starr?"

Alexa replaced her aids. "Yes?"

"I asked you how long you've been wearing hearing aids."

"I'm sorry. With my aids out and your back to me, I didn't hear you." The jurors got it.

"Are you satisfied, Ms. Lacey?" Judge Darnell asked.

The rest of the defendant's case was hardly worth the time it took to put on. Lacey and Baxter went through the drill trying to justify what couldn't be justified, trying to sew back their hypothesis to demonstrate this was a case of justifiable termination. But it had been torn to shreds and wasn't salvageable.

They did put on an economist who testified that, using his formula, Rafael's compensatory damages were no more than eight hundred and fifty-eight thousand dollars.

Closing arguments were relatively brief.

The Bank emphasized that the Federal Reserve had not officially vindicated Rafael, that his discussion with the auditor was absent from all discussions and communications with the Federal Reserve, and that his name appeared on some of the documents passed to the Bank of Taiwan.

That was no match for the plaintiff's closing.

After reviewing all the points gleaned from the testimony, Alexa reiterated that Rafael had been a whistleblower and was innocent of any wrongdoing.

"Rafael had absolutely nothing to gain from the illegal activity at TriWorld. Unlike the General Manager, who ordered him to act as an innocent messenger between the Bank of Taiwan and TriWorld, Rafael did not have a power of attorney for any accounts at TriWorld and took out no loans from Bank of Taiwan.

"Furthermore, that morning, as Rafael left TriWorld, agents of the Federal Reserve Bank of New York entered the bank.

"The General Manager – since fired and now unable to return to the world of banking – had made an appointment with representatives of the Federal Reserve during which they officially apprised him that the agency was aware of the illegal activity that TriWorld was engaged in, activity in violation of federal banking laws, activity which their auditor likely apprised them of following notification from Rafael Lamon.

"At that meeting, the General Manager, Bob Stamen, assured these representatives from the Federal Reserve that all had been taken care of, that TriWorld had conducted an internal investigation and the culprit had been identified and terminated. They told them that the bad guy was Rafael Lamon."

She closed with a simple question. "I'd like you all to think about one simple thing. See if you can answer this: If, in fact, Rafael Lamon was guilty of the illegal acts the Federal Reserve had discovered TriWorld was involved in, and if Bob Stamen knew that agents from the Federal Reserve would be coming to the Bank that morning as we learned he did, why didn't he simply hand Rafael over to them? Wouldn't it have made more sense to keep Rafael on the premises and hand him over to the Federal Reserve rather than send him away as fast as possible before they arrived?"

Lacey didn't seem to have her heart in her closing statement. It was as if she herself had become convinced that Rafael had done nothing wrong but was obligated to go through the motions of presenting a closing.

Following Lacey's lackluster and surprisingly dull summation, Judge Darnell gave the jury instructions on the law to be applied to the evidence.

As this was a civil case, all that was needed for Rafael to be awarded damages was agreement between three-fourths of the jury or nine jurors.

In the end, the jury unanimously voted that Rafael had been wrongfully and maliciously terminated for whistleblowing.

The judge received the verdict and concurred for the record, issuing a final judgment. Afterward, the four of them, Prince, Alexa, Rafael, and Viviana, had that drink of champagne together before Rafael and Viviana left to meet with Sofia and Joe for a celebratory dinner.

When they all said goodbye, Roger hugged Alexa, and they congratulated one another.

62

When Alexa arrived home, she realized she could do little more than lie down with the twins and listen as they babbled on for the few minutes they had with her before Ben picked them up for the weekend.

She had to drag herself up to say hello to him and goodbye to them.

She was sorry to see them go. She'd be lonely that weekend. She spent Saturday organizing Rafael's file, readying it for the coming punitive phase of the trial Roger's firm was working on, and returning client phone calls. After that, there was little to do.

She had a late massage and spent the evening relaxing with Chinese takeout. On Sunday morning, she went for a power walk and saw a movie with a friend. Sunday afternoon, she received a surprise phone call from Roger Prince.

"Just calling to say hi and congratulate you again," he said.

Alexa laughed. "And you."

"Alexa, I'd like to ask you out. You know, like a date. Maybe I could cook dinner. Or we could eat out if you prefer and maybe catch a movie."

Alexa was momentarily speechless. Then she heard herself say, "I'd like that when this is all over."

"Great. Okay, we'll wait until it's over," Roger agreed. "I guess it would be far too distracting otherwise. But you have to promise that we're on no matter what the outcome is."

"You've got my word."

When they hung up, Alexa took a long bath and thought about Roger Prince while relaxing in the hot tub. He certainly was different than Rafael.

The most obvious difference staring her in the face was Roger's lack of neediness. Whereas Rafael needed her with every step, Roger seemed self-reliant. In fact, during the trial, she had depended on him.

There were other differences, too. Roger obviously had adored his wife and most likely had never dreamed of being unfaithful. Granted, he'd been married far fewer years than Rafael. But Rafael had said that Viviana had always been the way she is. From that, Alexa inferred he had been unfaithful early on.

Alexa also doubted that Roger was as emotional a man as Rafael. *Was that a plus? What did any of it mean?*

Could a column of plusses create desire or love in her heart?

Her mind drifted back to the trial.

She was excited about the jury's finding for Rafael and anxious for the second part of the trial that would resume on Monday, all about how much to pay Rafael in punitive damages. Since the jurors had sent a clear message with their unanimous vote that they understood her client had, indeed, been wrongly and maliciously scapegoated for whistleblowing, all that was left was for them to decide how much money to award Rafael for TriWorld's breach of public policy.

Of course, the win still brought with it a hornet's nest of confusion about her relationship to Rafael.

Their last discussion about their personal life revolved

around marriage. Rafael had been firm: to him, a win meant leaving Viviana and marrying Alexa. It was pretty black and white.

Since then, Viviana had transformed into another woman, and Rafael had definitely taken notice. What that meant to his marriage proposal was yet to be seen.

Meanwhile, thanks to Sheyanne, Alexa had gained enough clarity to realize that her decision to marry Rafael or not to marry him would be based a hundred percent on her own feelings and not on her desire to protect Viviana. As it turned out, Viviana had been able to fend for herself and well, thank you.

Emotions aside, Alexa was first and foremost Rafael's attorney, and her prime concern was to represent her client to her best ability. She wanted TriWorld to pay a lot in punitive damages.

It was Viviana who called to thank Alexa for all she'd done. It was almost impossible to believe that Rafael hadn't called to thank her and say how thrilled he was that he'd won and discuss his award.

That was another difference between the two men.

63

Monday morning in court, Alexa's client looked refreshed and relaxed. Alexa was surprised to see that Viviana had not accompanied her husband.

Before court adjourned, Rafael asked if Alexa would have lunch with him. She had planned to spend that time going over things with Prince and so hesitated, but then agreed; her curiosity won out. Meanwhile, there was work to be done.

Roger addressed the jury.

He began by thanking the jury for finding that Rafael had been wrongfully and maliciously terminated.

"You not only found a just verdict, and not only helped make a wronged man whole,.More importantly, you sent a message to the defendant, a large corporation, a huge conglomerate, international in scope, that they cannot step on the toes of the little man without consequence.

Now, your job is to go one step – but a most important step – further. We must show TriWorld and other companies like TriWorld watching this case that when they step on those toes, the consequences can be dire.

"What is important to keep in mind is this: As you believe that TriWorld acted with malicious intent in wrongfully terminating Rafael Lamon, a whistleblower, they will be accountable to pay punitive damages. Punitive damages come into play where, as in this case, the defendant's actions are deemed to be against public policy. They're paid to deter the defendant and others from engaging in the type of conduct that damaged Rafael Lamon.

"I will be calling witnesses to the stand who will testify to the approximate net worth of TriWorld so that you can decide on an appropriate figure to award Rafael Lamon in damages.

It is impossible to know the company's true value – it's too massive.

But the question you will answer is this: what figure is appropriate for TriWorld's intentionally malicious wrongful termination of Rafael Lamon in violation of public policy?

Don't be intimidated by the very large numbers you will no doubt hear. I suggest you bring it down to numbers we've all dealt with in our lives. If TriWorld was valued at, say, one hundred thousand dollars, how much of that would you think they should have to pay Rafael Lamon for the damage they inflicted on his life? One hundred dollars? That's one percent of their total value. Ten thousand dollars? That would be ten percent. You might want to translate whatever percentage you think is fair into the figure you hear as comprising TriWorld's assets. I'm sure you will remember all you've heard so far in deciding."

He paused, then continued.

"I would very much like to thank each one of you for your patience to date and your sense of fairness."

"Your first witness?" Judge Darnell prompted.

"Your Honor, I call Paul Chodos to the stand."

Paul Chodos was in his mid-fifties, with salt-and-pepper hair in a crew cut. He wore a gray suit, a darker gray tie, and glasses. He was a financial expert.

Throughout his questioning of Chodos, Prince would be referring to a file of papers amassed with Chodos' assistance concerning TriWorld's financial information. It was neither complete nor very accurate. Detailed and accurate information about a corporation doing business on an international scale, at the level that TriWorld had been engaged in for decades, was – as Prince had told the jury – difficult, if not impossible, to come by.

How many millions upon millions of dollars did TriWorld have in its reserves?

How much cash did it have on hand? Where did the value of its stock fit in? It wasn't easy to obtain an accurate account of current assets and liabilities to ascertain net worth. But all the numbers were hefty enough to be impressive.

Chodos was seated and was about to be sworn in when Baxter and Lacey stood and addressed the Court. "Your Honor, may we approach the Bench?"

"Yes, come forward."

The seven attorneys gathered at the side of the judge's bench. "Your Honor, the defense would like to ask for a brief recess."

"Court has barely begun this morning. Why would you need a recess?" Judge Darnell asked.

"We would like to discuss the possibility of settlement."

Alexa and Prince stole a quick look at one another.

"Well, I suppose that's a good reason to take the court's time. I will call for a twenty-minute recess." As an afterthought, she said to Lacey, "Good luck," then she declared the twenty-minute recess and retired to her office.

Alexa motioned for Rafael to join the seven attorneys as they entered the side conference room. "They want to settle," Alexa said.

Seated around the Formica-topped table, Prince wasted no time. "Okay, talk," he said.

The attorney named Alvarez was his team's negotiator. "The Bank would like to settle."

"Right. That's why we're here," Prince answered.

"TriWorld is prepared to add two million to what your client has received."

Sitting alongside Rafael, Alexa felt him shuffle in his chair. She kicked him under the table.

"You're kidding," Prince chuckled. "Two mil? You think that jury would award only two million in punitives?" He chuckled.

"Okay, make it three million."

Prince looked over at Alexa. "Don't waste time," she said. "Right now, those twelve men and women would be all too happy to bankrupt TriWorld."

Alvarez frowned. "Our final offer is four million." Alexa saw Rafael put his trembling hands in his pocket. His face was drained of its color. She looked at Prince. He'd been looking at her for a sign. She was hesitant.

"We are authorized to wrap this up before the stock is affected. We're settling because the Board doesn't want to chance a dip in their stocks if the press gets the story, so we'd need a nondisclosure."

Alexa held her wrist up and made a show of looking at her watch. She moved her chair out. "Twenty million or we're going to the jury."

Rafael slid a few inches down in his chair and turned to the small window. Alvarez looked at Lacey. "We need to make a call," he said, bolting up from his seat, whipping out his phone, and strode out the door.

Lacey sat demurely, apparently completely detached from the situation. Prince looked at Alexa, and she was surprised to see tension in his expression. She was completely calm; she knew what Alvarez's answer would be. TriWorld had no choice. Alvarez gave it away when he spoke of TriWorld's stock prices. There was no doubt in her mind; news of a punitive award splashed in the papers would cause TriWorld stock to tumble, and that was to be avoided at almost all costs. The fact was, she had gone easy on them.

Alvarez reappeared in a few minutes, made a slight nod in Lacey's direction, then said to Alexa, "Okay, we have a deal. They okayed twenty million."

"Just a minute," Alexa said. "Mr. Prince and I need to discuss this offer with our client."

"Are you kidding?" Baxter said.

"It was your offer!" Lacey said.

All five defense attorneys looked irate. Alvarez shook his head and decided to take another line of defense. "Look, we won't go above that number. You know juries. Nothing is for sure. And we can always appeal. If we do, it will take years before your client sees anything. This is our final offer. And you'll all have to sign a nondisclosure agreement."

Prince looked at his watch. They now had five minutes left before they were expected back in the courtroom. "We'll see you in court with an answer."

Alexa, Prince, and Rafael left the conference room ahead of Lacey and her four gentleman cohorts. The three of them huddled against a wall. "What do you think?" Prince asked Rafael. "Do you want to take it? That's twenty million plus the two the jury already awarded you."

"Twenty-two million dollars?" Rafael was looking down. He whispered the figure. Then he looked up at Prince. "Are you kidding? Yes, I'll take it." He turned to Alexa. "Right?"

"I think so," she said mildly.

Rafael nodded. "Okay," Prince said.

In court, Prince told the judge a settlement had been reached.

Following that, the jury was thanked and excused, the paperwork completed, and court adjourned. The attorneys closed their files and legal pads and put everything away in their briefcases and attaches.

Trial was over.

64

As Alexa was gathering her files, Prince congratulated Rafael. Still in shock, Rafael thanked Prince for a job well done.

"It was my pleasure," Prince replied. "But Alexa was the star of the show." He called to Alexa, "We'll talk. I'll call you." and then he hurried out of the courtroom, attaché in hand.

Rafael walked out with Alexa. As they walked down the hall, she spoke. "Well, Rafael. Congratulations. You won. You're a rich man."

Rafael didn't respond. His teeth were clenched, his jaw, tight. His head was forward, and his shoulders were slung back. In short, he was tense.

Alexa found it a comical situation.

He was in a tight spot, and she knew it. He had more money than he'd ever dreamed of and one woman too many at the moment. No doubt that with this award, even after the lawyers got their share, Rafael would have enough left to make a nice settlement with Viviana and call off their marriage if he wanted to.

But did he want to?

Alexa appreciated his quandary, but she was aware that if he chose to leave his wife, the dilemma would then be hers.

Would she agree to marry Rafael without knowing him better, without living with him, without the children, without them having bonded at all?

With all his neediness and his inability to be a man without a woman for any period of time?

They had agreed they would decide the day after the case was over. That meant tomorrow.

They were the only ones at the elevator.

"How does it feel to be a rich man who never has to work again?"

Rafael threw his head back and sighed. "I don't believe it," he said. "Twenty million dollars?"

"Sshh! You can't tell anyone. No one! Not even family. That's part of the deal. You can't forget that– ever. And it's not twenty million; you're forgetting to add the compensatory damages."

They were walking into the crowded elevator as Rafael whispered, "Okay, okay. I won't tell anyone. I promise. I swear on my soul. But I can say how much I got besides the punitive damages, right?"

Alexa nodded. "Yes, that you can do."

"Okay." Exiting the elevator, Rafael said, "With my luck I'll crash on my way home and die."

It came time to go their separate ways and find their cars.

"I don't know what to say," Rafael stood humbly before Alexa. "You've done so much…" Though she knew Rafael was an emotional man, she was surprised to see him tear up. "You've saved my life."

"I made you rich," she said, trying to impart a tone of levity.

Rafael embraced her then. "You're an angel. A goddamned angel."

She pulled away. "This angel has to get going."

He kissed her chastely on her cheek and watched as she walked away.

When she got into her car, she listened to her messages.

The first two were from clients, but the third was from her brother Mike, calling from New York to say he'd be in town that afternoon. Alexa breathed a long sigh of relief. "Thank God!" she said under her breath.

Finally, she could share the emotional burden of her mother's declining health with the closest person to them both. She missed her brother and would be so glad to see him. And Mike was a doctor. He would be able to help make the best decisions for Giselle from here on. She could feel tension pour out of her just knowing he'd be there.

Following Mike's message was a message from Madlynn. Her voice sounded tight as she asked Alexa to call her. An alarm immediately went off in Alexa, propelling her to dial Giselle's home number that instant. There was no answer. Somewhat more panicked now, she dialed Madlynn's cell phone.

Madlynn answered on the second ring. "Hi, is everything okay?" Alexa asked. "Is Mom okay?"

"She's fine," Madlynn said slowly. Alexa detected a false note. "She's okay," she said again. They were both silent then for a moment, and Alexa waited for the pregnant pause to give birth to the reason for Madlynn's call.

"We're at Cedars. I had to call 911. She slipped and fell in the shower." Alexa's heart was pounding. She couldn't find her voice. "She fractured her hip. But she's okay now, really," Madlynn hurried to add. "The doctor has seen her. He gave her morphine. She didn't really need it."

"Oh, my God!" Alexa managed. "I'll be right there." Alexa hung up and called back the number her brother had called from. When he didn't answer, she prayed he was on the airplane on his way to LA. She left him a message, telling him that Giselle had fallen, broken her hip, and was at Cedars Sinai.

She turned her car towards the hospital on Third Street. She concentrated on getting to the hospital as fast as possible. She took shortcuts, taking side streets and avoiding the busy boulevards and avenues. Soon she was on Alden Drive. She swung into the valet zone and dashed into the emergency area. She found her mother lying down in a room with monitors attached to her and an IV drip.

"Mom, are you okay?" she asked as she rushed to Giselle's bedside.

To her astonishment, Giselle looked at Madlynn, then said, "Why shouldn't I be?" Then her mother looked from her to Madlynn. "What's happened? What's wrong with everyone? What's the fuss?" Giselle asked.

Madlynn spoke to Alexa. "A minute after the fall, she didn't feel any pain. It's the Alzheimers."

"I don't understand. She broke her hip, didn't she?"

Madlynn nodded impatiently. "Yes, but she has no short-term memory, so she doesn't remember pain from one minute to the next. Once they stabilized her hip, she couldn't understand why we were in the hospital. She wanted to go home."

Alexa realized she would never really know all there was to know about her mother's terrible disease. But with all the heartbreak, this absence of pain was the silver lining.

"So much of pain is memory," Madlynn added.

Alexa stayed with Giselle until she was admitted into a private room. Before she left, she told her mother that Mike would be there before nightfall. Giselle seemed jubilant to hear that. Alexa was surprised but glad that her mother remembered Mike, and then realized that Giselle had mistaken her brother for her deceased father.

She left the hospital emotionally spent.

The high of Rafael's settlement was replaced with a feeling of emptiness.

65

On her arrival home, Alexa was greeted by an empty house.

The children were still at school. Lupe was out and had not expected Alexa to be home so early, so she had not left a note. Alexa wandered into the kitchen and opened the refrigerator but had no appetite. She grabbed a bottle of water and the Aleve and went to her bedroom. She kicked off her heels, changed into her loosest pair of jeans and a T-shirt, and went out to the courtyard where she lay on a lounging chair.

With the trial over and victory theirs, the stress should have abated. Instead, her head was throbbing. She opened the bottle of Aleve and downed two pills with a swig of water.

Alexa had heard enough stories to know that a broken hip in someone older could mean a swift decline and often lead to death. Her own aunt had lived to be a spry eighty-nine, exercising regularly and in seemingly excellent health. But a fall and broken hip landed her in a rehab facility for months where she sat in a wheelchair and wasn't able to exercise or continue her usual diet or supplements. Within six months she had wasted away and contracted pneumonia. She died without ever returning home.

Add to that, Giselle's Alzheimers and Alexa was afraid to contemplate her mother's prognosis. Thank God Mike was almost home.

And then there was the question of what to do with Rafael.

He'd won his case, won millions of dollars, twenty-two of them to be precise.

Didn't that mean he should be needling her right now, begging her to marry him?

He certainly had enough money to ensure Viviana would live a comfortable life without him.

Where the hell was he?

Alexa was totally involved with that question until she faced the far more puzzling dilemma of what she would do if Rafael were standing there at that moment ready to marry her.

Would she say yes? How could she still not know? What was wrong with her?

She was a grown woman with children no less, already married and once divorced, who couldn't answer a simple question: *Did she want to marry Rafael?*

Suddenly, the answer seemed to float into her consciousness like a feather wafting through and settling softly on a cushion. *No. Of course not.*

True, their physical attraction was mutual and mythic. But other than that, their history was one of need: his for her.

Other than what she knew of him from their two encounters in bed, a few lunches, and discussing his case in her office and in court, Alexa knew nothing of Rafael.

She certainly wouldn't – couldn't –think of making such an unknown entity her children's stepfather or her husband.

She sat there wondering at how easy, what a total no-brainer the answer had been. *Why hadn't she seen it before?*

Relieved, she closed her eyes, feeling the burden of her stress lighten. The ringing of her cell phone startled her. She realized she had dozed off.

"We did it, counselor!"

"We sure did, counselor!"

"And so, now that it's over, I get to cook dinner for you. Or did you decide you'd rather not take a chance on my cooking?"

"As a matter of fact, I'm feeling extremely self-satisfied right now. I've decided to brave your cooking."

"Okay, then. Just say when."

"Um, I'm nursing a headache at the moment. Can I get back to you on that?"

"Absolutely. I'm sitting by the phone."

And just like that, she was about to have a dinner date with Roger Prince. She could definitely do worse. He was a sweet man… and cute with that smile that slanted over to the side.

She put her head back and closed her eyes again. Though still present, her headache had softened. She thought about Mr. Roger Prince, Attorney at Law.

He looked lean and strong. She closed her eyes and smiled. Roger wasn't needy; on the contrary, he was a caretaker, and she respected him. He was raising his son alone, and Alexa knew what that entailed. She might actually start to like lawyers.

Her phone rang again. This time it was Rafael.

"Hello, Alexa. I'm nearby. I need to talk to you. Can I come over for a short while?"

Needy Rafael! Oh well, Alexa thought. Better to talk it out now. There was no reason to wait until tomorrow as they'd planned. "Sure. Come over."

He was there within minutes. When Alexa opened the front door, he took her in his arms and hugged her tightly before she could utter a word. When they came apart, she noticed he held a bottle. "I brought champagne," he said. Alexa went to get the proper glasses. "Are the children home?" he asked.

"No, they're in school."

He stood at the table in the family room, waving the bottle in the air. "Alexa, I don't know what to do with myself. I can't believe it. I feel like it's a dream. One minute the Federal Reserve is breathing down my neck, and I'm scared shitless and broke; my life is not worth living, and I'm selling shoes, and the next minute I'm a millionaire. Twenty-two million dollars!"

"Believe it."

He shook his head, with a grin stretched to its max. "Viviana has arranged for a trip; a vacation."

Glasses in hand, Alexa joined him, and they sat at the table.

Her voice was smooth, nonchalant. "Oh? Where to?"

He popped the cork and poured the bubbling drink into the two flutes. "A cruise. Through the Mediterranean. Egypt, Turkey, Cyprus, Greece…" He put the bottle down and picked up his glass as Alexa watched him.

"Sounds like a great trip. How long will you be gone?" She asked, tongue in cheek.

Rafael shrugged without looking at her. She knew the man well enough to know there was a big smile under his mask of a straight face. "I don't know." He was trying to sound flip, as if he didn't care. "I think she said three weeks. Maybe four?" he shrugged. "I'm not sure."

Alexa picked up her glass. "To your trip," she said and touched Rafael's glass with hers.

They both took a sip, then Rafael spoke. "Alexa, I'm really at a loss. I don't know what's come over Viviana."

"What do you mean?" Alexa asked. She knew perfectly well what he meant. She didn't know what had come over the woman either. She'd apparently gone through a complete change.

"Well… like this trip," he said. "Viviana would never do anything like this. She wouldn't take the car in to be fixed or make dinner reservations. *A trip?* She actually arranged the whole thing as a surprise! She did it as soon as she found out I'd won the first part of the trial. Before the punitive part started."

"When do you leave?"

"In three days. She figured the trial would all be over by then. She didn't think we'd settle."

Alexa nodded. She always thought Viviana was a smart woman and was glad to see that she had fought for what was hers.

"So, I guess you and I will wait until you get back?" Alexa said, testing the waters.

"Absolutely. I'm glad you understand. I can't say no to Viviana about this trip. I think I'll be able to talk to her while we're gone, make her understand that we should divorce."

Sipping the champagne, Alexa almost choked at that comment. She had to stifle her laughter. Another woman may have reacted by throwing their champagne at Rafael and kicking him out of the house. But not Alexa; she found humor in the situation. Here she had been racking her brains out for weeks, months, actually thinking about marrying this man! It was too funny.

"Sure," she said.

"You'll do nicely, too; I'll see to that. Have you thought about what you'll spend your share of the award on?" Rafael asked. "It's several million dollars."

Alexa didn't hesitate. "Therapy," she said and downed her glass of champagne.

The End

TOPICS FOR THOUGHT

Having read the story of Alexa Starr and Rafael Lamon, here are some potential topics for you to think about and discuss:

1. Did you initially believe that Rafael was guilty or innocent? Why?
2. Try to argue the opposing viewpoint and discuss the points that support it.
3. Can you empathize with Alexa for wanting to help Rafael as much as she did?
4. If Alexa had been a male, do you think Rafael would have been counting on her as much as he did?
5. Were you surprised when Alexa was able to come up with the idea of "stopping the clock?"
6. Alexa said the idea of stopping the clock just came out unexpectedly. Have you ever had an idea spontaneously erupt in your mind that was perfect for that moment? Discuss.
7. Are you empathetic to Alexa's attraction to Rafael? Have you ever felt attracted to someone who was married or otherwise 'unavailable'? Discuss how you were affected.
8. Do you think she committed adultery when she slept

with Rafael, knowing he was married? If so, is that because of religious beliefs? Moral beliefs?

9. Did you initially assume Rafael had done something to merit being fired?
10. What do you think of Attorney Larry Bloom? Did he believe Rafael was guilty?
11. When did you come to understand that Stamen was responsible for the illegal activity?
12. Have you ever felt that you were unjustly treated? Discuss in depth.
13. Can you understand how Alexa felt when the expert attorney told her she could represent Rafael as well as anyone else?
14. Can you empathize with Ben (Alexa's husband) when she did everything he told her not to do? Did she make the right decisions based on the facts, or was she taking unnecessary risks with Rafael's life?
15. There was a lot of information about Alexa's private life and her family. Did that add to your enjoyment of the story, or do you think it was unnecessary and distracting?
16. Do you know anyone close to you who has suffered from dementia or Alzheimer's? Discuss how you felt and how it affected you and your friends/family.
17. If Rafael or Alexa had known earlier that Stamen had met with agents from the Federal Reserve the same morning that Rafael had been fired, what would have changed?
18. How did Viviana strike you? Was her makeover a surprise?
19. Did you follow the trial, or was it boring? Have you been involved as a party in a trial?
20. Have you ever sat on a jury? Discuss.

21. Did you like the idea of giving the jurors small numbers to decide on the amount to award Rafael for punitive damages based on the defendant's wealth?
22. How would you compare Rafael to Roger Prince?
23. Do you think Rafael intends to talk to Viviana about a divorce on their cruise?
24. Do you think Alexa Starr, the young, hearing-challenged attorney, would be a good character for future stories? Why?
25. Please discuss any aspect of the story you choose, which has not been highlighted above.

ABOUT THE AUTHOR

Guitta Karubian is a published author of poems and short stories. She was the past editor of an international magazine.

Target is her first novel featuring Alexa Starr, the hearing-challenged attorney. She has also authored the *Moon* trilogy, composed of three stand-alone novels: *Persian Moon, Moon Child,* and *Moonlight.*

Ms. Karubian majored in Sociology at UC Berkeley and received her Juris Doctorate from Southwestern University of Law.

She is the mother of two and currently lives in Los Angeles, California.

You can contact her at 123guitta@gmail.com. Please visit her online at GuittaKarubian.com.

Thank you,
Guitta

Made in United States
Orlando, FL
04 November 2026

90201510R00216